Black Music in Our Culture

Dominique-René de Lerma

Chairman, Black Music Committee
Indiana University

with contributions from

Thomas Jefferson Anderson, Jr.

Nicholas V. d'Angelo

Verna Arvey

David N. Baker, Jr.

William S. Cole

Leonard Feist

Rachel E. Foster

O. Anderson Fuller

John Hammond

Paul Klinge

Lena McLin

Portia K. Maultsby

Robert L. Morris

Russell Sanjek

Hale Smith

Eileen J. Southern

William Grant Still

Frank Suggs, Jr.

Richard M. Turner, III

Olly Wilson

and others

Black Music

in

Our Culture

CURRICULAR IDEAS ON THE SUBJECTS,
MATERIALS AND PROBLEMS

 The Kent State University Press

Contributors to this book have graciously allowed royalties to be donated to the Black Music Committee Scholarship Fund for Black students in music at Indiana University.

Contents

In Memoriam:
Martin Luther King, Jr.
On the second anniversary of the day
his dream became our full responsibility
4 April 1970

1. Preface

Much of the information included in this book was presented at a seminar, "Black Music in College and University Curricula" held at Indiana University from June 18 to 21, 1969. This seminar, the first in an annual series of related programs, was sponsored by the Indiana University Summer Sessions Office, the Indiana University Foundation, and the Irwin-Sweeney-Miller Foundation. It was planned by the Black Music Committee of Indiana University's School of Music which, at that time, consisted of Professors David N. Baker, Jr., and Austin B. Caswell, with me serving as chairman.[1]

We had hoped that the session would prove worthy of publication from the start, and accordingly secured permission of the distinguished participants to tape record their contributions for this purpose. The material presented herein includes an edited version of these proceedings.

Supplementing the seminar were three recitals, funded by the Indiana University Foundation. My primary goal for these programs included the return to campus of those musicians necessary for the performance of Professor Baker's exceptionally exciting cantata, *Black America*, so that it might be heard by those attending the seminar, as well as the many local people who wished to hear this most impressive work again. These three programs constituted the 117th, 118th and 119th recitals of Indiana University School of Music's 1969-1970 season:

I. A Recital of Spirituals and Chamber Music by Black Composers.

Quartet for Brasses _____ Ulysses Kay
    Fast
    Slow
    Fast

---

[1] The committee was subsequently enlarged to include Professors Robert H. Klotman and Robert Stoll, with Robert L. Morris as student representative, and Mrs. Sharon B. Thompson as secretary. Ex-officio members include Associate Dean of Music William B. Christ, Mrs. Martha Mosier (Administrative Assistant to the Dean of Music in Charge of Research), Rozelle Boyd (Assistant Dean of the university's Junior Division), and Vice-Chancellor Herman C. Hudson, who is in charge of Indiana University's Afro studies program.

Larry Wiseman, Walter Blanton, trumpets;
Michael Olsavsky, Jay Hildebrandt, trombones.

Dramatic Declamation: Rockin' Jerusalem! (from *Lyric
Suite*) _____ Robert Leigh Morris
    Ruby Jones, contralto; Robert L. Morris, piano.

Five Pieces for Soprano _____ David N. Baker
  If There Be Sorrow
  The Smile
  The Optimist
  A Song
  Parade to Hell
    Jan Albright, soprano; Douglas Murdock, piano.

Deep River _____ Harry T. Burleigh
Southland Sketches, No. 4 _____ Harry T. Burleigh
    Stephen Shipps, violin; Robert L. Morris, piano.

The Breath of a Rose _____ William Grant Still
    Helene Oatts, soprano; Robert L. Morris, piano.

Sonata for Violoncello _____ David N. Baker
    (Première performance)
  Fast
  Slow
  Fast
    Michael Peebles, violoncello; Gayle Cameron, piano.

II. A Concert of Jazz.

One for J. S. _____ David N. Baker
The Silver Chalice _____ David N. Baker
Son Mar _____ David N. Baker
Roly Poly _____ David N. Baker
Soft Summer Rain _____ David N. Baker
April B _____ David N. Baker
The I. U. Swing Machine _____ David N. Baker
  Indiana University Jazz Ensemble; David N. Baker,
  conductor.
    Walter Blanton, Larry Wiseman, Carl Schectman,
    Bob Farquer, Ed Smoot, trumpets; Rick Fecteau,
    Joe Hambrick, Bob Taylor, Jay Hildebrandt,
    trombone; Floyd Cooley, tuba; Paul De Marinis,
    Mary Taylor, Kim Hutchcroft, Don Hutchison,
    Harry Jansen, saxophones; Shelby Janes, piano;

Willie Ward, Kyle Tullis, double basses; Harry
Wilkinson, Victor Olsen, drums; Richard Markus,
vibes and percussion.

III.   Black America.

Black America: To the Memory of Martin Luther King;
a cantata _____ David N. Baker
   The Wretched of the Earth (Machinations, missionaries,
      money, Marines)
   Kaleidoscope
   125th Street
   Martyrs (Malcolm, Medgar and Martin)
      Indiana University Jazz Ensemble; Janice
      Albright, Linda Anderson, Beverly
      McElroy, sopranos; Robert Ingram, tenor;
      David Arnold, baritone; David N. Baker, conductor.

Credit for the first program belongs to Robert Leigh Morris, a graduate student in choral music at Indiana University (subsequently appointed to the Black Music Committee). The hour-long cantata, *Black America*, was presented twice on the same evening in order to accommodate the large number of people who could not be seated for the first performance.

Beginning with registration, which attracted the 93 persons whose names are given in Appendix 7, it was evident this was not going to be a traditional meeting of professional musicians. Old friends greeted each other in a manner which may almost be the property of the Blacks, and new friendships were established with a minimum of hesitation and a maximum of warmth. As the sessions progressed, emotional bonds and fervor became still more evident, culminating with a final dinner and an informal talk by Wilfred C. Bain, distinguished Dean of Indiana University's School of Music.

The many approaches to the topic suggested the wide diversity of the area, from spirituals to electronic music, from relatively conservative individuals to those dressed in African styles. Even so, we found ourselves incapable for this seminar of considering one important aspect of current-day music: soul. A particularly alert professor, whose schedule prevented his attendance, cited this lacuna in a letter:

I am both impressed and disturbed by the type of thing you have planned. I am impressed by the thoroughness of your plans in this very needed field, and by the fact that you are bringing together so many excellent people for a consultation. However, I am distressed at the omissions in the type of subjects that you will be discussing. I do not notice any reference to soul music or to gospel music. Undoubtedly you will be considering this type of music, but it seems to me that the thrust of Black music study should not be on highly developed art forms and/or composers who have made it in the "Establishment." It seems to me that what Black people want in the studies of Black music is related to unique spontaneity and improvisation in music: qualities that are not usually present or emphasized in school of music curricula. In other words, I feel that your approach is going to have to be much more radical than your publicity would seem to indicate.

At one point in the seminar, I indicated a kind of terror in an awareness of thinking constantly in terms of composers and of alphabetical or chronological arrangement. In working with the same areas in which these approaches are normally valid, the materials do not always cry out from mismanagement. One of the things about dealing with Black music and culture, however, is that traditional techniques in any aspect might sometimes be totally lacking in validity. It is unfortunate that an experienced educator may owe his success partly to the habit of following pre-ordained concepts, to which he adds new information (which only weighs down the pre-conceptions). Because he must constantly be dealing with new ideas, of all people an educator must be in a position to approach innovations through techniques suggested by the materials themselves, and not by habitual reactions. I accept this blame personally, not sharing it with my fellow committeemen, because I designed the contours of this seminar, but I pass these comments on to present and future teachers for their consideration.

The matter of teaching soul, gospel and jazz music presents very distinct problems, to which present academic techniques and attitudes do not fully relate. This problem of the educators merits a great deal of additional consideration, as the seminar participants indicate.

On the other hand, we cannot discard those figures who fit more closely into the academy's "mainstream" (the ghetto citizen would be wryly amused to see Thomas A. Dorsey or Booker T. as being regarded out of the mainstream). If we are to develop a definition of Black music, and if we are to know what this potent culture really is, we simply have to consider those whose names appear on concert programs as well.

There is a certain amount of impatience to define what elements constitute a Black music style. The interest in this definition exists for one of several reasons. If we cannot prove to the rest of the world that this music has qualities which are unique, we can hardly answer some of the reservations which are expressed about giving special attention to the subject. There is also the matter of ego: individualism, even on a racial level, provides identity (and Blacks have been seeking the extent of their identity for many years, in many ways). Perhaps the most important justification for a definition is musicological. Forgetting the racial prides which we might feel and looking at the material in terms of our profession, we know we should be able to isolate stylistic qualities, and there is adventure and challenge in examining an area which has not properly secured this attention. (Or is my concern for this area a symptom of the fact that I have regarded this an obligation in the past, and am now forcing that habit again?)

Perhaps we can all express intuitive ideas about a Black musical style. Depending on the range of material we have examined or heard, we may not be sure if these ideas will spread out to include music by contemporary native Africans, Black Latin Americans, Samuel Coleridge-Taylor, John Carter, Charlie Parker, Olly Wilson, Thomas Dorsey, Roscoe Mitchell, shouts and hollers, Leadbelly, Oliver Nelson, or Aretha Franklin. My correspondent refers to spontaneity and improvisation. When the time comes that some concept of this style can be established, even if it cannot fully embrace Saint-Georges or Akim Euba on equal terms with John Coltrane or George Walker, spontaneity and improvisation will not be missing.

It is true that these qualities are normally not emphasized in the academic world but, as I suggest later, I think some curricular habits may have to be broken so that the educational system can be kept alive and vital. Such a change will emphasize, by the way, that the location of the recapitulation in a Mozart quartet or the identification of a Schönberg tone row has not gotten to the heart of the music.

The development of this seminar was not the first action of the Black Music Committee. Our initial work was the identification of the Black composers, whose race was hidden in the past by the discretion of non-discrimination (a kind of guilt-complex symptom), or who were unknown because they were beyond the pale, so to speak. This survey, which also had to make specific citation of their entire known output, was funded by the National Endowment for the Humanities, and will result in the publication of *Black Music; A Preliminary Register of the Composers and Their Works*, to be issued by Kent State University Press.

That was our first venture; the 1969 seminar was the second. It was not designed, by the way, so much to disseminate information as to explore the area, as indicated in the title. Actual training seminars, in various areas, were initiated with the 1970 sessions.

To some extent the seminar was frustrating to all of us; the area is too large for all questions to be answered, for all viewpoints to be registered and discussed. Nonetheless, here are the goals as they were stated at the inception of the seminar, not all of which we were able to consider:

We will speak of functional music. I wonder if the Black composer always creates music for the same reason as the non-Black, if there is some residual of the fact that music is always closer to life for the Black. Is he active in composition because published music is not always readily available which relates to Black choirs, pianists and bands?

We know that there is nothing in music that can be called a "sacred style." This is manifest no less with Palestrina than with Mozart or Verdi or Stravinsky. Church music is not always in a language other than that of the people. With Black music, this brings two factors together: jazz and spirituals. Can it be that these two have attracted the Black composer because for so long these seemed the only avenues of expression open to him?

Jazz has admitted its unsophisticated roots, but now we know it has a long culture of its own. Even in the training of jazz musicians, we have moved a long way from the instrumentalists whose genius overshadowed their failings with traditional embouchure considerations, with Hanon, Jeanjean or Lafosse. Players today might be very conversant with Stockhausen or Xenakis, not to mention the jazz giants of the past. Should those teaching a course in contemporary music see to it that the history of jazz is included, even at the expense of dropping some composers from the syllabus? Is jazz important enough an area that a special course, graduate or undergraduate, should be offered and, if so, how does one actually teach a subject wherein performance counts for more than notation?

If the Black composer wishes to contribute to the main stream of western music (or, as it might at times be, third stream), does that decision mean he is negating his race? Does he regard the string quartet or opera as a medium of the Whites? Perhaps not; after all, he has not looked on the piano as being Italian, or the saxophone as Belgian. Does he then have the right to free access, to use any materials—even electronic—for his creations? Can the "Black experience" be expressed with these choices, or does the composer relate to his race automatically? What has been the impact of serial writing, aleatory music or electronic sounds on the Black avant-garde? (In fact, hasn't chance music been old hat to the Black performer for more than this century?)

We have seen how non-musical elements of a given culture may be reflected in the music of a nation or a race. Slavic languages, lacking articles, may find less use for pickups when set to music than German. Italian, with stresses in place of accents, needs less to convert spoken language into vocal music. French vowels subtly reflect a possible national interest in the way wind instruments may disguise their gender. Accents in English are often on the first syllable, and cannot help but produce a music which reflects this syncopation. What of Black music? Despite dialects, from the lilt of the southern Bahaman to the colorful and direct speech of the ghetto "dude," the language is English. Is there some other element in Black culture which has influenced our music? Perhaps dance? Let us discover if there has been substantial cross-breeding between these art forms, which have traditionally permitted improvisation and a direct expression from the performer.

If these aspects are to be absorbed in existing classes, and if more important areas might merit special courses of study, what materials may be used for this teaching? One can speak just so long about names, forms, influences, idioms, trends and titles. The real communication is the music itself; lectures are after the fact, not before it. We know that new texts must be written and that existing histories must be rewritten, but we will not have reached the music itself, even then. Those engaged in teaching aspects of this culture must all have asked themselves if there really is enough published and recorded music to satisfy the needs of the classes, and if the radio and concert hall provide the supplementary listening and performing opportunities which are needed. Now that Willi Apel has cared for what used to be called the "dark ages of music history" (i.e., the fourteenth century), do we not find that the Black Age is even darker? We need to hear from those in the publishing and recording industry, to know the problems and potential solutions, and we need to hear from the teacher who is trying to cope with these difficulties.

We need also to hear from the student. Is he disillusioned with the Back-to-Africa movement? Does he regard spirituals as something, like the minstrel shows, from the past? He may be more concerned with securing a job than considering the relevancy of sixteenth-century Black-Brazilian composers. We must know how he thinks and feels, even if every one of his ideas cannot be acted on, so we can at least be sensitive to these sentiments as they develop when he becomes part of the new establishment. Student interests bear symp-

toms of a new regime, and they will remind us that we must constantly be able
to reevaluate thinking habits before we fall into the despair which occasions
the elderly, unimaginative mind. In fact, a true teacher is one who stimulates
reevaluations from his students; habits need no teacher.

By this time we will have considered the materials and their distribution,
and we will have seen what is desired by those who may soon be offering what
we might have ignored. The time then comes for practical considerations.
Is the assumption of some students that special programs in Black studies
which should be offered by a Black professor an extraordinary one? If the name
of Dallapiccola could be uttered in a classroom only by an Italian professor,
or that of Cabezón by a Spaniard, these names would rarely be mentioned
in many schools. And yet, Black students want an authority from their own
race. How many Black musicologists or theorists with a Ph.D. do we know?
Several important questions are available for each one who exists. Are there
more Blacks in education than in these areas because it was long thought,
even by him, that this was "his place?" I suspect that few Black colleges offer
a major in musicology or in theory, particularly on the graduate level. If this is
true, a cycle without end is created. With respect to all of this, let us see what
role might be possible with funding, scholarship programs, and institutional
grants.

Not one person whose opinions or ideas expressed herein is necessarily rep-
resenting the institution or organization from which he comes. There is a
great deal of merit in having the opportunity to "rap," free from concerns of
institutional image, and I think we all took advantage of this. We were thus
able to hyperbolate and develop ideas in the process of discussing them with
others. I have exercised editorial rights to extract material which might have
been particularly strong in this respect, but only when the train of thought
would not suffer.

We must understand that it is often important to consider matters which
are not directly musical or curricular, and there are two reasons for this. One
is historical, the other is sociological. Musicologists have never felt inhibited
about discussing factors which have been of some effect on music. It is usually important, for example, to indicate the problems Mozart or Bach had with
the clergy, yet doing this does not prove the historian to be anti-clerical. At
this particular time in American history, however, there can be in some circles
an automatic reaction on the part of the public that the writer, if he deals
boldly with Black culture, is too far left, too militant, too sympathetic with

violence. This very "danger" makes it (falsely) safer to study earlier ages; conservative people or institutions may feel a good bit more comfortable with isorhythmic motets or even the texts of the *canti carnascialeschi* than with recent folk music or poetry of the Blacks.

As for the sociological reason, and with no disrespect to Elliott Carter or Pierre Boulez, it is safer to study their music than that of Charles Bell or Joseph Jarman. Black arts seem to be from the start part of the entire social fabric of the people. Music is rarely an end in itself, as it so often is (or was) with Western cultures. When we really get down to it, almost all Black music may be *Gebrauchsmusik*, and every singer and performer and composer no less a philosopher. This is part of the total involvement which White youth seeks today, possibly not understanding that the idea comes from the Blacks, like so many others current today. This has made pop music cover the distance it has from the texts of Frank Sinatra to those of James Brown. The poet Nikki Giovanni has stated, "There is no difference between the warrior, the poet, and the people. Like Stokely is a poet, and so is Rap Brown."[2]

Before long, we may be surfeited with justifications for Black emphasis. By that time, corporate prejudice, real or innocent, must be only a historical shame. This will be the time for that intense vitality which open channels should provide. This book is an apologia by its very title, but it is also designed as a positive move toward the future.

As the final draft was being prepared, *Time* produced a special issue (April 6, 1970) entitled "Black America 1970." Therein is reported the results of a poll which indicates that 97 percent of the Blacks feel that they might make real progress if more of their race were better educated. Sixty-seven percent plan to go to college (and note that half of Black America is under 20 years of age). James W. Bryant, program advisor for special projects in education of the Ford Foundation, reports in *Survey of Black American Doctorates*[3] that the majority of Blacks who now hold doctorates were trained as undergraduates in predominately Black colleges. If previous estimates for the future are true, supported by non-racial admissions policies, many of the formerly White schools will become darker and should therefore be preparing very quickly for this change. *Time*'s survey indicates that 85 percent of those interviewed are

---

[2] Quoted in "The undaunted pursuit of fury" in *Time*, April 6, 1970, p.98.

[3] Published by the Ford Foundation, February 1970.

in favor of Black studies programs, which poses a curricular challenge to the nation's universities.

Bryant reports that 0.8 percent of all Ph.D. degrees awarded between 1964 and 1968 were won by Blacks, and *Time* states that only one percent of the faculties in 80 public universities are Black. For every four Black Ph.D. professors, only one teaches in a White school. If Blacks wish to be taught by teachers of their own race, the compromise of the schools may have to be far greater than I suspect the institutions will permit. Perhaps the easiest immediate solution is to develop stop-gap arrangements from among those qualified persons presently available, but all possible steps should be taken right away to secure, train and graduate Black Ph.D. scholars.

Had Black culture been recognized for what it is, there would be no need of the compensation for the false cultural inferiority which exists today. The militant struggle of the Blacks to close ranks and unite would appear rather sophomoric had the race been given access to its heritage in the past. This was not the case, however, and the only course of action open is the one being taken. The study of Black culture, perhaps not so immediately important as the development of Blacks in business and economics, is nonetheless an extraordinarily important factor in healing the social wounds of the United States. It is of no consequence what color the students of any given school are, I think it is obligatory that American students learn to respect the unique Black genius by developing an awareness of this culture, and to learn that very much which we think of as being American music is, in fact, Afro-American music. This educational process can transform Black intuition and hope into known facts and cultural security.

Blacks need to see themselves as leaders. There may not be an abundance of Black education majors, but there are far more teachers than conductors, than musicologists, than music theorists, than deans. Whites should realize what it feels like to find someone of another race, at a time when racial identity is enormously important, in a position of leadership.

Bryant indicates that, by 1973, the number of Ph.D. degrees earned by Blacks may rise by 20 percent but, even so, it will mean that only two of every one hundred doctorates will be held by Blacks. It is certainly not going to be easy to have the personnel resources we need, and the honest support and interests of the Whites will be essential.

This book cannot make any attempt to answer all of the questions, or even to pose them. It may hope for nothing more than a stimulus within its restricted area. If it accomplishes that much, all of us who have been engaged in its development will be gratified.

As a final note, I apologize to the seminar participants who were not properly identified by name in the tape transcript and to those who, as a matter of format, are not cited with their titles in the seminar coverage. Distinct appreciation is due to every person from this seminar, who allowed these contributions to be included in this book. I am also deeply in debt to the members of the Black Music Committee at Indiana University, to Mrs. Martha Mosier, Associate Dean William B. Christ and Dean Wilfred C. Bain, to all of Indiana University's School of Music, for the assistance and encouragement they have given us in these ventures, to Dr. Jane G. Flener, Assistant Director of Libraries, for her cooperation and interest, and to Howard Allen, Director of the Kent State University Press, and his splendid staff for many factors related to the development of this book and our other efforts. Gratitude is also expressed to Mr. and Mrs. Harry Elzinga and Mrs. Penny Archer who transcribed the seminar tapes, and particularly to Ben Cheesman for his help in preparing the final drafts.

Note: On July 20, 1970, as this book was going to press, Indiana University was informed by the National Endowment for the Humanities that funding will be provided for the establishment of a Black Music Center in Bloomington on September 1, 1970. The Executive Board consists of Dominique-René de Lerma as Director, David N. Baker, Jr., as Associate Director, Herndon Spillman as Assistant to the Director and Research Associate, and John Taylor as Research Associate. An honorary committee of outstanding musicians under the chairmanship of Thomas Jefferson Anderson, Jr., will serve in an advisory capacity. Predominantly Black American in membership, the committee also includes representatives from Latin America, Europe and Africa. Unique in design and international in scope, the Black Music Center will be a research and reference library for the study of the various manifestations of Black musical cultures.

2. Indiana University's Black Music Committee

David N. Baker, Jr.

● David Baker, head of the jazz studies program at Indiana University, has a rich background in music, despite his youth. Following graduation from Crispus Attucks High School in Indianapolis (the same school which produced Wes Montgomery, Slide Hampton, and J. J. Johnson), he completed his bachelor's and master's degrees at Indiana University. His work as trombonist with the George Russell Sextet is documented on numerous recordings. He has also recorded with many other groups and, in the past few years, has been active as a jazz cellist. Even though he is very widely known as an outstanding jazz performer and composer, his work as a non-jazz composer displays a broad talent of exceptional quality. I particularly regard his dramatic cantata, *Black America*, as one of the most powerful truly Black works I have ever heard, but mention should also be made of his cello sonata (premiered by Michael Peebles and Gayle Cameron during our seminar) and the concerto for violin and jazz band (which Josef Gingold performed at Indiana University on April 5, 1970). Dave is a warm, deeply human person, with whom all people can instantly relate (if he can be located, which is rarely easy), with a ready wit and an incisive understanding of his role as a Black musician.

BAKER: It is my pleasurable task to give you a progress report on what we've been doing, about some of the things that have taken place, some of the people we've talked to, some of the ideas and attitudes which have been manifest, some of the types of music Black composers are writing, something about the programs and societies we've encountered, and something about Black music in general. I'd like to give you first a little bit of the background which launched our work.

For all practical purposes, the real interest was born with the death of Martin Luther King. On the morning after the assassination, Indiana University's president asked for a memorial service. It was deemed proper that there should be some music by a Black composer, which our faculty Berkshire Quartet could play, but our library seemed to have no appropriate music.[1]

---

[1] The Berkshire Quartet selected David Baker's own *Pastorale* for strings, which had been written some years earlier.

This came as a sort of revelation to us. All of a sudden, there was an awakening of the consciences of many people, certainly those of this university. Almost immediately, Dean Wilfred C. Bain selected a committee, charged with the task of exploring activities in which his school of music might play a role.

About this time I was at a social gathering, and everybody was suddenly concerned with brotherhood. At dinner, it was suggested that we should have something similar to our Latin American Music Center.[2] Someone said to me that it would be nice to have such a thing, but you could play through all the non-jazz works by Black composers in one hour. That made me angry, and I proceeded to explain to him that there were more compositions by Black composers than he could ever imagine. He said, "Name five." I knew he didn't know more about it than I did, so I proceeded to lay some names on him, but I knew all along that probably no one really knew how many of us there were or what we had done.

We became quite concerned about finding who the Black composers were and, in traveling across the country, I found that there's not much knowledge about this, even among other Black composers. If you're in Los Angeles, do you know what's happening in Chicago, or in New York? Who are the Black composers in your own city, or who work in your own idiom? This is the basis for our big research project, which will result in the publication of our *Black Music*.

I have to admit that we were very naïve when we started off, and we've had to revamp our notions constantly. We began with a visit to Dr. Roscoe Poland, past president of the National Association of Negro Musicians, who lives in Indianapolis. I went through his files to find people's names, as a starting point. None of the young Black composers we subsequently identified were cited. To a large extent, the names were those of performers, which is not what we were after at this point. Following this, every time we talked to a composer, we always asked for names of others. The list has grown considerably, and now totals more than 700 persons, yet we may not even now have all the most important people.

---

2 Indiana University's Latin American Music Center was established in 1963 by the Rockefeller Foundation as a research and reference center for music of the Latin Americas. The center, which has been directed from its inception by Dr. Juan Orrego-Salas, has exceptionally large holdings of published music and recordings on deposit with the School of Music Library. Included within this collection are works of many Black composers. The catalog of the center's holdings may be secured from its offices at Indiana University.

The next trip was to Chicago. We talked to members of the AACM (more on this later), to many of the gospel composers in the area, to Mrs. Lena Mc-Lin, and others. We found there was an obvious distrust at first (and particularly from the younger men) of the "Establishment." It didn't make any difference that it was a Brother who was taking care of it, there was a real distrust. When we first went out, Dr. Caswell and I went together, thinking it would be easier to do research this way. The Brothers pulled me aside and asked, "What are they doing, sending somebody to watch over you?" You dig? Well, this was one of the first attitudes we had to deal with, and we eventually found that Austin could talk to some people, but I'd have to take care of the others.

The next problem was how to go about reconciling all of the different areas, and if we should make some decision about who gets included in the end. All right, you've got on one hand a non-jazz composer, and you can cite his manuscripts and publications, his symphonies and his string quartets, but what do you do with the jazz musician who has seventy-five short tunes? Is he equally important? Then we're faced with the fact that almost anybody now who plays has written some music, because he knows better what he wants to express as a performer. And we get to gospel music, where people are more arrangers than actual composers. Well, they're all there, and we're keeping them, along with everything we can get on their background, their philosophies, and every single title they've ever written.

More touchy is trying to get a composer to identify his style, insofar as that's possible. And from there we move into the question of what is Black in their music, and that brings up the philosophy.

There are certain societies which should be mentioned. In Chicago, there's the group of Black jazz musicians called AACM, the Association for the Advancement of Creative Musicians, a real hip bunch. Their goals, a set of beautiful aims, will give you an idea of what they're after:

1) To cultivate young musicians and to create music of a high artistic level for the general public through the presentation of programs designed to magnify the importance of creative music.

2) To create an atmosphere conducive to artistic endeavors for the artistically inclined by maintaining a workshop for the express purpose of bringing talented youngsters together.

3) To conduct free training programs for young, aspiring musicians.

4) To contribute financially to charitable organizations.

5) To provide a source of employment for worthy, creative musicians.

6) To set an example of high moral standards for musicians, and to uplift the public image of creative musicians.

7) To increase mutual respect between creative artists and musical tradesmen (booking agents, managers, promoters, instrument manufacturers, etc.).

8) To uphold the tradition of elevated cultured musicians, handed down from the past.

9) To stimulate spiritual growth in creative artists through participation in programs, concerts, recitals, etc.

The manner by which these aims have been manifest include the issue of recordings under the Delmark and Nessa labels,[3] participation in conferences and concerts, both within and outside the immediate community, publication of an irregularly issued periodical, *The New Regime*, and free instruction in theory, instrumental and vocal music to children and youths of Chicago's inner city.

When I asked if the AACM had anything to do with Black power, the group's first president, Richard Abrams, replied, "Yes, it does in the sense that we intend to take over our own destinies, to be our own agents, and to play our own music." This does not suggest parochialism or dogma. Each member is free to be the individual he wishes to be, and to express himself by whatever techniques or styles serve these needs. Influences might be traced as easily to Johnny Desmond and Ornette Coleman as to Earle Brown, Karlheinz Stockhausen, the streets of Chicago, or General Motors.

Another association is in New York, a high-powered group of young composers, and one of the more important groups in the country: The Society of Black Composers. Many of you know about this. We have one member here at our seminar, Hale Smith. Another member of the group, Steve Chambers, has provided the following description of their work:

> The Society of Black Composers comes into being at a very critical point in the day-to-day history of the Black liberation struggle which has been going on in this country for some four-hundred odd years. The cultural movement of this struggle holds equal importance with the political-economic movement. The Society of Black Composers is one of several significant cultural organizations that has recently come into being to play

---

[3] These recordings contain avant-garde jazz works by AACM members Richard Abrams, Lester Bowie, Anthony Braxton, Joseph Jarman and Roscoe Mitchell. Delmark records can be secured from 7 West Grand, and Nessa records can be secured from 5875 North Glenwood, both in Chicago.

a very vital role within the Black cultural movement, and to perpetuate those unique and poignant contributions by Black creative artists—composers in this instance—in the rehabilitation and redevelopment of the spiritual and moral selfness of Black communities at large, in this city, state and, indeed, this nation. One of the essential functions of a Black cultural movement is first to crystalize the ever-present cultural elements of the Black experience, and then to implement programs that will project these elements to the world scene, to bring about the reordering and rededication of a people's destiny in regard to their spiritual, moral entity.

Bringing new Black composers and emerging Black communities closer together is one of the society's primary objectives. This particular phase of operation will aid in bringing about a clearer perspective in regard to the composer and his image vis-à-vis the Black community, his overall relationship to that community, the relevancy and distribution of his work to the community, and his financial support by and because of the community. Another very important objective of the society is to project the work of Black composers throughout the general community so as to correct and eliminate eventually those distorted concepts that have prevailed in regard to all Black creative artists and our cultural identity. This identity will occur when we commence to establish and initiate a collective cultural, spiritual and philosophical ideology that is and will be commensurable to the overall Black cultural movement. Black cultural nationalism is a concept that can and will give us Black creative artists identity, purpose and direction, these in turn telling us who we are, what we must do, and how best we can do it. Indeed, if art is really about the recreation of one's environmental context, and if that context is permeated with an abundance of negatives, rampant racism, hypocrisies and various manifestations of economic, political, cultural genocide, then Black creative artists (poets, writers, musicians, dancers, actors and painters) must become warriors, moving against the minds rather than the institutions that perpetuate such negatives, to exist within that environmental context.

Another such group is MECA, in St. Louis—the Metropolitan Educational Cultural Association. It has two subdivisions: AIR (Artists in Residence) and BAG (Black Artists' Group). BAG, which is headed by Julius Hemphill, one of my former students, has goals not totally unlike AACM. They have a community center where evening concerts are presented without profit. They provide instruments and lessons for the neighborhood kids at their own expense. They beg and borrow instruments[4] for the kids, from all sources. By

---

[4] Donations of instruments from socially-oriented instrument manufacturers would doubtless be accepted by BAG and AACM, as well as other such groups which might

presenting their image as artists, it is a little easier for these kids to have heroes again.

The oldest group is certainly the National Association of Negro Musicians, which probably most of you belong to.

I'd like now to give you some of the answers most generally provided when I asked what Black music was. We'll no doubt build on these in the sessions of this seminar:

1) Essentially, music by Black composers and performed by Blacks,

2) Music stemming from the Black experience and reflecting that culture in any of its forms,

3) Non-provincial interests with a wide latitude of aesthetic principles, or

4) Music with an emotional strength not common in White music, free from White intellectualisms and verbosity.

When I asked for more specific things, the first thing to come up was rhythm. That was followed by intuitive thoughts regarding energy, a particular approach to narrative, the use of folk elements, spontaneity and improvisation, and inherent social functions. Many suggested that Black and African music never violated the body and its natural flow, and almost everyone brought up matters of inflection: the cadence of conversation, speech imitation, pitch variation, vocal music qualities, smears, slurs. Related to many of these are ideas about microtones and cross rhythms, polymeter, the primacy of rhythm and its flow, a spirituality, and blues scales with their resulting vertical structures.

I asked for specific innovations, especially from jazz. What emerged was a feeling that a new use for rhythm would have to be considered, for Black music is often based on the constant conflict of rhythms. It was also said that jazz gave popularity to certain instruments in non-jazz areas, and the range of all of the instruments has been widened: trumpet players now play two and three octaves higher than before. Furthermore, instruments do things technically which would never have been done before, such as the trombone taking the role of the saxophone. Instrumental performance has become very virtuosic, and the dramatic possibilities of all instruments are broader. Much of this came about because Black musicians couldn't afford lessons from teachers who told them what should or could not be done, so they had to invent—like

---

exist in other cities. Individuals might also wish to search their attics and closets for instruments that might be put to better use.

Wes Montgomery. Nobody told him how to play his instrument. Jazz provided the impetus for aleatory music, liberating the imagination of people like David Tudor, Lukas Foss and John Cage, and improvisation became respectable again. Harmony has certainly been changed because of jazz, and there has been an introduction of additive forms, rather than developmental forms, to Western musical thought. We have led music away from the propagation of standards and aesthetic concepts of the European middle class. We have exposed the symphony orchestra as a historical and social anachronism.

QUESTION: May we have more information on MECA?

CASWELL: This organization is sponsored by both municipal and federal funds for the St. Louis area, and is headed by Dr. Custer. Its purposes are not basically racial, but cultural, for all ages and groups. It sponsors a number of organizations of which BAG is one aimed at the city's Blacks.

FULLER: During these interviews, was anything revealed to explain the rise and wane of interest in Black composers?

BAKER: That is a very stimulating question, and I'm afraid I never even thought about it before. I know some Whites are surprised to find that there have been militant movements before this. Maybe there is a relationship. This certainly would be something for someone to consider seriously.

SMITH: I am very concerned with the question Dr. Fuller just raised. The work of these earlier men make it easier for all of us to do what we do. A few years ago I wrote to William Grant Still to express my appreciation for opening the doors for us. The younger practitioners are too often either not aware of what changes were made, or they tend to overlook them because the changes don't address themselves to current problems they think, but I regard them as very pertinent.

QUESTION: I think probably the biggest problem appears when you try to have some contact with music of a decade or two ago. It is terribly difficult to try to find recorded music or manuscripts, or published music from the past, which makes it difficult for the young Black composer who wants to look back to those roots. He's got no records to listen to of any particular consequence or, at least, of any bulk. He can't buy the score. All of this points to the need for research that would uncover manuscripts and anything else that would make it possible to come in contact with the music.

SUTHERN: Through a $10,000 grant from the Esso Foundation, we were able to solve that particular problem. In some cases we've been able to trace down some things, and back in attics and so forth we've come up with the manuscripts. We've been able to go one step further because we have on our staff a pianist-in-residence whose brother, George Walker, is a very fine composer. Through the help of this foundation, I've been able to offer her and other performers a stipend for learning and performing the music.

HAMMOND: Has any study been made of the decline of the Negro popular musician with the rise of the American Federation of Musicians? This is a particularly fascinating subject in New York. Back before 1920, when Local 802 was established in New York (and I'm a good union man myself), in the field of society music in general it was Negroes who had reign. Florenz Ziegfield had a Negro conductor for the Ziegfield Follies. In popular music there was far more use of the Negro musician before 1920 than in the two decades after. I think this subject might be very interesting to go into in considerable detail. In New York we had a so-called integrated union (it wasn't, really). In other cities they had separate unions which actually barred the Negro musician from Class-A jobs. Some of these unions may even exist today. It seems to me that this would be a very good idea for future discussion and research.

MACK: I'm also a musician, formerly of 208 (the reverse of 802) in Chicago. Our local subsequently became integrated with the Chicago Local 10, and is now Local 10-208. This goes along with the attitude you spoke of a while ago. Not only with reference to Black musicians, but White ones also, the jazz musician lost the principle of what his role was. He was an entertainer. He descended not from the great masses of the past like all real musicians, but from the court jesters. The more he started to ignore this role and to look upon the music as a vehicle by which he expressed his talent, the less he was appreciated. We saw this in the late 30's and early 40's. We came to a point where even the greatest jazz artist couldn't play at normal clubs because there was less and less of the entertainment value. Then too, there is a growing alienation of the artist and the musician from the audience in other ways. Significant composers, such as Ralph Shapey, may not have a single published work. What's the normal route of publication? The publishers. It's often much easier to get printed anything which can be used for educational purposes (any march or arrangement) than any really significant music.

BAKER: I think probably one of the things that's certainly been a problem in my own thinking about the position of a jazz musician as an entertainer is that nobody expects a string quartet to entertain in the same sense of the word. They play music. That's all that anybody should be required to do as far as I'm concerned. I feel absolutely no need to do any more than communicate. Music has its own reason for being.

SMITH: I don't feel that educational music necessarily has to be junk. Perhaps much of it has been, but we have to consider several factors. The publisher is in the business to make money. He is going to gravitate naturally to those products which will give him a reasonable return on his dollar. One thing many publishers have not done, however, is self-subsidization. Through income derived from less elevated products, it is possible to subsidize the more esoteric and the avant-garde works. These forward-looking works are really the stimulae which create a basis for the development of further popular tastes. We are in danger of weakening musical life because the really vital substances coming from the sub-strata of society are not given enough serious attention, and the production and propagation of popular music is largely in the hands of illiterates—musical illiterates—and people who have absolutely no interest in artistic values. That's not only the fault of the publishers, it's partly the fault of the recording companies and the educational institutions who fail in their responsibility to create a relationship between their curricula and the world. One of the best ways for any composer, Black or White, to get himself published on a national scale is through the area of educational music. If we don't create our audiences at the level where they are receiving their education and when their tastes are being formed, we're cutting our own throats. This goes for the performing musician, the composer, the publisher, and the record company. There are more and more jazz musicians, for instance, who are taking time going to schools, playing for the youngsters. I'm talking about elementary, junior high and senior high schools, as well as the college level. That also goes for performers from non-jazz. I have recommended to an number of composers that their stylistic integrity need not be compromised whatever by the production of music for education. We would go a long way before we found something of a higher artistic level than Bartók's *Mikrokosmos*, for instance.

WEIDNER: How deeply are you going into the eighteenth and nineteenth century in your research?

DE LERMA: Bridgetower is going to be included. Saint-Georges will be there.

If we can find anybody from the Renaissance in Naples who was Black, he will be entered. These will not be twentieth century musicians in every instance, but Dave has greater access to those composers who are living for his interviews.

LEE: Do you make a difference between the arranger and the composer, or do you run across any arrangers who were also out-and-out creators?

BAKER: This was one of the first problems we encountered. We decided to include the arrangers. To treat them as less creative than an "out-and-out" composer is a value judgment which we would like to avoid. Besides, you can't leave arrangers out when you're dealing with Black music.

QUESTION: Is there any provision made that might give credence to the assertion that Beethoven was of African lineage?

DE LERMA: Beethoven's ancestry was known to be Flemish. As a result, he might have some degree of a Spanish background, and that can open the doors for a lot. If enough were known about the roots of his family, some distant Black relative might emerge from the woodpile, but it would be very distant and hardly worth the trouble. I don't think Beethoven had a "Black experience." The question is highly speculative and based mostly, I'm afraid, on hope. There is enough talent without weakening the cause with an idea that, at best, is tenuous.

HINDERAS: I've been very interested in the background of Gottschalk because I have a very good friend, Jeanne Behrend, who has researched his background and who has edited his diary. I've always told Jeanne that I suspected Gottschalk had Negro blood. I suppose I really wanted to claim him because he was America's first concert pianist. At first she vehemently denied this, and then she became very interested in the subject. She talked with relatives of Gottschalk and examined his diaries, but in no instance could she really come up with a definitive answer. To an even greater extent, I think this is true with Beethoven.

MORRISON: I'm an elementary public school teacher from Indianapolis. I'm on a personal crusade with the boys and girls I teach, and I've had quite a lot of resistance. I'm so glad to be here and hear the things you have said, and I hope you will not stop at the college level. The elementary child needs this too. Many of our children are never exposed to the real Black music. I've been in some other seminars with some very astute professors in charge, and I got nothing from it. They admitted they didn't know the Negroes, the Black musicians who are composers. I really think we need to know. I think the Western approach has been overdone. We must admit that jazz is ours, it is American, and that it should be used and taught and appreciated. I hope a resumé of this meeting can be made available to the music departments of our school systems.

QUESTION: We are all from the Establishment, be it Black or White. It sounds to me as though you've been dealing rather exclusively with the producers of music. I happen to be interested in and in favor of the Black militancy in the country, and the inner-city consumer. Have you done anything with the people who are not erudite, who are not educated, who may be in a sense dropouts, who are really consuming and can give us perhaps a definition of what Black music is to them?

BAKER: This is a very valid point. Our present work, however, is the full identification of the producer of the music. Someone will have to consider your approach and all of its ramifications, but our approach now is to handle the producers.

DILLARD: I'm wondering how we're going to get down this information to the ghetto, for example, or in the Negro church. These are the persons who will use the music, and you have suggested to reach them through the teachers. I say that too. I try to get my students to understand that we are here talking about this thing, but it's no good unless we are going to get at that person down there, those out there, who are interested in music that is not even approaching what we are talking about this morning. We had a concert pianist at our university who spoke on Black music. I'm still asking myself if the students at our college really got the point. There was about 40 of 1,400 there, and the rest don't give a hoot about this thing you're talking about.

BAKER: Well, I think that when you're dealing with any kind of document that purports to do a job, you almost have to restrict the type of job it's going to do and adhere to whatever rules you've set up. Ours, just now, is to locate Black composers. If we try to do more than that now, we'll fail. There are plans afoot related to the inner-city, not within the scope of this book, in which we plan to be active. But don't think our committee plans to solve all Black music problems. We're working with an institution which has charged us with certain tasks to which Indiana University can properly relate. There are enough problems for all of you to have your own committees.

SMITH: I'm concerned about the fragmentation which exists in the schools, not to mention the lack of relationship between courses and the real world. Things are broken down to such an extent that a student might take theory classes, harmony classes, ear training classes, and what have you, and make no relationship between these subjects, which are actually indivisible. If a piano teacher asks his student a question about the form of a work he is studying, he may very possibly wonder why part of his form and analysis class is being brought into his piano lessons. If they don't have the connections made within that limited area, how can they care for the wider areas? Regardless of what one might think of the current soul musicians, these students should be made to understand the very many points of relationship between products of James Brown and those of Mozart, or Schönberg. There are many concrete points of relationship. In too many cases, the faculty is deficient in this knowledge. I would like to make another point about the Society of Black Composers. This is a group of men with widely divergent attitudes. When Mr. Baker was reading the aims of that organization, I was able to identify the person who wrote it though his language. He may not reflect the feelings of some men in the group, but that's not important. What is valuable is that they have gotten together with the idea of disseminating the music, of performing it, of using the Black musicians that are very active in New York. One aspect of this is to demonstrate that there is a large pool of very proficient Negro performers in that city. And our programs make no distinction in terms of style. A typical program might have music by Howard Swanson, Ulysses Kay, Ornette Coleman and Joe Chambers.

⬤ Two particular ideas have been presented in this discussion which might merit attention. Although peripheral areas may arise later, I can see value in two research projects, both with distinctly social overtones. First is the matter which Dr. Fuller brought up, supplemented by Mr. Hammond. There have been those periods when, almost in spurts, Black freedom and power seemed about to break forth. Did these come about because of the specific personalities involved? Does the reason rest to any extent in White patronage or support? In music, what role did the American Federation of Musicians (or, rather, the locals) play? Reference might be made to the comments of Dr. Anderson which open the panel discussion in Chapter 6, particularly his mention of Shirley Graham's article. We might even be able to chart the degree of interest in Black culture through a graphic representation of years when the major monographs appeared, which are now being reprinted at such a rate that this fact alone signals the intensity of today's interests.

The second topic would be more difficult to treat. An unidentified questioner, followed in part by the problem raised by Professor Dillard, focusses attention on the consumer of music. We in music have fallen heirs to a rather unfortunate situation: Those who want music are expected to come to us; we do not go to them. Recorded music and that which is on the radio or television does reach them more easily, but we would have a difficult time trying to develop really new audiences if we continue thinking the world of opera, chamber music or the symphony orchestra is so superb that young adults from the ghetto are saving their money so they can manage an occasional concert. I suspect that the people who go to concerts might look on the experience as a necessary or valuable part of their lives, but no new audiences are being created. Part of this is due, of course, to the matter that David Baker pointed out, that the orchestra is an anachronism. Such a statement has enough evidence for support without additional documentation, despite the fact that we may still hold Mozart and Brahms, Monteverdi and Schubert, Bach and Mahler, all close to our hearts. We can also have warm devotion for Chaucer and Shakespeare, but the museum aspects of their cultures come into focus when we think properly of our own century. Natalie Hinderas has shown[5] there is hope for Mozart and Beethoven in the ghetto, but we are not all properly blessed with people of her ability and imagination. In effect, this is a real challenge to education, to find out first of all why the musically uneducated likes music, and I mean the inner-city consumer. What qualities in rhythm, melody or harmony attract him, and what psychological effects do these produce? The answer can provide more than a mere study. It can alert composers and performers to factors which can contribute to their desire to communicate. Perhaps we have all been guilty of living too securely in our ivory tower, not really understanding exactly what we have been doing. Of course, it would come as a shock to the academic world if it should be discovered that a de-intellectualization of music would actually elevate it.

---

[5] Quoted in *American musical digest* (New York), v.1, no.6, p.6.

3. Some Curricular and Philosophical Challenges from Black Music[1]

Let us admit without hesitation that less is generally known and taught about music composed by Blacks than any aspect of non-Oriental music. The information is lacking among public school teachers, college professors, chamber music coaches, musicologists, recitalists and conductors, and there has not been too much help coming from the publishers, jobbers or librarians. If we go to ethnic scholars we can secure some assistance, but far from enough to provide us with sufficient data to sketch even a historical outline of any substance, much less to develop a syllabus or plan a concert.

The doctoral student at his qualifying examinations may be ready to discuss any aspect of Greek theory, renaissance performance practice, song settings of Goethe texts, style characteristics of French music, eighteenth-century concerts in London, or serial techniques in late Stravinsky, but if you ask him merely to name five Black composers, living or dead, he will be at a loss. Not to name titles of their works, mind you. Not to whistle a tune from any of these compositions. And, if you asked such an outlandish question, your colleagues on the committee would be horrified. Why?

There may be a music educator from the inner city more concerned getting his students to listen to the *Peer Gynt suite*, the *Messiah*, or *1812* than developing their cultural awareness through Duke Ellington, James Brown or T. J. Anderson.

Perhaps we can find a student who wishes to write a term paper or a dissertation on Scott Joplin, but can we find a teacher who would encourage him? Can we find one who can guide the student over the bibliographic and subject complications of such a project?

If we want to include nineteenth-century Italian art songs in a program,

[1]This chapter, in its earlier versions, has been read before the 1970 winter meeting of the Music Library Association in Toronto, the Music Educators National Conference meeting in Chicago, and at a symposium on Black music held in Geneva, New York, at the Hobart and William Smith Colleges.

we know already some of the literature or certain reference books which can help. If we have trouble finding publications, we can call on the publisher or dealer for assistance, and there is, incidentally, a substantial increase in expertise within these circles. But if the songs we are after are by Black Americans, all of these resources become subjected to great strain. Can your librarian help any better?

Why is there such a huge hiatus in this area, without which no definition of American music is accurate? It is easier to find music by Gossec or Elgar than it is to find works of William Grant Still, Arthur Cunningham or John Carter.

We have passed the period when racial identification was regarded as inconsequential. Twenty years ago in some circles, it was not thought polite or important to mention "Colored" or "Negro" when speaking to a Black citizen. Of course, this was in liberal communities where the races had some degree of reason to communiciate; segregationists had no qualms about reference to race. Twenty years ago, the liberal was regarded as a good man. We now know that his type of liberalism had some shortcomings. He was a sort of great White father, too noble to be prejudiced, too tolerant to discriminate, and too color-blind to notice that the world was not always as white as he was.

Things have changed, but that liberal may now be your president, your conductor, your senator, your dean, your principal. He is the same as he was two decades ago, but the world is not. He is somewhat like the college graduate of 1950, who knew that Bartók was a contemporary composer who had been dead only five years. He still thinks the same way, despite the fact that Bartók is as old now as Ravel was then. A retired choral director told me just a few years ago that he could not understand what was wrong with high school students today. His efforts to produce *H. M. S. Pinafore* in a school recently failed, yet his production in 1924 was an extraordinary success. The older liberal has this same kind of problem. He might have thought himself radical at one time, and freed himself therefore from the obligation to renew approaches constantly, to reevaluate the present almost daily.

Tell him you want to teach a course in Black music. He may say, "Your interest in Negro music is racism in reverse." He is afraid to say Black because he thinks of panthers and power, and because he was conditioned like so many Blacks to think black is not a complimentary color. Speak to him about isolating Danish operas, Polish string quartets, or even Nigerian folksongs, and he will be more receptive. But when you speak Black, you are talking about his country, his society, his century. The liberal is one who will admit all men to his society, but to *his* society, and on *his* terms. This is not integration, it is unconditional surrender. No man should have to sell his birthright or cultural heritage to be accepted. A world must have room for all cultures, and their existence and the pride of their practitioners must stimulate an interplay that makes a society dynamic and positive, not subject to backlash or polarization, no matter who encourages this.

The liberal might as easily say, "What does it matter what race wrote it? If it is *good* music, that is enough." Then, because the music has not been published, performed or studied, it is no good? If the music is really not significant, who has made the evaluation? Where did he hear the works, where did he see the scores, where did he study the history? He is assuming, I guess, that right wins by its own virtue, without a champion, without a publisher, without a performance. Perhaps, if it has one, the problem of Black music is that it is out of the mainstream. But originality should be a merit. A society which lives in segregation develops its own culture. If that culture does not fit the liberal scheme, this should not make it inferior. On the contrary, and with aesthetics taking second place to the social importance of music, that makes it important.

"Why Black music? Why not purple music?" This question is often asked, although if the one who poses it has a better understanding of music history, he might ask, "Why not Irish music?" Well, of course: if one is teaching in an Irish ghetto (an interesting juxtaposition of words) the culture of that community cannot be overlooked. In this circumstance, Irish music becomes very relevant.

It might also be said that Black music belongs to ethnomusicology, but one of my points is that this discipline should not be removed from the history-literature-musicology complex. Even if it is to remain distinct, and we admit that a large amount of social music can fit there, we must confess that Hale Smith or George Walker fits in ethnic studies about as comfortably as does Donizetti.

I have recently returned from an extensive trip in Europe. As I travelled through Germany in particular, I could not help but think of the rich history so many of these cities have witnessed: Hamburg, Munich, Cologne, Frankfurt, Bonn, Darmstadt. To admit humility is not to admit sentimentality, but even this can be allowed a Latin. And then a heretical thought came to mind. Do I, my colleagues and our students know these cities and their composers so well because of *Musikwissenschaft* (note, I did not say musicology), or because they really are so important? Had musicology developed in Africa, would those cities be obscure, and would we then know the musical histories of Nairobi, Nakuru, Lusaka, Kampala and Luanda? Has our attention been geographically oriented by a kind of innocent racism, or is music finally and completely German, or European? These are the composers we know, the music we study and perform. From these works come our techniques of analysis, of notation, and our definition of our art. Do we therefore accept only those non-European works which conform to our vast network of preconceptions? Then let us not pretend to be international. Let us admit that our knowledge is either prejudicial or parochial. Black America is going to change this; this is part of the Black man's burden, and we do not always have to look to the militant Blacks to see evidence of this change.

Take, for example, the first edition of the American Musicological Society's *Guidelines for the Doctor of Philosophy Degree in Musicology*, issued in December of 1969. The society's Committee on Curriculum and Accreditation, which drew up the document, was not in total accord. It was Alexander Ringer who posed the following challenge:

> While in full agreement that the musical event forms indeed the prime *object* of musicological study, I would add that the ultimate *objective* of musicology, as of all other humanistic fields of inquiry, must be a better understanding of man, gained in this case through in-depth investigation of the products of his musical imagination, past and present and wherever they may be found. In short, I am inclined to view the musicologist as a scholar whose specific concern with music enhances human knowledge at large and, in so doing, ensures continuing "relevance" of a field that has by and large been characterized by an unusually large degree of esotericism.

Dr. Ringer's sentiments suggest in my mind that he is what might be termed a "soul musicologist."

We simply must admit that Black music belongs in the curriculum now, and not just in predominately Black schools or in graduate musicology courses, either. This is an important and vital aspect of American culture, just as the impact of the Black experience is a major element in any social definition of the United States. This music belongs in undergraduate courses and, if it is not incorporated within the pre-college music studies, we will have White students who lack formal contact with dynamic musical ideas, and Blacks who, perhaps unaware of the extraordinary musical genius of their race, will forsake a potential career.

The standard network of classes and credits, in the eyes of the Blacks, gives total attention to White western music. In college, this study ends not with a bachelor of music degree, but with a bachelor of White music. The textbooks, the aesthetic concepts, the lectures, the examples, the analytical techniques all justify this viewpoint. We must admit without hesitation that such course work presents a very constricted and confining picture of music, its means and its goals. Redefinitions came about because of John Cage, not jazz, not African tribal music, not ghetto music. The school says to the Black student, "We will admit you into our school to study our music. You may have deficiencies because you are, as we gently call it, culturally disadvantaged. You do not know about four-part writing or Roman-numeral analysis, you do not know about this White composer or that, and you make very strange sounds on your saxophone. Of course, it is *our* music you will study because your music is not really that important: you know, spirituals and jazz and things like that."

How remarkable it is that the musical accomplishments of the Blacks can be simply stated, and let us confess they are often so glibly summarized. This is all the more surprising when the Blacks themselves admit they do not fully know their cultural heritage, *which is exactly why they want to study it in an educational institution.* Demonstrations, ultimatums and sit-ins may manifest traditional sophomorisms, but they prove the ardor of the students' faith in the colleges, fired up to desperate measures by extraordinary and multi-faceted frustrations. Within the *Statement of Basic Aims and Objectives of the Organization of Afro-American Unity*,[2] it is said that "our culture and our history are as old as man himself and yet we know almost nothing of it. We must capture our heritage and our identity if we are ever to liberate ourselves from the bonds of white supremacy." Stokely Carmichael and Charles Hamilton, in *Black Power Now; The Politics of Liberation in America*[3] say that "African-American history means a long history, beginning on the continent of Africa, a history not taught in the standard textbooks of this country. It is absolutely essential that Black people know this history, that they know their cultural roots, that they develop an awareness of their cultural history." As first editor of *Crisis*, the journal of the National Association for the Advancement of Colored People, W. E. B. DuBois—one of the great minds of this century—made a point of citing as many of the cultural accomplishments of his people as he

---

[2] Quoted by George Breitman in *The last year of Malcolm X; the evolution of a revolutionary*, New York: Schocken Books, 1968, p.111.

[3] Harmondsworth (Eng.): Penguin Books, 1969, p.52.

could find, a search sources (not potentials) made difficult at the start of this century. The passionate thirst for this knowledge is present with almost any Black American, and the need for it by White America is critical.

The new president of Hunter College, Mrs. Jacqueline Wexler, has taken a stand on this related to the question of an open admissions policy. In her interview with *Time*,[4] she stated that discrimination on the basis of prior preparation is tantamount to economic discrimination, that the poor and less culturally refined should be taught as eagerly as the deaf or blind. And when she refers to "cultural deprivation" she means not only Blacks and Puerto Ricans, but Whites who have not had the opportunity to learn about non-Western culture. The lack of information about any culture is tragic, both to the people that culture has produced, and to those whom it might not have directly touched, but educators must know that James Baldwin was right when, in *The Fire Next Time*, he said "White Americans have supposed 'Europe' and 'civilization' to be synonyms—which they are not—and have been distrustful of other standards and other sources of vitality."[5]

The new generation is forcing reevaluations, and the Blacks are in the vanguard. University administrators and music supervisors are asking themselves now why certain courses are being offered. What really justifies the curricular structures we all know so well—perhaps, from habit, too well? Tradition and social need are major factors, possibly not always distinct, but let us note that Washington and Newark are now mostly Black populated, that more than one-third of the citizens of Detroit, Baltimore, Cleveland and St. Louis are Black, and that at least a quarter of the residents of Oakland, Cincinnati, Philadelphia and Chicago are of this race. Sixty-five percent of Black America lives in the urban centers. During the last decade, the White population of these cities fell by 2.1 million, and that of the Blacks rose by 2.6 million. It seems social need may be very strong, right now, in the largest cities of the United States. For these majorities, as well as the White minorities, Black music may presently be more significant that the polyphonic Lied, a Sousa march, or the *Dance of the Hours*. Does that sound like heresy?

The source has been lost but, at a conference which took place within the past two years, a White participant made some comments which might be even more heretical:

---

[4] "The lady is not for drowning," v.95, no. 3 (January 19, 1970) p.51.

[5] Middlesex (Eng.): Penguin Books, 1965, p.80.

I have no sympathy for those administrators or teachers who are opposing such things as Afro-studies programs on the undergraduate level; these administrators and teachers have watched for four decades the corruption of the university ideal by the admission of courses which are far inferior intellectually and culturally to anything proposed for Black students. It is certainly duplicity—or maybe racism—for these same administrators who will allow courses, even majors and minors, in such sub-intellectual—I would say anti-intellectual—fields as 'education' to refuse absolutely *anything* which can be verbalized into the curriculum.

When the teacher has administrative approval to begin instruction in Black music, he faces the problem of bibliography. Perhaps the appendices in this book will begin to fill that need. There are other resource projects undertaken which might help. My bibliography, *The Black-American Musical Heritage* was published in the summer of 1969 by the Midwest Chapter of the Music Library Association.[6] The national offices of this society, aware that the publication was totally exhausted within two weeks, is now preparing a second edition which may be available before 1971. Almost 700 titles are included in this bibliography. Subsequent research has presently raised that total to 2,000 entries, which may be doubled before the third edition is ready for publication. These materials don't have to be used just by people working in Black music; there is good material for traditional areas of study.

With a small contribution from the Black Music Committee, Professor Ernest Dyson (Federal City College) is planning an extensive discography on all Black music, including "jazz, spirituals, and things like that."

Finding scores by Black composers is not so easy. There is the customary difficulty of not knowing who publishes what if, indeed, a specific title or composer is known. An extensive biographic bibliography is being developed by the Black Music Committee at Indiana University. It is our hope that this book will facilitate other library acquisition programs, research, concert and teaching programs. Royalties from the sale of this book, by the way, will be immediately directed into a special scholarship for Black students in music at Indiana University, where the Music Library is well on its way to owning everything published by or about a Black composer.

A sample of the composers included will give an idea of the extent of Black creativity. Perhaps we already know about the Chevalier de Saint-Georges, who

---

[6] Kent (Ohio): Kent State University, School of Library Science, 1969 (Explorations in music librarianship, 3).

was of distinct influence on the history of the violin sonata in the eighteenth century, even if only one work of his has been reprinted in the past two hundred years, and we may know of George Bridgetower for whom Beethoven wrote the *Kreuzter Sonata*. The classic figures should not be unknown: Samuel Coleridge-Taylor, William Dawson, William Grant Still, Robert Nathaniel Dett, Clarence Cameron White, Harry Burleigh. Then there are the younger established figures, such as Ulysses Kay, Howard Swanson, Olly Wilson, Hale Smith, T. J. Anderson, Julia Perry, and the jazz or jazz-influenced composers whose names are familiar: John Lewis, J. J. Johnson, George Russell, Duke Ellington, John Coltrane, but what about Blind Tom Bethune (as remarkable a prodigy as music has known), Chuck Berry (to whom the Beatles pay hommage), Charles Bell (a particularly articulate and significant young man), James Weldon Johnson (a founder of the National Association for the Advancement of Colored People, and an unquestionably brilliant intellect), Akim Euba and Fela Sowanda (both contemporary figures from Africa), Lena McLin (a warm and bright light from Chicago's school system), Carman Moore (who is also music critic of the *Village Voice*), Benjamin Patterson (former president of the Society of Black Composers), Amadeo Roldán (one of the most important composers in Cuba's musical history), George Walker (an extraordinarily accomplished pianist and composer), and Roque Cordero (Panama's leading composer). You know of David Baker, whose non-jazz works are in the repertoires of the Berkshire String Quartet, Josef Gingold, and János Starker?

And there are surprises: Langston Hughes (better known as a poet), the actor Stepin Fetchit, *Life*'s photographer Gordon Parks, Dubose Heyward (who wrote the play *Porgy*) and Jester Hairston (from the cast of radio's *Amos and Andy*). Not only can we find tunes like *I'm Just Wild about Harry, Carry me Back to Old Virginie, I'll be Glad When You're Dead You Rascal You, When the Lights Come on Again All Over the World* and *One of These Days You're Gonna Miss Me Honey*, there is electronic music, serial music, piano concertos, operas, near-East jazz. It is not as simple as "jazz and spirituals and things like that," even though these are valid areas for study. There are teaching pieces for piano, songs for children's voices, band music for the high schools, chance music—even works for sopranos and frogs, or for the audience alone. And these composers generally insist that their creations are Black, that this music expresses the Black existence.

But what is all this? Is it merely paying attention to a (rather strong) minority whose past bears, we all know, evidence of white America's greatest shame and whose present state is often handicapped by a continuation of this germ? Far more than this. This music is not of that type of nationalism which escorts a foreign tourist around, showing him the things he wants to see. Particularly with the new composer, it can be music very alien to western concepts (but, we will observe, if things move as they have in the past, it will not be long before many Whites follow the cleared paths as has been their habit, forcing the Blacks to break new trails for their identity). I do not suggest that the entire avant-garde movement was born in the ghetto, because the traditional vanguard (if such a combination of terms can exist) had little knowledge of Black music, but there is no doubt but what the music of the Blacks is barometric.

As "mainstream" music and music teaching becomes more aware of this, we should observe changes in ideas, in techniques and in materials. New personalities will emerge from the Blacks, not just in areas where they have been active in the past, but in positions of leadership: scholars, conductors, deans, principals, supervisors. Music will move off the nineteenth-century concert stage, and the bands will leave the football field so that music can be presented where the people are. There will be less emphasis on the European concepts of form, melody and instrumentation. The effect of this, subject to the rate of influence, can be enormous on the teaching profession. Ethnomusicology will become more popular and will be forced to examine its materials more as real music and less as artifacts of exotic cultures. Educators will have to acknowledge they have not been developing what Franz Fanton called the "entire, universal man," for the Black sentiment is not pro-Black, but pro-individual; the focus will be on people, not on forms. We will see long hair, for example, as a departure from the tradition, but the choice of the indivudal. Abstractions of nationalism will give way to basic, universal morality, rather than the reverse. Schools will become personalized and will stimulate the potentials of the individual, rather than perpetuate their own standards.

This in effect is a revolution. It is being sponsored by people who might not all have degrees, but whose innate wisdom and whose experience are posing the challenge. Equally important, they are being followed by the prophetic minority of our generation and the potential leaders of a younger group. These trends need more than sympathy from the established figures. The channels we understand must be kept flexible and open, not out of fear, but because our very role is not compatible with regressive sentiments. And for once, music is forced to the forefront.

The spirit of this challenge was outlined by John A. Killens in *Black Man's*

Burden[7] who said, "The American Negro can be the bridge between the West and Africa-Asia. We Black Americans can serve as a bridge to mutual understanding . . . To rid the world of 'niggers' is the Black man's burden, human reconstruction is the grand objective."

_____

[7]New York: Trident Press, 1965, p.176.

4. *Black Music in Church and School*

Lena McLin

● Mrs. Lena McLin is a member of the faculty at Chicago's Kenwood High School. She is also exceptionally active as a church musician and in opera. When I heard the warm reports from Professors Baker and Caswell, I knew we had to secure her for the seminar. My reason was mostly, I'm afraid, selfish. It is next to impossible to communicate with her by mail. She openly admitted that she rarely has time to read letters sent to her. Most of our pre-seminar contacts, then, were by phone. The last time I spoke to her, she had twenty-two days to write a libretto, compose the music, and produce an opera that was already scheduled. I told her it sounded like *Don Giovanni* or *La clemenza di Tito*, but she is embarrassed by any suggestion that she is gifted. Meanwhile, of course, she continues to write vital music, so fast that she could never account for her *opera omnia* for even one year.

Her visit to Bloomington was enhanced by the presence of her chorus and several student composers, sent as a courtesy of Don Minaglia, supervisor of music for Chicago's public schools. The talent she has developed in these students is really exceptional, and it is very encouraging to find someone so fully dedicated to education, whose basic orientation is totally social.

McLIN: In our school, as in other systems, we are very concerned with teaching and bringing to the forefront the contribution of the American Black man. We do not wish to instill any hostility because of past injustice; we want to build now, for the future, so we have to be careful about how the materials are presented. I think it is the duty of any public school teacher to make a presentation in a manner that creates not an emotional resentment, but that makes a contribution. This is what we've tried to do at Kenwood.

Our method of teaching the humanities course is not by isolated facts. We don't believe in reports on Beethoven just for that sake alone. That's dull and boring, and such routine tasks are killing the idea of education. People who do that are really way back. We do think, however, that young people need to know what has happened, so when we talk about Beethoven, we don't overlook Bridgetower. We try to correlate *our* history this way. And we don't overlook anyone: we may start with James Brown, Aretha Franklin, or Barbra Streisand. It doesn't matter where we start. What does matter is how we present to young people the unknown contribution of Black people.

It isn't always easy. We don't have enough recordings of our music. We don't have adequate representation in publication. William Grant Still, one of our most prolific and dynamic composers, has a very beautiful work, *And They Lynched Him on a Tree*, which is very hard to find. Some young person who reads about Dr. Still and would like to hear this work is frustrated.

So I thought of a little idea for presenting Black history to students through music. The idea of this particular example is flexible, and I really would like for some of you to use it if you like. You can add as many people as you wish. If you're in a particular location and an outstanding Black leader is there you would like to include, this can be done in the narration. The work is called "I'm somebody, I am." The poem is by William Holmes Bordis. I wrote the music. This can be performed in costume if you wish, so that one of the singers is dressed like the person he is to represent.

I'M SOMEBODY, I AM *(excerpt)*   *by* Lena Johnson McLin[1]

---

[1] The text employed in this excerpt is by the composer. Formal publication of the entire composition is pending.

NARRATOR (with deep expression): I'm a poet laureate in Gwendolyn Brooks; I'm a fighter for rights in Jesse Jackson and Ralph Abernathy; I'm a composer in Nathaniel Dett, William Grant Still, Ulysses Kay, and Margaret Bonds;

I'm Mr. Football in Gale Sayers; I'm a dancer, singer, and Soul Sister in Aretha Franklin; I'm a world famous soprano, who opened the new Metropolitan Opera House in an opera written especially for my voice, in Leontyne Price;

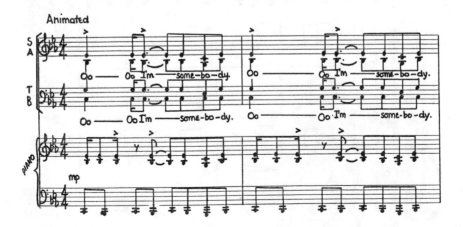

I'm the little man who walked with the leader of leaders, Dr. Martin Luther King, Jr.! (in loud voice) I'm somebody, I am!

We feel that in this we are really creating, we are telling history. Also, we are creating a feeling of dignity in our status, and we're not painting a one-sided picture. You see, we're like everybody else, we're some of everything. Everything that's here, we are that.

In our program at Kenwood, and in the Chicago high schools, we have a course called "music major." This is a course in which we approach everything creatively. And, since I like to dabble around with composing, I have my students dabbling around with it. Out of this we may find some really fine talent, but we don't always get all of the people we want. Anyway, the students are required to write a composition as their final examination. This gets them personally involved in the problems of the creator, in trying to find the materials of music which will express their own individual needs.

These are a few of the ideas I think teachers need to think about in their instruction.

The other part of my life is centered around the church, and this means gospel songs. Musicians would find it very difficult to get a church job that doesn't involve the gospel choir, even in the most prominent Black churches. As serious musicians, we have to face this fact.

Secondly, we have to do something to record this idiom, to document those things in performance which notation can't indicate, or doesn't. We certainly should have some uniform way of putting it down. It shouldn't be like the period into the middle of the nineteenth century when there was no recording of the tremendous folk music of the Black man. I know that some of us avoid the gospel, thinking it makes us look small. This is the same thing the spiritual went through, but it managed to survive the disdain and disrespect of the second generations. I think Mr. James Brown and Miss Aretha Franklin have captured very vividly and very beautifully what goes on in some of our churches, and I think too that the day has come where we ought to stop being ashamed of any folk contributions!

The gospel song started about the time of Ma Rainey and Thomas Dorsey, entering the churches about then. I try to make clear to young people and to church people some rather simple definitions. A spiritual is a folk song, originated by the Black American, which must have a *personal* relationship with the deity. When I sing *Sometimes I Feel Like a Motherless Child*, this is a spiritual. I said the spiritual is also a folk song. It's been handed down from generation to generation, and it is still with us.

Many people don't talk about the jubilee because everything that comes off the press is called a spiritual, but there is a difference. The jubilee does not express a personal relationship. *Ezekiel Saw the Wheel* is a jubilee.

Gospel songs are composed, but the singer expresses this music in a personal style, free, unrestricted in any way. The singer may add or take away (you can't do that with the spiritual), but the basic line remains the same. There are three types of spirituals: the short, syncopated, segmented type (like *Little Lamb, Little Lamb*), the call and response form (such as *Have You Got Religion?*) and the long narrative type (like *Deep River*), but there is only one kind of gospel song. Whether it is narrative, call and response or segmented, it depends on the ability of the singer to interpret, to "worry" the notes. It can't be sung straight. That's not living the experience.

These, then, are my ideas about the obligations we have in teaching and in the churches. Music and our history must be presented to the young people so they have a part of it, and so that the part they have is that portion which will be a foundation for the future. And that musical history which we have in our churches must be preserved and respected.

● The seminar was not designed foremost as a conference which would lend itself to publication. Despite that fact, many of the talks and panel discussions can be represented in this manner. At the same time, oral tradition meaning what it does to Black arts obligates editing out some of the spontaneity of the discussions, and it is not possible to represent here the sounds of Mrs. McLin's music, or the sound of her students' excellent voices.

A greater problem exists with respect to David Baker's talk on "Liturgical uses of jazz," which was rich with musical illustrations. In summary, he illustrated how the church has begun to accept the music of the people, based to some extent on its willingness to enjoy architectural and technological advantages of recent times. Through *contrafacta*, however, an eternal sacred or secular style never really existed. Like Luther, he pleaded for the church to make room for music of the people, no matter in what form the style was cast.

His first illustration was of Joseph Kyagambiddwa's African oratorio, *The Martyrs of Uganda*, a work which was performed for the first time in Rome in 1964, in conjunction with the sanctification of these late nineteenth-century martyrs. The composer, a native of Uganda (born in 1923), created the work in the tradition of African music.

His second example came from his own *Lutheran Mass*, followed by excerpts from his *22nd Psalm*, and *The Beatitudes*, as well as a portion of his *Black America*. He apologized for using his own works to illustrate his talk, saying that they do not represent the best of the genre, but he was using them "because I have access to them, and besides, I like 'em."

Concluding his talk were two works by Saul Edwards, from Indianapolis, *This Shall Be a Sign*, and *The Baby King*.

5. An Experience in Jazz History

John Hammond

● John Hammond is one of the most refreshing personalities in the music business. He is also, regardless of his modesty, one of the most powerful. Because he has been very closely allied with the history of jazz for more than forty years, he has maintained a personal and working relationship with most of the major Black jazzmen, from Bessie Smith through Aretha Franklin. Those at the seminar were stunned to realize the very major role he has played in jazz history, yet his facinating talk does not cover half the names. Persons wishing more information should consult Ernest F. Dyson's article, "The man who discovered everybody" in the February 1 (1970) issue of the *Washington Post* (p.K1-2).

HAMMOND: I think it's wonderful that Indiana University's School of Music has had this Black music conference because it's practically the first one that I've ever heard of, and I've been in this business making records since 1931. That's 38 years. The role of the Black musician has been overlooked far too long. It is high time that educators and interested persons get together to discuss the matters and see what can be done.

I would like to talk a little bit about the history of jazz, its roots and the society from which it emerged, and how I believe that records serve the real history of jazz since 1917.

The general public first learned about jazz in a rather roundabout way. Jazz recordings were put out by Victor and Columbia in 1917 by the Original Dixieland Jazz Band, a group of New Orleans musicians with rather rigid rules. There wasn't really much improvisation in this, but at least the music was not written and there was a certain amount of excitement. It was a small group which came to New York from New Orleans in 1917. Although it had been in existence down there before, mainly with wonderful Black musicians like Buddy Bolden, King Oliver and various others, it was the Whites, as usual, who stole the thunder of the Negro musician and were the first to perform it on records. It's true that a year or so before, W. C. Handy had gotten together a band for Columbia playing *St. Louis Blues* and *Memphis Blues* and some of his other things, but all this music was written. There wasn't a note of improvisation in it, and it really was a perversion of what we think of and know of as jazz.

The roots of jazz probably go back to the late nineteenth century when ragtime was popular. There was a wonderful composer from Missouri, Scott Joplin. And there was also an extraordinary Black piano player who was born in 1883, Eubie Blake. I can talk about Eubie because I've just made a two-record album of works, some of which he wrote as early as 1895. He's still an active composer. He's probably the best stride piano player alive today, and I was astounded to find that one of the things he recorded was a *Charleston Rag* which he had composed in 1896. He also composed many rags before Scott Joplin's *Maple Leaf Rag* of 1899. So ragtime is one of the roots. Blues certainly was one of the most important foundations of jazz and, as we know from listening to pop music, rock and roll and R & B, blues is now enjoying a really sensational renaissance.

There is of course also church music, and I am thinking of gospels, which weren't always called such. I guess the jubilees go back on records to 1896 when the Fisk Jubilee Singers made a tour in Europe and then came back and recorded on those old round cylinders about twenty selections which had been a sensation in London, Paris and Berlin. But the general public never heard very much about the jubilee. They knew about spirituals from the watered-down arranged versions of Negro sacred music that was performed by great concert artists, including Roland Hayes (an extraordinary singer, still alive, well in his eighties).

I first became interested in jazz in the early 20's. I was born in 1910, so I'd say maybe the first jazz musicians I heard live were from around 1922 and 1923. Ironically, I didn't hear those musicians in New York, because there was no jazz that an eleven or twelve-year-old kid could hear there. I was on a trip to London in 1923 with my family and there were two things which happened in a place called Lyon's Corner House. They had an American orchestra, and within this was a band called The Georgians which may have been the most outstanding small White jazz band that had been assembled up to that time. Jimmy Dorsey was in it, for example. Every afternoon at five you would have your ice cream sodas or tea, or whatever they served, and listen to a forty-five minute concert of improvised jazz. That was the first time I heard jazz, and it changed my life.

At the same time there was a Negro show (they didn't call it Black in those days) called *From Dixie to Broadway* that was playing at the London Pavillion. Since they had matinées I was able to sneak away from my family and see Florence Mills and hear a rather sensational pit band which had in it on baritone and soprano saxophone Sidney Bechet.

When I got back to America, I started looking around record shops for Negro jazz and I found to my horror that the places I went, the record stores in downtown New York, didn't stock them because in those days records were made by markets. There was a popular market and in 1920 the record business found out there was a Negro market. It was then that the Okeh Record Company put out a blues record by a singer from Baltimore, Mamie Smith. Bechet was on those first records, but you couldn't get them in downtown New York. You had to go up to Harlem or the various Black ghettos in other boroughs of New York before you could even listen to such a record. Well, I was 12 and I had no fears, so I started going around to these stores. I guess the two most influential records as far as my life goes came out in 1923. One was by a pianist named James P. Johnson, who had put out a double-faced record with *Worried and Lonesome Blues*, and on the other side was *Weeping Blues*. This was the first time I'd ever heard an instrumental blues, played in this instance by one of the most extraordinary pianists who ever lived. He was Fats Waller's teacher and perhaps in his heyday every bit as good both a composer and pianist as Fats was. In that same year, Bessie Smith recorded a record called *Reckless Blues*, backed by *St. Louis Blues*. I liked Bessie, although I couldn't quite understand an earthy blues shouter at the age of 12, but I sure could understand the trumpet obbligato which was played by a man I'd never heard of—Louis Armstrong. I guess it was the next year that Louis Armstrong started recording under his own name with a small Chicago band, the Savoy Five. Then, in 1924, he had come for a while to join the Fletcher Henderson orchestra in New York. So the first year you can hear Black improvised jazz on records is 1920.

Okeh had the field to itself for the first three years, and then Columbia (owned by the Columbia Gramophone Company in England) started with Bessie Smith, who was found singing in Selma, Alabama, by one of their scouts. Although her records were never sold in White stores, the sales were more than a half-million. For those days, this was a tremendous sale. The first Bessie Smith records came off for 85c, and then the subsequent ones were 75c, and that was a lot of money for the Black community then. But Bessie reached them completely. She was the complete artist. I was lucky enough to record her finally in 1933. Of all the people I've ever recorded, I suppose she gave me more of a thrill. She was an extraordinary artist, and if jazz is ever to be studied, the 160 sides she made for Columbia (all of which are going to be released within the next year) probably will be the best example of what jazz is really all about. Bessie had a huge and powerful voice, with no need for microphones when they were available. She captured an audience both with her soul and her volume. She was enough of a musician that she worked as an ensemble artist with some of the greatest musicians that ever recorded—people like Coleman Hawkins, Joe Smith (her favorite trumpet player, including Louis Armstrong), and Fletcher Henderson. Luckily, Henderson was replaced by James P. Johnson who usually worked by himself. Jimmy was an extraordinary artist. His records, I'm happy to say, are still on the market.

When I first became interested in jazz, there was no such thing as integration. There were very few places where the White public went, where Negro musicians could be heard. We had a completely segregated society in those days, just as segregated in New York as it was in the South. Once in a while those bars were broken. There was a hall in New York called the Roseland Ballroom which would bring in bands like McKinney's Cotton Pickers for the White dancing public, but it was strictly a White public. Negroes were barred as customers. Even the very posh Harlem night clubs and those in Chicago discouraged Negro patronage, even in the heart of the ghetto. The Cotton Club in New York, where Duke Ellington, Cab Calloway, Jimmie Lunceford and the Blue Rhythm Band made their fame, had an exclusively White audience, although everyone else but the owners were Black. It was very rough for a Negro musician to make even a quarterway decent living in those days.

At an earlier session I brought up the fact that before 1920 the Negro musician was actually better off than after 1920 because the Negro musicians in New York had their own club, the Clef Club, in which James P. Johnson, Clarence Williams and other old timers were the guiding forces. These musicians had a lot of work, although they may have worked for very little, but I know that all the society parties given around World War I in New York were played by what even the square society folks thought were the best musicians, and those best musicians were always Black. When the American Federation of Musicians formed Local 802, the situation changed. I don't know if it was conscious or not, but the White musicians got a lot of the jobs the Blacks held before, and it was very hard for the Black musicians to get back into that market.

I mentioned that Florenz Ziegfield had several of the great Black arrangers, and that the conductor of his band was Black. That was soon changed, however. One of the places where Black musicians could get work was in the burlesque circuits, because burlesque—that very lowly but lively art—did have Black and White shows, and the White shows had the usual horrible five-piece pit band, but the Black shows carried their own musicians. It was terribly revealing for a kid like me to see the difference in the quality of the music. I can remember hearing Fletcher Henderson's band at Minsky's Republic Burlesque Theater in a Black and White show. It wasn't the whole band; the pit wasn't big enough for more than seven or eight men, but you heard some of the greatest music that's ever been heard in the theater. The result immediately made itself evident in the dancers who had been disspirited during the White section of the show, but who were really swinging in the Black section of the show.

The record business really served as one of the principal places of employ-ment for Negro jazz musicians. They didn't accompany the White artists, the Eddie Cantors, the Ted Lewises. They played for innumerable Black singers and comedians. Literally hundred of Black bands were recorded by the various record companies up until about 1928, when the record business started a very sharp decline. Other places where Black musicians were able to play were in the tent shows and carnivals that toured the South, the Northeast and the Mid-west. There was a Negro theater circuit called the Theater Bookers' Offices As-sociation which was known in around 48 theaters throughout the country where Negro shows were able to get practically a year's work. The economic and physical conditions in these theaters were pretty frightful. Among Ne-gro performers the TBOA was known as Tough On Black Asses, but this was a very large field where the Black musicians could work.

We have the history of jazz on records from the first dixieland band records, from the emergence of the so-called Chicago jazz style which came in the mid 20's, we have also that brief but horrible period when Paul Whiteman foisted something called symphonic jazz on the public. He did have some great solo-ists in his band, like Joe Venuti and Bix Biederbecke, but he had the world's worst rhythm section and horrible, creeching strings, playing the most appal-ling arrangements you could conceive of. But he lit onto something that did save his hide for a long time, and that something was called George Gershwin. Whiteman had commissioned Gershwin to write the *Rhapsody in Blue*. This was not really jazz, but it did have a little more rhythmic excitement than most extended works from those days, and it caused a sensation when it was intro-duced in New York's Aeolian Hall in the 20's. Fortunately it did not have too much effect on the history of jazz because, if it had had the success that Whiteman hoped for, I don't think we'd be having our conference here at Indiana University.

Much of the early part of jazz which fascinated me was the improvised jazz that was cut in Chicago. The most important of these figures was Louis Armstrong who had followed King Oliver up from New Orleans. But Louis, a marvelously ebullient guy, was such an unbelievable master of his instrument that poor old Joe Oliver, who was no slouch himself, finally had to take a back-seat. Then Louis pulled out to go to New York for a brief stay with Fletcher Henderson's band at the Club Alabam, then came back to Chicago and formed his own group. For a while he had his wife Lil Hardin play the piano. She was a ragtime pianist who always reminded me of Minnie Mouse's playing in the early Disney movies. But about 1927 a young guy from Pittsburgh went to Chicago, Earl Hines—probably the most sophisticated jazz musician of his time. He was a formidable technician, he was far more adventurous harmonically than any piano player prior to him, and he and Louis made some of the greatest jazz records of all. But Louis Armstrong, I think, was the first Black jazz musician who had an enormous impact on the White musicians of the day.

In New York, we had the Fletcher Henderson band, which was probably the greatest jazz band, certainly of the 20's, and very possibly of the 30's. This was a band of elite musicians, people like Buster Bailey, Coleman Hawkins, after 1928 John Kirby on bass, a wonderful drummer named Walter Johnson, and marvelous trombone players J. C. Higgenbottom and Sandy Williams. They were really a group of all-star musicians. Although they didn't do well financially, they were envied by all the musicians who did have security. Fletcher's home in New York for years was the Roseland Ballroom, and he played there opposite Jean Goldkette's band, a White band which got the money Henderson's band didn't. Fletcher was as much avant-garde in those days as a man like Archie Shepp is today, or Ornette Coleman. There were a lot of Fletcher Henderson records made in the 20's. Not all of these were good, because it was the publisher who controlled how tunes would be played.

Publishers would normally pay for the arrangements, and frequently pay to have their tunes recorded. They did not allow any liberties to be taken with those tunes; they had to be played straight. Since Fletcher did have a following from the White public, most of the records he made were of pop tunes. If you were lucky, there might be an eight-bar solo by Coleman Hawkins, or a small solo by Charlie Green or some of the other soloists, but they were pretty straight and not very exciting.

The big band era didn't actually start until the 30's. There were big bands on records, but they were pretty commercial on the whole. There's an exception to all this in Duke Ellington. He made his first records on an Indiana label in 1926. Those records, Gennett, can no longer be found anywhere. Very soon after that, he recorded for practically every label there was, well over a hundred. Duke is one of the people who really lasted in this business, and there aren't many of them. He was able to get into records because he was the property of a publisher, Irving and Jack Mills. Mills very often paid for these recording sessions because he published all of the tunes, so Duke could write his own ticket with a publisher who was also his manager. He started on records with an eight-piece band called The Washingtonians, a terribly important group in the history of jazz. Around 1928 or '29, it became a twelve-piece band (four rhythms, four reeds, and five brasses). It never swung like Fletcher Henderson's, but Ellington was a genius as a composer, and early things like *Mood Indigo, Black and Tan Fantasy, East St. Louis Toodle-do* are still some of the great works to be found in jazz. If you don't believe they have lasted, go to any of the dives in London or Paris or New York ,and you'll find strippers still dancing to a lot of Duke's early music.

The Black man never has really had his proper place in the business side of the record industry. There was a Black company formed by a publisher named Pace in New York, called the Black Swan label. Fletcher Henderson was his musical director, and they had some quite wonderful artists on it like Ethel Waters, the Henderson band, and various popular and blues singers of the day. But they didn't have the proper economic backing and the company folded within a year and a half. It was bought by a furniture company in Grafton, Wisconsin, called The New York Furniture Company, which made records primarily for the Negro market: race records on the Paramount label. For many years the Paramount label (which had no Black ownership, but almost exclusively Black artists) was a tremendous means for the employment of Black musicians. Some of the greatest early blues singers were on the Paramount label. As a matter of fact, Paramount's contribution to music was far greater than the Black Swan records because the Black Swan catalog contained almost nothing but pretty commercial things, aimed at the upper-class Negro public, rather than the ghetto public where the real sales of records would be. People like Ma Rainey, Ida Cox, Trixie Smith, and an extraordinary blind street singer by the name of Blind Lemon Jefferson were among the great artists on the Paramount label. Paramount died in 1932 unfortunately, but a lot of those records are being reissued on the Riverside label now and can be found if you hunt for them.

I guess until Motown started some eight or nine years ago, the Black Swan was the only record company entirely controlled by Black capital that had ever been launched. Now there are quite a few more.

The record business was a very important factor in preserving jazz, but in 1928 radio came in and this was the beginning of the end, it looked, for the record business—first the radio, then the 1929 financial collapse. Of about 70 or 80 active labels around 1923 and 1925, by 1931 there were exactly four left. Since jazz was extremely marginal as far as profitability was concerned even in those days, the first kind of records they stopped making was jazz. It might have been a permanent casualty if it hadn't been for the acceptance of jazz in England. It's quite amazing how much England fashions American tastes in music. In 1931, when no jazz was being recorded in this country, the three biggest labels in England all had very active jazz series of the great American jazz artists, both Black and White. They were just screaming for more products, and nobody would give it to them. This is more or less how I came into the record business.

I have a sister now married to Benny Goodman, but in those days she was the wife of a Tory member of the British Parliament. I used to go to England every year or two, and I became very friendly with people in the record business. In 1931, I became the American correspondent for the biggest record magazine in England, *The Gramophone*. I got to know a lot of the English musicians who were fascinated with American jazz. It was obvious to the British, listening to the records that were being put out, that the greatest musicians in the jazz world were the Black-American musicians, yet they couldn't read about what these musicians were doing because none of the U.S. publications—including the Negro press—bothered to write about this. The American trade papers for music rarely even mentioned the Black musicians. They asked me if I would write a regular column for them just detailing what was happening in the Black communities around the country. Since I had sort of an independent income, I decided I would. I used to spend a lot of time in Harlem, in Chicago, and in the deep South. I started writing a column first for *The Gramophone*, and then for *The Melody Maker*. Suddenly, when I went back to England in 1933, the English Columbia Record Company asked me if I would become their American recording director and record jazz for them which would be issued in the U.S. by the American Columbia Company, then in bankruptcy. The year before, I had done a record session for American Columbia of Fletcher Henderson's band. It was my first commercial record session, and I had done some things privately financed in 1931.

The band arrived an hour and a half late, being on what we called CPT (Colored People's Time), and we only had 45 minutes to finish the session, but in that 45 minutes we made two marvelous selections: *Honeysuckle Rose, King Porter Stomp*, and a thing I'm sorry to say I let get through called *Underneath the Harlem Moon*. W. C. Handy's daughter was singing on it, and she insisted on using the exact words in the lyrics, which included "that's how darkies were born." I had a fit, but Miss Handy said it had to be included.

In Europe, unlike America, the intellectuals in music appreciated the unique role of jazz. One of the most famous music critics of the day, who was also a composer, Constant Lambert, was most enthusiastic. Another supporter was the composer and jazz bass player, Patrick (or "Spike") Hughes. They sort of discovered Armstrong, Ellington, Fats Waller, and all the other people in America who were thought of as entertainers and clowns, and not recognized for the fantastic talent they had. European musicians who came over here were tremendously impressed with the originality and vitality of the Negro jazz musicians. Maurice Ravel would spend hours at the Grand Terrace in Chicago listening to Earl Hines. Walter Gieseking, a really splendid "classical" pianist, was so moved by Negro jazz that he actually wrote a jazz suite which, alas, he never recorded but which I heard him play, and his debt to Earl Hines was just unbelievable.

We had extraordinary Negro jazz musicians in those days. In 1932, I went to Fats Waller's 28th birthday party; Fats would be only 65 if he were alive today. Unfortunately, he died in 1943. At this party, after he had about a fifth of gin, he sat down at the piano and played the entire score of *Petrushka*! Then Reginald Forsythe, a Black English musician, joined him in a four-hand performance of the Delius opera, *Village Romeo and Juliet*. Fats, who had to be a clown in order to make a living in this country, could actually have been an extraordinary, all-around musician. The American public wasn't ready for that, and certainly the managers who know how to make a buck out of Fats wanted to have him retain the entertainer image. There were any number of Black musicians frustrated like that.

James P. Johnson was another musician who had a good knowledge of form and arranging. He wrote an opera in 1939 with Langston Hughes, *The Organizer*, which was put on by a reasonably left-wing group in New York, because they were the only people who appreciated the artistry of these two great men. It was a marvelous work, just short of an hour in duration. I don't believe it ever had another performance since 1939, but any educator interested in the contribution of the American Negro to jazz should certainly get hold of the score. I recorded the only tune from that show which was ever recorded, *Hungry Blues*. It is in the James P. Johnson album that is now out. This says an awful lot of things about society that just weren't allowed to be said by the White folks and the reactionaries that supervised the record business in those days.

A big year in my life was 1933. I started recording for the British market, hundreds of recordings which were later all released in this country. Early that year I had been in a little place in Harlem called Monette's Place. Monette Moore was a pretty good blues singer of the 20's at a place called the Morocco Club. Some mobster in Harlem decided that he'd back her in her own speakeasy. She asked me to come to opening night, so I went and drank my usual lemonade. She was very busy greeting all the celebrities who were there: Clifton Webb, Carl Van Vechten, and all the Whites who used to spend time in Harlem. But there was a girl singing, just about 17. And her name was Billie Holiday. I was about the first White guy who heard her sing. She had just gotten out of jail. I listened to her, and I couldn't believe what I heard. This was a vocalist who was a horn player, who was everything—I mean she had a complete style of her own. I'd never heard anything like it! I started to talk to Billie and the wonderful pianist with her, a girl called Dot Hill. Billie said, "Maybe, you know my old man, Clarence Holiday." Clarence was the guitar player with Fletcher Henderson's band. I couldn't believe that Clarence would have a talented daughter like this (because I knew immediately she was a star) and wouldn't brag about it! This will give you a small idea of Billie's social background. (Incidentally, we're going to do a movie on her, so I've been digging a lot into her background in Baltimore, before she came to New York.) Anyway, the next day I went to the Congress Ballroom where Fletcher was playing and told Clarence, "I heard your daughter Billie last night. She's the greatest thing I've ever heard!" He frowned at me, so I waited until intermission. Then he told me, "John, for God's sake don't talk about Billie in front of the guys! They'll think I'm old!" He explained to me that he was 14 when she was born, and Billie's mother (whom he married three years later) was 13. Billie was a girl completely outside of the social fabric, and a lot of her desperation and anger and deep feeling came through in her music. I wasn't able to get her recorded immediately because nobody was recording, but I was able to get Benny Goodman to use her on one of his first record sessions in 1933. These were the first records she ever made: *Riffin' the Scotch*, and *Your*

Mother's Son-in-Law. It was a year and a half before I could persuade anybody to get her back into a studio again, but we made up for that with a vengeance in 1935.

While working for the British, I was able to get Benny Goodman's first recording band together. I'll never forget that session because I was trying to get Benny to use Coleman Hawkins and other great jazz musicians who were around. But Benny was worried. "John, you know I worship these guys, but if I play with Negro musicians I'll never get another job on the radio." It was that rough. I believed him, but I didn't stop trying. So the first session we made was with all White folks. We did have some good ones, like Jack Teagarden, Joe Sullivan and Gene Krupa. By the time of the second sessions, Benny decided to take a chance and he added Negro musicians. This was at a time when Black and White musicians could not play together in public. By 1935, he had been recording for two years, originally for the British, and then for Irving Mills. Benny got a band together, first at the Billy Rose Music Hall in New York (all White), and then for the National Biscuit Company (also White). In 1933, I had listened to a radio program and heard a Chicago pianist named Teddy Wilson. I was so excited about Teddy that I sent Benny Carter to bring him to New York, and I got Benny and Teddy Wilson together in the record studio in 1934 for Columbia Records' *Moonglow*. Teddy was the first pianist Benny ever heard who could keep up with him technically. He thought it would be wonderful to play with him, and we got a trio together with Gene Krupa which would pave the way through records for these three to play together live. Benny was under contract to Victor, and I got Teddy to sign with Brunswick, and through these arrangements I managed to get Billie Holiday on records again. In June of 1935, I got Billie and Teddy in a band with Cozy Cole (drums), John Kirby (bass), Clarence Trueheart (Chick Webb's guitarist), Roy Eldridge (trumpet), Ben Webster (tenor sax) and Benny Goodman. We made four sides. There have been five or six real highlights for me in the record studio, and this certainly was one. Goodman was in the session because the only way Brunswick would let Teddy record with Benny for Victor was if he would return the favor for Brunswick, which he was doing.

This was the beginning of integration on records. Before this, there were maybe only five or six times the Blacks and Whites had played together on recordings. Fats Waller had played with Ted Lewis in 1931, four of the best sides that miserable band ever made. Eddie Condon, from Chicago, insisted on using Negro musicians. Louis Armstrong once had Joe Sullivan, a White guy, on piano. Milton Mezzro used to play with Black bands on occasion, but not very well. And Bubba Miley, Duke's great growl trumpet player, used to play with Leo Reisman, a society band leader for Victor, for special effects. All of this was done very secretly because the public wasn't ready to see Black and White together. But then in 1935 the Goodman Trio records came out. If anything, they were more successful than the Goodman band records, although the band records paved the way for the big band era, and Goodman changed American tastes, certainly the relationships between publishers and band leaders, because Benny had Fletcher Henderson do his arrangements. This was part of the deal for the National Biscuit Company radio show. Benny had a budget for eight arrangements a week, and this was how he built his library. Fletcher knew just about how much they could get away with. Benny used a lot of solos, playing only the first chorus pretty straight. The records sold, and Benny could call the tune. After 1936 the publishers could no longer say how to play, and this changed quite a lot of things.

The first time the trio was allowed to appear live was at a concert of the Chicago Hot Jazz Society in 1936, at the Congress Hotel. Everybody was scared. The owner, a nice guy, said, "Gee, I don't know if the public will take it." Of course it was the biggest hit of the concert. Benny was managed by MCA and they felt it would be rough. "We'll never be able to book a band with a Negro performer, you know." But Benny insisted, and they tried it. Out of this came the quartet, and from that the sextet—guys like Tommy Dorsey, Charlie Barnett—and a lot of other big bands soon had one or two Negroes in the band. I think Benny had as many as six. It was a breakthrough, but only a start. The record companies have done more I think than any other part of the amusement business to break down prejudice, but there's a whole lot more to do.

One of the reasons I'm so happy to be at this conference is that I really know now that the record industry is going to have to get together, all the big, progressive companies, and make a substantial catalog. I know there are at least five companies that can work on a project like this, because not only a lot of jazz has been preserved, but almost all of the blues is on record. The early work in the field of art songs, chamber and symphonic music has unfortunately not been preserved at all.

We know jazz is in a pretty sorry economic state now. The number of clubs where guys can work is shrinking constantly. The frustrations of the Black music are almost greater now than they were in the 20's and 30's. The field of motion pictures has offered an escape for some. We do have people like Oliver Nelson, Benny Golson, Quincy Jones and Herbie Hancock (that great pianist with Miles Davis) who are taking over sound scoring in Hollywood. I have a feeling the very talented and persistent Black musician will make it, but we're paying a terrible penalty for the status of jazz in this country. I go around to a lot of jazz competitions at various universities in the country, and I see fewer and fewer Black kids trying music anymore. They aim for industry and professions which are more open now than they used to be. It is very depressing to me that the heritage of Black music is perhaps being threatened by the fact that there's just not enough kids going into music now.

QUESTION: What avant garde jazz is Columbia Records engaged in recording now?

HAMMOND: I'm recording Archie Shepp and Sonny Murray on Monday. We ought to have a lot of fun. Although I'm director of talent acquisitions and an executive producer at Columbia, I do not make the final decisions. Sometimes I have to fight hard for an Aretha Franklin or Bob Dylan, who are not in this specialized field of pure jazz, who therefore present the possibility of an enormous profit. In jazz it is minimal, even with the biggest artists like Miles Davis and Thelonius Monk. The records may only break even. I've been recording with Sonny Murray, and you know the business will hesitate to make concessions when numbers might last 18 minutes and might not even get much air play, even in the underground. I'm sorry we've never recorded Cecil Taylor. He is a genius, but he is being recorded. Archie Shepp is under contract to Impulse. Albert Ayler and a lot of these guys are being recorded. One of the problems is that Columbia is a huge operation. We need to sell about 15,000 copies a year of a recording with the accounting system we have, the money it costs to package the thing, the kind of editing we do, the studio time, and the rest. We not only do our own recordings, but our studios are available to our competitors. The business really needs the smaller companies too.

QUESTION: Would you tell us about your initial contact with Miles Davis?

HAMMOND: I'll be horribly frank. Miles made it on other labels. Prestige really financed his early years, and he made wonderful records for them. Teo Macero, who produced both Miles and Monk, was able to sell the Sales and A & R departments at Columbia on the advisability of signing Miles. Happily, he has an enormous amount of artistic freedom at Columbia. If he wants to spend $30,000 on an album, like the things he did with Gil Evans, he can do it, and it's paid off. He's a giant in the field, and will continue to be.

Monk is a different problem. Of course, he is an enormously talented composer. Teo is trying to use him with a big band, with arrangements by Oliver Nelson. We'll see how that works. I'm skeptical.

I should mention that I've done a certain amount of work with John Handy, who is a marvelous musician. His first album sold about 25,000 copies. I did Don Ellis, this Electric Bath album which got the *Downbeat* award for the best record of 1968, but I know Columbia's not going to make any money on it. It sold remarkably well for a jazz album, more than 30,000, but the costs that went into this album were about $28,000, and record companies don't make anywhere near a dollar a record in profit. I also recorded Denny Zeitland, who is an avant-garde pianist (and a psychiatrist!) and there were some darn good albums there, too.

QUESTION: Will we be able to get some of the older records again, this time on stereo?

HAMMOND: Well, the record business is really all-stereo now. Those of us with a conscience hate to rechannel a record for stereo because all it does is louse up the original sound, yet the dealers and rack jobbers will not stock records unless they are stereo. We tried rechannel jobs on some of our old issues, but now we're putting on the original, authentic recording. We know the public. If they want them badly enough, they'll get it.

QUESTION: Is the intellectualization of jazz destroying it, in your opinion?

HAMMOND: It's true that jazz has become more intellectual and less obviously rhythmic (if it is impossible to have "intellectual rhythm"). It's not for dancing anymore, that's for sure. The potential public is thereby cut down, but I think jazz has to go its own way. No one can dictate to musicians for very long.

QUESTION: I'm curious about what you would have to say about Art Tatum.

HAMMOND: He was a semi-blind pianist from Toledo who hit New York in 1932. I heard him then in a speakeasy uptown. There had never been anybody with the kind of technique he had; it was just astonishing. I don't believe any "classical" pianist has a better, more fleet technique than Tatum had. I first had him on a program when I was disc jockey in New York on WEVD in

1932. He was always a marvelous ensemble musician, but he made it on records as a solo artist. Just three weeks ago I received a tape of some things he had cut in 1941 in Harlem, in after-hours joints. This may be the only time he ever recorded with an all-Black audience. He was drunk part of the time, and he sings two of the damnest blues you've ever heard; they're just marvelous. Also with him on these after-hours sessions were people like Frankie Newton, a good bass player and a marvelous singer. This is a side of Tatum that the record public has never seen, and this should be out quite soon. But he did a lot of recording in recent years for Verve, and some really excellent things for Twentieth Century just a couple of years before he died.

QUESTION: Within the economic framework at Columbia, what is the fate of other Black music on record?

HAMMOND: I've said I hoped forward-looking companies in the record business would get together and serve the community by recording the major works of Black composers from the turn of the century. We can't do it expecting to make a buck. It might be done within the framework of a large company like Columbia, particularly if foundations will underwrite the costs. The possibility of doing Dave Baker's *Black America* may be another matter. Under the new union rules, we no longer have a symphonic rate and the costs of a 44-piece orchestra and chorus would be almost prohibitive in this country. The only hope may be to record it in Europe. Smaller works, without the tremendous outlay of musicians, whose albums might cost around $30,000 is another story.

QUESTION: What about an orchestra of composers on a cooperative basis?

HAMMOND: I think it makes sense, but of course the players don't get paid then, do they? A major company can't do anything like this. Smaller companies can manage it. The union doesn't bother cracking down on them, but we'd lose our license.

QUESTION: What chance do you think there is that this music, relegated to a corner, will be handled in the future as a race-labeled concept? Will Black music still receive secondary consideration and have secondary criteria applied to it?

HAMMOND: That depends on some things not directly related to music. It depends on what way society is going to go. A few more racist elections and the answer would be a firm yes. Within the music business itself, I know our company is employing Black men in considerable numbers for promotion, and not just for the Negro market. And we have two excellent Black producers. This is a start. One other thing which will keep the race record concept away is the fact that there are too many aware and alert youths, Black and White. I also feel that the more educational institutions which get into Black studies programs will help.

QUESTION: Does Columbia have any plans to issue more records of Black artists from the 20's, like Ethel Waters?

HAMMOND: Yes, we've got an Ethel Waters album now with two separate records. One is out with Ethel doing show tunes, and the other of blues. We've got a problem, because she is now part of the Billy Graham Crusade, and some of the early records were what might have been called pornographic then. I prefer to call them earthy, but she has indicated her desire that we move with caution. I hope eventually we can get her permission.

QUESTION: Your archives are full of Black music. I suspect other companies have valuable things stored. In view of the fact that release of these recordings is dependent on the exigencies of the commercial market, in view of the fact that the Black community uses music not as something that can be totally dependent on the commercial interests but as something which is an integral part of its expression, and also in view of the fact that at least one of the things I see coming out of this institute is the formation of a center for the propagation and preservation of the artistic output of the Black community, do you as an individual (I know you can't speak for Columbia Records on this just now) think there would be a possibility of working out something? If the center does develop, can these various archival collections be made available to the educational institutions?

HAMMOND: I think it is a superb idea. There are probably only three companies that would have this kind of archive. The only ones existing today that were in the business in the 20's are Victor and Columbia. There are some independent labels which reissue some of the things that were on Paramount and Gennett. For a while, Decca had access to the Gennett catalog. Then Riverside, part of the ABC Paramount, has the Gennett rights. Columbia started in 1889, but didn't record Black music until 1896—the Fisk Jubilee Singers. Those will be terribly valuable recordings. They sound awful, but the spirit is there. The blues market started in 1920. Here, there are only three companies to deal with, and I think this is the kind of thing that Victor, Columbia and Decca could get together on, and they should be very happy to make these things available.

QUESTION: What about things recorded in the 50's which were not released, because people were afraid they wouldn't sell?

HAMMOND: Then there is the question of the union. The A.F. of M. might be leery of allowing these records to an institution where they could be recorded, re-recorded and played without trust fund percentages. Before 1941, you don't have to worry.

EDWARDS: I've had the privilege of working with Cannonball Adderley. I remember he and his brother Nat have done some avant-garde things. Are they doing anything for Columbia?

HAMMOND: Unfortunately, they have never been under contract to Columbia. They are on Capitol, I believe, and of course they have a marvelous Viennese pianist Josef Zawinul, who is doing a lot of their writing.

SANJEK: They have commissioned a number of works, by the way, which are being recorded in Europe for distribution on a label they own, but which will be available from Capitol.

HAMMON: I am delighted.

QUESTION: Who do you think is responsible for be-bop?

HAMMOND: The first time I was conscious of bop was in the old days at Minton's. Monk was around, and Charlie Christian had as much to do with it as anybody, even though he died in 1942, but the real beginnings of bop were in those days of 1941 at Minton's. Dizzy was involved because he was sick of being cut by Roy Eldridge. He wanted to do his own thing, and he did.

QUESTION: Is Columbia engaged in the recording of jug and washboard bands?

HAMMOND: After 1928 it was, and so was Victor. These groups used non-union musicians, which was one reason, frankly. They may have been paid a jug of gin. They were utterly and completely exploited, and this is why there are so many jug and washboard bands on records. I think the best one was the Washboard Serenaders. It was a lot more sophisticated than the others, mainly because they had a great pianist. The records sold maybe two or three thousand copies to the Negro market. I think Victor is coming out with new releases of the Washboard Serenaders, which I would urge you to get. We have some of our best washboard things in our album *The sound of Harlem*, which is a re-issue of three LP's with some of the greatest sounds of the Harlem night clubs from the 20's and 30's.

QUESTION: I heard a statistic which might be wrong that Bessie Smith sold 8,000,000 records between 1927 and her death in 1937.

HAMMOND: Oh no. Bessie's sales were all between 1923 and 1928. She probably sold between six and seven million records during that time. Between 1928 and our first Bessie Smith reissue on 78's, I doubt if 20,000 records were sold. Our first reissue was about 1938, the second 78 package was in 1940. We issued the big Bessie Smith story early in the 50's. That has sold phenomenally well. In fact, the total sales of these four albums is well over a half million in this country alone. We've had another extraordinary success with the Delta blues musician, Robert Johnson. His records came out between 1936 and 1938, and I don't think they sold over 700 then. In fact, I don't believe they were ever sold excepting in the deep South, but I got them for review at the time. One of the first things I did when I came back to Columbia was to put out an album called *The King of the Delta Blues*, and this is now being resurfaced. You know, the biggest sale on college campuses is the old blues. I have a son who makes records for Atlantic. He does his best to be a rural Mississippi Black man. I don't know how successful he'll be, but he's a good guitar and har-monica player. A lot of kids are having tremendous success, and my son was the first guy in the area. He started in 1961, before Black kids were interested in the blues. It's only in the last few years, thanks to the Rolling Stones and Eng-land's recognition of people like Chuck Berry, Muddy Waters and Howlin' Wolf, and the great natural American blues artists, that America is finally get-ting to know these people. It isn't the American public that did this; it was the English artists. Even the Beatles will tell you that Chuck Berry was one of their big influences.

QUESTION: May we work for a moment in a non-jazz area to take advantage of your presence? I don't know what the arrangement is between the recording companies and orchestras such as the Philadelphia Orchestra or the New York Philharmonic but, if they are under contract to record periodically, is it possible to suggest to these orchestras that they use our Black music? How many recordings do we need of the Beethoven symphonies, for example? Why can't we have our Black music recorded by these orchestras?

HAMMOND: I would like to see an orchestra that has a feeling for Black music record these things rather than our lily-white orchestras. In popular music, we have managed to break down racial barriers to a degree, but it is worse than ever in "classical" music. For four years, I was head of the Discrimination Committee of the New York Urban League, and we tackled all of the orchestras and theaters in New York. In the Radio City Music Hall, for example, they now have about ten percent of their permanently employed musicians who are Black. The New York Philharmonic has one token, but magnificent, violinist in Sanford Allen, who's been with them for eight years. These people will not bend until public pressure forces them, even with a sympathetic guy like Lennie Bernstein as conductor. I'm vice-president of the Symphony of the New World, one of the really integrated symphony orchestras in this country. We have 38 good Black musicians. We chose them because they're good. I think an orchestra like this should record the works of Black composers, and there's foundation money which might be gotten for it. And I'm hoping that one of these days there will be a real Black-owned record company, sensitive to the cultural needs of our country, because we're not going to go all the way with the present structure.

BAKER: This concept of an orchestra with a feel for Black music: Black music at this point encompasses every color in the rainbow. I don't think it's that important for an orchestra to have a "feel" for the music. Let's just get a performance.

HAMMOND: You're absolutely right, of course. I meant a social feel as well as a musical one, because I think we're going to have to develop Black musicians in other orchestras so that the major orchestras are going to *have* to take them.

SMITH: I'd like to make one comment regarding Dave's statement which might be a mild contradiction. One conductor told me he thought an ostinato passage in my *Contours* was a kind of boogie-woogie, and it has no relationship whatever to boogie-woogie. Even so, when the players are working with a jazz-based piece, it would help if they would have had some jazz experience and not approach everything up-tight. The New Haven orchestra doesn't have any Black persons, but it has people who understand jazz, and *Contours* was well played by them.

HAMMOND: And when you have a Joe Wilder on first trumpet, a Warren Smith on timpani, an Art Davis as first bass, and a Kermit Moore as first cellist, as you do in the Symphony of the New World, you will get a whole lot more understanding than you would elsewhere.

LEE: There is a lot of music in the "classical" field which is not recognizably Black. If the conductor thought of playing a work of yours, but never saw your face, he might never know you were Black. But anyway, isn't this a start, even if a White orchestra were to play the music? Debussy wasn't always played well either.

HAMMOND: Well Sylvia, we are thankful for our good young Black conductors, like your husband Everett Lee, like James De Priest, and the few others.

COLE: The question really is that we've got to put pressure on the large orchestra. There are three excellent Black people in the Pittsburgh Symphony.

HAMMOND: Yes, and one of these has just placed a suit against one of the Big Four because they rejected him.

COLE: It's my feeling that what really should be done is that Black people should produce Black musicians and do their own thing, like the Symphony of the New World.

HAMMOND: Well, I wouldn't want to withdraw the eleven Black men who are playing in the "regular" orchestras. I think it is important for the orchestras and for the players to have them there.

● John Hammond proved himself to be a captivating speaker but, more importantly, his contribution to jazz history has been very profound. He is at the top of his business and ranks with any person of any race in terms of what he has done for the Black musical community. Very frequently jazz historians think only of interviews with performers, composers and other historians. Even outside of jazz, it would be well to remember the very important role played by partners of the artists, including those colleagues engaged in publication and in recording.

The question of currently unavailable recordings was in the minds of many people. The one who was spokesman for this group was not, unfortunately, identified. Within the latitude permitted by laws and company policies, it does seem possible that the industry would be receptive to these special needs, and this point will be developed in the final chapter.

6. Black Composers and the Avant-Garde

Thomas Jefferson Anderson, Jr.

Hale Smith

Olly Wilson

● To regard Black music as consisting of "jazz, spirituals and things like that" suggests not only a lack of respect for these traditions (which are certainly as powerful as sixteenth-century motets and eighteenth-century *divertimenti*), but a lack of knowledge about what is taking place in the music of today. We were fortunate enough to attract three of the most important and articulate composers of their generation who, in addressing themselves to the question of the modern Black composer, will make it evident that these are men of genuine creative substance.

I first met Dr. Anderson through my good friend, Leonard Klein, when we were all in Oklahoma. In addition to contacts at concerts in that state, we spent one day talking by a lake north of Langston University, where Dr. Anderson was serving as music departmental chairman. When Dr. Klein and I left for Indiana University (Dr. Klein is now at Mills College), T. J. left for Tennessee State University, in Nashville. Although we corresponded with some degree of frequency, it was not until the research of the Black Music Committee began that I was able to see him again. By this time it was obvious that he was well on his way to the top of his field (he has since been appointed Composer-in-Residence for the Atlanta Symphony Orchestra).

Dr. Wilson took a summer's leave from Oberlin College a few years ago to accept an appointment at Indiana University. We met at one of Dean Bain's large parties, and I expressed to him my great interest in Black music. This was in the early days of our committee, probably in 1968, although it seems much longer ago than that. He later took time from his busy schedule to visit with me, and to provide some orientation on current trends and ideas in Black music. Since our seminar, he has accepted a position with the University of California at Berkeley.

Hale Smith is one of the most published of all Black composers, and has a rich background in most areas of music and music publishing. I met him first at my home, one day before the seminar began, although we had been in correspondence for some time before that. He is certainly well known in musical circles and has been increasingly active of late as a panelist and lecturer.

Dr. Caswell, who chaired this session, is one of these musicologists whose interests are broad enough to encompass early music as well as jazz. After a week of teaching at Indiana University, he is found on Sunday mornings as music director of a progressive church in Bloomington, conducting jazz masses one week, and Bach cantatas the next.

CASWELL: The purpose of this forum is to consider the avant-garde elements of composition as they relate to the Black cultural traditions. Too often we have associated the Black influence on music as stemming from past traditions only, from the spiritual, folk music, earlier jazz. This afternoon's discussion is to see what influence the Black composer is having upon the more recent facets of composition.

ANDERSON: This is an attitude which is not only reflective of my opinion, but the opinion of many in the Black community: When one thinks of the avant-garde, one immediately thinks of revolutionary composers, those with a new musical language, those who are involved in experimentation, or anything outside of the establishment. If we take this as a definition, and since we can already assume that all Black composers have always been outside the establishment, one logically reaches the conclusion that all Black composers are avant garde. Now on first thought, this may seem a bit facetious, but I can assure you that I say this in all seriousness. Those of you who laugh would immediately suggest the name of Ulysses Kay as being one that would be an exception. I grant you that Kay has made a tremendous impact in terms of the establishment in music. However, if you look at the Pan American Union's *Composers of the Americas*, where there is a bibliography of his works and publications, you can see that Ulysses Kay is very limited in terms of publications and recordings. Therefore, one has to conclude that Kay has only made an indentation on the visual establishment, but not the musical establishment at all. To say that Ulysses Kay is as good as any of his contemporaries is to miss the point, for he certainly is as good as any other composer writing today. However, Kay's activity within musical circles shows that he does not belong to the tradition of having-to-be-better, clearly a tradition which has prevailed throughout the society.

I was reading an article by Shirley Graham, the widow of W. E. B. DuBois, perhaps our most illustrious leader. It was titled "Spirituals to Symphonies" and appeared in *Etude* in 1936. In this particular article, she discussed the tremendous growth of potential in Black serious composers and the works of Florence B. Price, William Dawson, and Nathaniel Dett. What she actually came out with is a conclusion that we stood on the threshhold in 1936 of a renaissance period in which Black artists would move into the society and greatly enrich the cultural heritage of the country. It is ironic that some thirty-three years later we're still standing on that threshhold and, in fact, I think the case can be made that we have actually slipped back in terms of position. Instead of America's music being vitalized, in the last thirty-three years it has taken the road of imitation and is basically a poor imitation of European music lacking in rhythmic imagination, harmonic intensity, and also tends to be overly intellectualized.

Now, to develop further the point of all Black composers being avant garde, one has to realize that the Black composer comes out of an aesthetic. Whether he is aware of it or not is not too important, for it's his duty to show the social and environmental relationships. Secondly, since Blacks feel the pressure of the system (political, economical and social), is it not therefore normal to assume that Blacks would be more sensitive in the art forms? Third, the total range of the avant garde in America always finds Blacks to the left. If we had a convention of conservative composers, I would dare say that all of the conservative composers in this country would immediately place the Black composers who also attended such a convention to the left; for in considering intra-group variations of Whites, one has to assume that the intra-group variations are quite broad, while the intra-group variations of Blacks are quite small. And I would suggest that this variation is due to the fact that Blacks have been more responsive to social issues in their music. Fourth, composition does not reflect the feeling of the times, but is a response sociologically in terms of one's emotions in a particular time and a particular place. It's impossible to imagine a Sistine Chapel without a church with great finance. The affluent society can always produce pop and op art because it has money. Now what I'm saying here is that the study of music is not a history, but a social commentary on the human reaction to the environmental factors which relate to the individual. Therefore, the composer does not make a conscious choice, but selects unconsciously adaptations of things that exist in the society.

To define the Black avant garde further, we would say these are the composers who have suffered the Negro experience in America. And the rate of this expression is therefore a quantitative measurement in terms of its relative relationship to Black people. My good friend, the late poet M. B. Tolson, put it another way in his book *The Harlem Gallery*. "Poor boy blue, the great White world and the Black bourgeois have shoved the Negro artists into a White and non-White dichotomy: the Afro-American dilemma in the arts, the dialectic of to be or not to be a Negro." This sense of being pulled from one pole to another is not only characteristic of the Black artist, but is characteristic of the society, for there should be a dichotomy in the existence of all White artists in the society. Can the White artist of today see the existence of Blacks in this country and not be affected by his own humanity?

When we look at the culture in which we are a part, we have to become overly concerned in the economic basis because that's where it's rooted, and one has to examine the sub-culture. Now I use the term "sub-culture" only to imply a small portion of a larger group, a sub-division. It has nothing to do with a value judgment. The economic basis of the Black community has been put out in governmental statistics and it's funny that in one way the government turned out to be a benefactor (that's in the publication of figures) and in another way turned out to be a suppressor of human rights (I'm thinking in terms of the Justice Department's lack of prosecution of the laws in which relate to open housing and fair employment), and yet we still have to be aware that this dual role which is shared by the federal government has a great effect on us. By 1970 the percentage of Black families in poverty will be between 30.6 and 32.9 percent, compared to between 10.8 and 12 percent for White families. This figure is increasing. In 1966 Blacks had not achieved the employment status of Whites in 1940. Because we bear the brunt of the disproportionate processes in terms of jobs and money, we have been basically absorbed in our living. Thus, there is the same basis for Appalachian folk music and the blues of Harlem soul music, proportionately.

We live in a machine civilization, and all machine civilizations pride themselves in their efficiency. Webern represents the maximum in terms of time concept. African music, on the other hand, has no time consciousness. Webern's symphony, opus 21, would take approximately ten minutes to perform. Yet an African festival in which the participants do the right thing at the right time, sometimes goes on for days. In the machine civilization it is inevitable that the artists tend to reflect other institutions and, therefore, they too are time oriented. What composer doesn't put on his score the amount of time this piece would take to be performed? What conductor doesn't look at this timing first to see how long his audience has to suffer through the contemporary work? Since the anatomy of the society is structured this way, we have become overly specialized. The arts have become compartmentalized and highly structured. Therefore, we have produced schools: impressionism, expressionism, and so forth. These are the results.

Before technology won over, art forms were most important because they relate to the whole fiber of the individual. And when we understand this, we understand truly what Black music is all about. Indians in America have no event without singing and dancing. African societies couldn't have a hunt without its being related to religion, singing and dancing. The statement of LeRoi Jones seems to sum up what I'm talking about: "Black music is total reality." By this we mean that the environmental understanding is related to the metaphysical torment which grows out of universal suffering and that the religious experience of the Black church is a classic example of dialectic theater.

Within the Black community there exists many points of fascination. In the area of instrumental music (marching bands, dance halls and clubs) one constantly sees experimentation. Musicians basically self taught develop abilities on the basis of accident, or as a means of developing self expression. We see the development of new techniques to fit one's own personality or peculiar needs. Instrumental music is very much related to voice in that the music is sung and not played. And another term which I'd like to interject is "inspired intensity." I don't know if this exists in any other music, but this is a fusion of achieving the highest degree of expressive powers within a framework of limited technical facility or skill. I think we constantly see musicians who are limited in terms of background because of the lack of economic privileges, who are basically self taught, or ill-taught in many cases, and who actually develop this means of communication through the development of expressive powers which transcend their limitation in terms of ability. In the area of vocal music, word inflections for dramatic intent can be seen. Tonal colors of the voice and the use of wide vibrato is constantly seen for increasing emotional effect. These contributions have been made to the mainstream of the avant-garde movement in the country, and an examination of sources would clearly show these points: There are new methods of tone production which have been a part of the Black tradition for years. Tonal effects (mutes, distortion of tone, physical tricks) are quite common. The extended ranges of instruments, either by trick fiingerings or mouthpiece pressures, are another by-product of the environment, and the greater use of the unestablished instruments (things like the tenor saxophone, the electric guitar) are quite common, of course again relating to playing the instruments that are available—this heterogeneous grouping of instruments.

In conclusion, the social and psychological infringements of the Black experience make the Negro composer unique. Whether he is a liberal or conservative is not important. His role in the society is only significant because his perspective is Black. These are the composers involved in the fundamental issues of existence.

WILSON: Art is experience consciously transformed. If an artist is honest with himself, transforming his experience is precisely what he does, consciously or not. Since his experience is a Black one, this is the only thing he can represent. Now the manifestations of this experience are going to vary even within the spectrum of Blackness, at different times, at different geographical positions, and at different levels of the sociological ladder. In spite of these variations, all Black people are united because of their Blackness. LeRoi Jones, in *Blues people*, talks about this very cogently, particularly regarding the various movements in jazz after 1940. The same kind of thing could be found by looking at Black musicians who have had experience in the jazz tradition and are involved at the same time in the mainstream of Western "art" music. And even here there would be differences in the reflection of this Black experience.

What is Black music? I don't think that's one of the basic things we're trying to grapple with. In order to do this, we would have to start with African music. This has already been done to a limited extent by A. M. Jones, the ethnomusicologist, in his book *Studies in African music*. It's from this kind of study that the notion of time, which T. J. pointed out, became apparent. The Afro-American experience is different. The original African concept of art as life, and the concept of the musician as the bearer of truth and history—this philosophical heritage was broken down by forcefully moving people from one continent to another. At the same time, certain vestiges of African means of musical expression were maintained, and these are illustrated in Gunther Schuller's *Early jazz*.

SMITH: Things both of my colleagues have said relate to certain devices common to the avant garde. It isn't very clear to those who are not familiar with the subject that certain methods of tone production, of instrumental manipulation have come about through players not having had traditional training and through their trying to express something that is a part of their own background and yearnings. This has been most often done by the jazz player. There are certain players who have developed mastery within the accepted ranges of that term—for instance, Eric Dolphy, who had a thorough mastery of his instruments as far as classic technique is concerned, but who went beyond that because it was not possible for him to express what he had to say in terms of techniques he had learned as a younger person. What makes the use of a device by a Black composer different from that of a White composer's use? The fertilizing element in an individual's background, in the case of a socially conscious Black composer, tends to give his work a greater intensity, although there are a number of non-Black composers who have produced very vital music.

CASWELL: We are all quite fully aware of the uses of Black material in traditional composition, for example the use of spiritual tunes, or harmonic patterns which come from jazz. There are obvious devices. In today's kinds of work with electronic, serial and aleatory music, I'd like to ask if you feel the Black experience and the Black attitude toward music can apply.

ANDERSON: The newer forms generally come late in a person's musical training. By the time a Black youth gets to the university, where he might pick up one of these advanced forms, the roots of his life style, of his Blackness, are already formed. This would just be superimposed on what he already has as an enrichment, which he personally may choose to take or reject. I know of no Black school that has an electronic studio, so basically it's true that Black youths are being informed of developments in electronic music, but they might not be able to participate. In many ways, the choice will be made on the basis of experiences. If these experiences are not provided, certainly their choices will not reflect them.

WILSON: You must remember that any kind of system (for example, serial) or media (for example, electronic) is simply that. It's a means by which one may project himself. It can also shape what is projected, but this is up to the composer. I think that the composer who is intellectually honest with himself will project that which is in him, so that he will transcend the media. A medium will simply enable him to do it in a different way, but it won't change the basic impulse.

CASWELL: Would you relate this to your work for chorus and electronic sounds, *In Memoriam to Martin Luther King*?

WILSON: I was going through a profound emotional crisis at the time of his assassination. We all were. It made me aware of a lot of things that I had not been fully sensitive to before. I wanted to write a piece which would reflect some of the intensity of my feelings, and something about the multi-faceted character of the man. Unfortunately, some people put Martin Luther King down because he was a pacificist. Too many people forget that, viewed in the context of the social situation of the late 50's, Martin Luther King was extremely militant; it took a great deal of militancy to go again and again and again, to meet the dogs and the racist cops, yet he did it. He had such a tremendous amount of power. I wanted to express some of this in the *In Memorium*. The text is derived from refrains from Martin Luther King's speeches. You know, in the tradition of the Black church, the minister often states a motive as a refrain, says something elaborating that subject, then comes back to the refrain. I used the refrains from his speeches as a text. The electronic medium is an extension of the choral medium, so that at times they are matching one another.

CASWELL: What would you say to a person who professes to see no Black musical elements in your techniques aside from the obvious dedication and subject matter?

WILSON: Nothing.

CHAPMAN: It seems in a sense it's irrelevant to talk about what is Black music. There are many similarities between African and European music. There are lots of divergencies, but you have many similarities in the use of things like thirds and fifths and counterpoint. You even have response in common. You can't talk about any one African style. There are many different ones. African music of Ethiopia is influenced by the Middle East. Sub-Saharan pygmy music uses counterpoint, almost like fourteenth century Europe in some ways. Quite a heavy emphasis on rhythm appears on the west coast, but as you go further east there is less. I'm not sure I could tell the difference between Burleigh's *Southland Sketches* and a work by John Powell, who was a White racist.

SMITH: The distinction between cultures is most clear on the primitive level. The closer people are to the soil and the more isolated or insulated they are, the more clearly established are their musical styles. These elements become more diffuse the more the person is in contact with neighboring groups and societies. On the North American continent the Black musical definition is most clear in that music of the Black man who is closest to the soil or in the lower cultural or economic levels. In spite of television, radio and the phonograph, there are people who have had less direct contact with the technical means of expression than their economically more fortunate brothers and sisters. You will find blues singers out of Mississippi or singers in the various store-front churches which come as close as anything can to the essence of the Black experience through music. But when the Black musician acquires technical know-how and to the extent that he uses these tools and is influenced by the music of other societies, he becomes less easily identifiable.

WILSON: I take issue with just about everything you said, Miss Chapman. When we talk about the Black experience and the Afro-American cultural heritage, I think this is clearly demonstrable empirically. You take a group of Black teenagers and they will recognize the Blackness of James Brown right away. There is something peculiarly Black about our musical expression. This does not mean White people cannot learn it (the history of music has certainly demonstrated that). This does not mean that someone like Leontyne Price cannot learn a European tradition. It is true that there are cultural differences in African tribes, but there are larger similarities. For example, it is aberrant rather than usual for an African tribe not to use drums consistently. Not only drums, but groups of drums. If non-Mediterranean regions of Europe can still bear effects of the Greek and Roman cultures, maybe this is something which will explain African similarities. I know the Bantu moved from one area of Africa to another. It may have happened with others, perhaps on a fairly large scale, and this would explain the many similarities which make these people more allied with each other than with another part of the world. I wouldn't be able to argue in terms of the basic thrust of all your comments because of time, but I think it can be illustrated that there is a cultural unified expression in music of the Black people.

ANDERSON: I think it's certainly apparent to Black people that we live in a society which has totally controlled the educational system. It's also true that the Black youth have been subjected to dehumanization by the educational process. If we are ever to establish any meaning, we have to take control of the educational process and throw out the textbooks which have demoralized and brainwashed both the Black and White youth. I think that this revolutionary attitude will produce a new set of values. It's impossible for us to sit here now and discuss this and that because we're not steeped in the tradition of objective thinking. We have not had the time to evaluate the material—even the idea of this conference is unique. It will take many experiences like this, much research and a lot of reevaluation of the music. In fact, a lot of performances. This is by way of objecting to your initial remark that it is irrelevant to talk about what is Black music.

CASWELL: I know this is a hard task, but we will have to be in a position to define Black music to some degree, unless we're just going to say it is music written by Black people.

WILSON: I think that is precisely what we're going to have to do, for the reasons T. J. has outlined. We're just going to have to say that Black music is simply music written by Black people. We can talk about certain idioms, about jazz, gospel, soul, African music, early Afro-American music, but it is difficult to pinpoint the music of the contemporary composer the same way. Implicit behind this is the inference that there is a way for Black composers to compose, you see, and that if you do not compose this way, you are not Black. Well, I totally reject this. That idea is harmful to the development of any art in any kind of situation. I'll use whatever I want, whatever there is, whatever media, whatever techniques, whatever style—the whole world. Half of it came from my ancestors anyway.

SMITH: If we attempt to make a list of characteristics which are prevalent in the musical expressions of Black culture, we are barking up a dead tree. Those of us who have been trained in the study of European music history are very much aware of different attitudes in comparing the German and French composers. That doesn't mean you can identify nationality always, but we do find attitudes with which these two nations approach the arts. It's a matter of cultural definition, and I think we can do the same thing with Black music, without trying to make a list that would care for all situations.

ANDERSON: We seem to get bogged down in giving things names. It seems to me that what we are trying to do there is bring out that the contribution of Black expressivity is integral in terms of their overall expressivity in American society. We are saying that the expressive contribution of the minority in American society will give a truer picture of the overall expressive view of American society. It has nothing to do with separating Black music on this hand and White music on that. This would be ridiculous. The Black Music Committee here is saying that there is a significant contribution to music which has been ignored in the past, and that music happens to be the music of minority people, and those people happen to be Black.

LEE: Concert goers are not always musically educated. Even among us who are here today, can we be sure we could tell Gunther Schuller's music from Olly Wilson's, or T. J. Anderson's, or Hale Smith's? Is it audible that a work is by a Black man? Is it Black music by a Black man, White music by a Black man? What difference does it make whether a Scotch-American has used some bagpipe tunes or not? The Spanish-descended person doesn't always write with Spanish dance rhythms.

ANDERSON: When we get into the problem of definition, we begin overly intellectualizing, and when we intellectualize, we stop being human. I think this is one of the problems of the society. We see countless deaths in Vietnam every day, and we overly intellectualize that peace is being negotiated. This process of always rationalizing instead of emotionally reacting to peoples and their conditions is a bag, and White folks have been trapped in it for years. I don't want to see us get caught up in it now! I think we have to address ourselves to being what we are, responding emotionally to what we want to respond to, and if somebody wants to define and explain it, that's all right. As a Black composer, I'm more interested in addressing myself to the problems of the ghetto. The plight of the symphony orchestras, I don't give a damn about, because basically it's a continuation of the paternalistic system in that Whites control it financially. It's an institution. Today they talked about there being only eleven Blacks in the American orchestras, like if we practice a little harder, maybe later on we'll be a part of it. I mean, let it die! It's dying anyway. If a symphony orchestra doesn't become meaningful to the times, let it die. What I'm saying is the society has to change, and the society has to change in that it has to become humane, and the obligation of the Black people is to make the society become humane. I think that's what we have to address ourselves to.

SMITH: But T. J., excuse me but you didn't answer the question.

ANDERSON: Why should I have to define Black music? It's not important. The main thing is to try to get it presented, to get past the pressures that would hinder it.

WILSON: I would prefer to believe that you are in fact a result of all your experiences, so that a Black man cannot exist outside of his Blackness. That's why I say when I write a piece, if I'm honest with myself, and I profoundly think I am, it obviously reveals my Blackness, whether it is demonstrable or not, whether you hear it or not. It could be that your ears aren't good enough. You see what I mean? It could be that there are subtle things in the music which are not demonstrable, but at the same time are Black anyway.

LEE: Yes, but you can transcend all this. A man's nothing but a man, whether he is Black or White, after he gets to a certain level in his music.

WILSON: Transcend to what? A man is a result of all his experiences. It's impossible for anybody else to have the same experiences I've had, irrespective of his color. Nobody else could have the same set of experiences.

SCHULLER: I'm concerned about whether the Black composers and musicians are seriously thinking about how they might preserve these contributions. If it is true that in a country like the United States there's an automatic acculturation process, which Black people are trying to resist, when you move from integration to something called Black Power or Black identity, is there a similar kind of Black identity movement among Black composers to preserve that multi-faceted heritage, which Olly delineated so well, in order to keep that vitality, that special quality, that Blackness in the music? If it is not possible, it's conceivable that all this in time will be integrated and be no longer distinguishable. I'm thinking for example of the Japanese composers. After the war they all went very industriously to Darmstadt and picked up the new techniques to such an extent that you couldn't tell they were Japanese. Significantly though, with the younger generation of Japanese there is now a concern about not losing the extraordinary beauties of their ancient ceremonial music. They want to preserve it historically on tapes and recordings statistically, but also to preserve it as an identifiable strain of their own Japaneseness, without making it a nationalistic cause, just because it's something beautiful and worthwhile that some people feel should not be lost. I feel the same way obviously about the Black heritage of music. Should we not be thinking about preserving these elements?

DE LERMA: Before this important question is answered, I think it would be appropriate for us to acknowledge the presence of a man who has left no aspect of twentieth-century music untouched, who took time from a horrendous schedule to visit us today, to whom this conference already is already deeply in debt, Gunther Schuller.

ANDERSON: We have been moving in this direction, Mr. Schuller, before your arrival. Questions were posed to Mr. Hammond about making the coffers of the various record companies available to the formation of a Black music center. I think that's largely what this whole conference is aiming towards. I think there is this long-term interest, which a number of people have had for many years, but we've never gotten together before. This is one of the things we hope will come out of the conference—a center where the essence of all kinds of the Black musical expression will be preserved and propagated.

SCHULLER: May I ask one more question? I have been in the presence of very violently militant Black people who have said that the only worthwhile Black music is soul music, that this is the only manifestation of Black music that is legitimate. They have gone so far as to accuse other Black composers who happen not to be involved with soul music that they have simply been absorbed into the White culture, and that they are traitors. They're obviously taking a hard and, in my view, a very narrow line. But what do I say? I must admit that I was a little bit speechless. What do you say to a man like that who has a certain kind of statistical backing by the very ironic fact that a large portion of the White people in the United States, for very good reasons, are unable to comprehend Olly Wilson's music, but are immediately able to react to James Brown?

ANDERSON: Since I teach in a Black institution, I face this charge constantly on the part of my students, and I always tell them they have a Blacker-than-thou attitude. Certainly the Black experience is diverse and there's room for everyone. If the revolutionary spirit means anything, it certainly means *freedom*, because that's what is oppressing us at this present time: the lack of freedom. I see the development in many different areas on the part of Black composers, so we have room for Olly Wilson, James Brown and Hale Smith. In fact, we need this diversity. I think it's very important to maintain it.

SMITH: I'd like to make a statement regarding this, Gunther. I think that the persons who take that hard line—and I've come in contact with them also, as perhaps most of us have—first of all are in my opinion underdeveloped musically and they're rationalizing away this weakness, or they're not musicians at all. They're probably basically politicians or people thinking in terms of the social structure and would like to subvert music to their own purposes. All of us, I think, are aware of what happens to music or any art when it is subordinated to political purposes. The decline of music in Soviet Russia is a pretty good example. The decline of music in Nazi Germany is perhaps even more dramatic. I am a Black composer who has extensive experience in jazz and non-jazz areas. When I write of these experiences, my way of sensing rhythm, pitch relationships, formal balances, and so on, are influenced by my background. The fact that a lot of my music would come off much better if it were played by performers with jazz backgrounds doesn't mean that I'm writing jazz, but it does mean that it's written by a person who had had that type of experience, who thinks that way.

WILSON: Gunther, I would suggest that you say nothing when someone asks you this question. There's nothing you can say. Very few people who say that to you may say the same thing to me. One other idea. When we start talking about the study of jazz, we have to recognize that we are dealing with a different kind of idiom. The analytical procedures which are proper for some music are not necessarily proper, complete enough or adequate for jazz. It's impossible for one to study early blues, for example, outside of the context of the oral tradition of Black literature. People erroneously say there is no Black literature, you know, but there's a wealth of it in the oral tradition. The same with music. In order to study that, we have to do it in conjunction with a linguist who knows about words and ideas, preferably someone who's Black. That's what we're involved with at Oberlin. In terms of jazz, again I think there are new types of analytic procedures which one has to develop, particularly suited for this music. This does not mean we have to throw everything else away. Of course not. But it does mean that there are some things about the music we may not be aware of because we have tried to apply the wrong analytical techniques. The issue here, you see, is identification of the music. The need for new techniques in analysis really becomes obvious after the work of A. M. Jones in African music, and of Gunther Schuller in jazz.

SMITH: Whether I think of it consciously or not, one can find extensive examples of ragtime and Charleston rhythms in my music, without it's ever being made an obvious thing. That's my own personal relationship to the preservation of the traditions you're talking about, Gunther.

DE LERMA: The only definition we could accept *pro tempore* is that any work written by a Black composer is Black music. I'm happy the panel feels this way also. This is not an analytical definition. It is a working one. Before worrying about a definition, I think one should know why it is wanted. Our need was strictly bibliographic, so it is a retrospective one, not a philosophical one. In effect, this means, "This has been done and this is the state of things as they are." Other definitions may prove acceptable to one group, but not to another, so these would be of little consequence to us. And I'm very reluctant to accept any *a priori* definition which is not retrospective. One other thing, I'm sure we have all encountered Black militants and White militants, in various degrees. I'm sorry that our membership here these few days is as unified as it is, but I believe there is hope for our cause as well as that of the militant—the Black militant. The White liberal (the unconscious racist) is not hopeless. He is not really sensitive to the ramifications of the issue. It is easy to be outside of the issue, to work with the beauty of renaissance choral music for example, and avoid the whole twentieth century. I'm not ready to ditch anyone's past (that's why we are here, to become better aware of the Black heritage) but it must relate to our own times first. I do hope that encounters any of us experience can be constructive, which will be encouraging and truthful. Emotionalism has already done its damage.

HAMMOND: Is it an inhibiting factor for Black composers to write symphonic music, knowing that this will be played for a small minority of Black people, performed in the great mass by White people?[1]

ANDERSON: I haven't had that experience yet so I can't comment on it.

SMITH: The point here, John, is that there won't be a mass anywhere. When the composer is busy writing, he shouldn't be concerned with who's going to be listening to it, and he shouldn't be concerned about who's going to play it except insofar as he is writing for a specific set of circumstances. But, you know, we can't count on a mass of performances of anything we do, no matter what color we are.

CASWELL: Perhaps the synthesizers will play a role?

WILSON: No, I think to the contrary; it might just be the opposite. When somebody says Olly Wilson writes electronic music, immediately that turns people off. They say, "Electronic music? That's anti-human," or "It's going to replace the performer." This works against you.

CASWELL: Hale, did you say a composer shouldn't think about who is going to

---

1 [In speaking of "the great mass," I feel Mr. Hammond meant this as "the majority." This interpretation was not realized by the speakers. Ed.]

perform his work, or if it is going to be performed at all? Is that what you said?

SMITH: When he's busy writing, he should be concerned with the problems of writing, not who's going to listen to it. He shouldn't be concerned with who's going to play it unless he is writing for a specific body of instrumentalists. The actual job of putting notes on paper is hard enough by itself.

CASWELL: Do you know of any important Black composers who are not published? When you submit a manuscript to a publishing company, do you indicate, "I'm a Black composer," or what?

FEIST: I can state unequivocally that no publisher I've ever known ever took race into consideration in examining a manuscript.

● This was a tremendously important and provocative session. It started off with a virile *sforzando*, thanks to Dr. Anderson's extraordinarily important remarks (which, I might add, were impromptu). He proved himself once again to be verbally articulate, an unexpected quality for a composer, and wonderfully straight forward. The remarks following a spontaneous burst of applause further qualified and amplified his comments. I hope that all persons interested in the subject will consider repeatedly the ideas brought up by these three leading Black composers.

I regret that it is not possible here to include a recording of Dr. Wilson's *In Memoriam to Martin Luther King*. This work is a long way from music we had heard earlier, a difference due partly to the fact that electronic sounds were employed. The composer mentioned that the "electronic medium is an extension of the choral medium," which is certainly manifestly true. Space and sonority are two very important elements of this terse composition, which is not yet commercially available.

The whole question of what is Black music blossomed forth again, and this was not the last time the matter was raised, nor will it be the last. Even though a computer analysis of all Black musical expressions may eventually be possible, I doubt that the matter will be solved to everyone's satisfaction.

More crucial, perhaps, is the question of what is Black? A history of the men and women who descended from the slaves will certainly indicate that substantial progress has already been made toward real integration. Even so, society has forced a separation without clear-cut definitions. What really makes a person Black? The color of one's skin certainly cannot be a real measurement, because many of this race are quite light. My own Afro-Castillian (Moorish-Spanish) heritage has given me darker skin than many whose Blackness was only recently introduced, if one wishes to look at it from that side of the woodpile. Is it a matter of philosophy? Then many who appear to be Black are less so than their more militant neighbors. If we were to find out, for example, that a very distant relative of any composer was of African blood, would that make the composer a Black musician? Suppose the figure were Béla Bartók, Igor Stravinsky, or Carl Nielsen? If it is philosophy that counts, then Leonard Bernstein might be greeted with open arms. It is a matter of who is making the definition. A Black Panther would probably not agree with Thurgood Marshall, and some Southern governors would disagree with these. Perhaps it is the "Experience" which makes it, yet this is substantially different in comparing one who has lived in Harlem all his life with one from Mississippi, or a successful jazz figure who has enjoyed employment in Paris and Stockholm for a decade or two. If we cannot define the race, how can we define the music? This is why I feel more resolved than ever to say that Black music, as our committee uses the term, simply means music written by one who claims to be Black. More precise definitions I leave for others.

It was really an unexpected honor to have Gunther Schuller arrive, even if he could stay for only part of one day. We had hoped to get him as a speaker, but his schedule would not permit it. Instead he came as a listener. He did bring up the matter of a center which would preserve the heritage, and he asked about possible reactions to those young Blacks who refuse to relate to anything before James Brown and other soul singers. In supplement to the responses he got, I call attention again to the tested ideas of Natalie Hinderas (cited at the end of Chapter 2) which suggests that it may be possible to prove that Mozart, Bach and Beethoven (not to mention Anderson, Smith and Wilson) were human beings also, to whom even the non-German or non-Austrian can relate.

And then, as Dr. Wilson pointed out, under the stimulus of the writings of Arthur Morris Jones and Gunther Schuller, the techniques we have for analysis and evaluation of music are terribly parochial. Trying to apply them to jazz or African music, for example, only proves their weaknesses. If we end up with conclusions as a result of this test, it will surely smack of institutional racism, if not just unscholarly pedantry. This challenge is one of the most potent of the entire movement, and merits immediate attention from musicologists and theorists of free spirits.

7. Negro Dance and Its Influence on Negro Music

Verna Arvey

● Verna Arvey, probably known to everyone as Mrs. William Grant Still, is a person of many significant talents. Perhaps she established herself first as an authority on the dance, but she has been a faithful librettist to her husband for many songs and operas, and she is an accomplished music historian and pianist. It was an unexpected pleasure when we found that it would be possible to attract Dr. and Mrs. Still to our seminar, and it was of great value to us to have an authority who could trace the dance from Africa, through Latin America and to the American ballet scene.

When we study the Negro dance through the ages, we may well get a clue as to the reason for the great vitality and fascination of Negro music, for in so many instances Negro folk music and some sort of physical movement have been inseparable. In at least one African tribe, the Dan on the Ivory Coast, only one word is used to indicate dance, song, and instrumental music: *tā*. The Dan say that music (meaning music *and* dance) is literally that which imparts vitality to a man. Ezra Pound wrote, "Music begins to atrophy when it departs too far from the dance. Poetry begins to atrophy when it gets too far from music. But this must not be taken as implying that all music is dance music, or all poetry is lyrical. Bach and Mozart are never too far from physical movement." In a related comment, Margaret Glenn said, "No national music can exist long without national dance, and it is evident that the Puritan movement in England, by killing the dance, dealt a heavy blow to the national music."

We all understand that these statements may not be universally true, but even if they contain only a small percentage of truth, it is easy to comprehend the infectious quality of most Negro folk music, so much of which as a matter of course has been automatically an accompaniment to the dance. In fact, "Kid" Thompson, husband of the late Florence Mills, told me that in our own show business, the Negro singers who were hired had to be able to dance, as well as sing: Florence Mills, Ethel Waters, Hattie McDaniel—these were not exceptions to the rule, although we don't think of them as dancers. Today this guideline still holds in many instances. Singers like Shirley Bassy, Barbara Mc Nair and Sammy Davis, Jr., can and do dance and sing. In the cases where specific dances are done to specific music, movements have undoubtedly been influenced by the music, and vice-versa. One might call it a true wedding of music and dance.

These two, music and dance, have also been influenced by another factor: costumes. In certain formal European dances, movements were inhibited by the clothing worn by the dancers, hence the dance music was also inhibited. This was not generally true of African dancers, despite their often cumbersome headdresses, dance masks, and such, so their bodies were freer to move at will. This surely accounts for the distinctive character of some of their dance movements and, in turn, for the character of the accompanying music. In passing, it should be noted that the African melodies followed the African words of the song, while movements were influenced by the costume.

Dancing in Africa varies (like the music) from tribe to tribe, and region to region, ranging from a rather self-conscious slow shuffle to the spectacular movements of the tall Watusi. Some are most interesting in their formations and in the originality of their steps and movements.

Of great importance is the fact that Africa's music and dances are used for every significant development in the life of a human being, and in the daily and seasonal life of a tribe.

In most cases throughout Africa and the Western hemisphere, the great unifying element in much of the native dancing is the drum, and in those instances where drums do not predominate, some other percussive device is used to mark the rhythm. Henry Cowell once said there was a question as to just what constitutes a rhythm, implying that even non-rhythms can be considered rhythms. I do not agree with this idea; a rhythm has to be recognizable as a rhythm before it can be one. The Negro dance and dance music down through the ages have certainly exemplified rhythm above all. And as long as this distinctive quality exists, it will endure as a truly creative form of expression, pertinent to all facets of life.

For instance, among the people of the Dan, there is a festival music and dancing after the excision rite for girls (girls as well as boys are circumcised in the various tribes). The girls have learned the songs and dance in the bush while their wounds were healing. They return to the village where they sing and dance, accompanied by several adult women and some young men. The girls and women wear jingling ankle bells while the boys beat drums as they dance. In another Dan village, the young girls sing in the Malinké language and do a sword dance at the conclusion of the excision rites.

In Ruanda, in the heart of Africa, vocal and instrumental music are distinct in style, although vocal music goes along with the dance and hand clapping in many instances. This may be exemplified by some of the popular songs of the Lake Kivu region of the Kasenyi territory, where women and girls sing and dance during marriage celebrations with responsorial solo and choir alternations. At times in this music, one can hear intervals reminiscent of Negro spirituals.

The music of the Pygmies is equal in interest to that of other African groups. They too have songs and dances for the hunt, for wakes, and for daily events. So also the Giriyama tribe of East Africa, whose complicated dance steps are most interesting, or the Tonga tribe of northern Rhodesia, which makes use often of the calabash, resonating a one-string bow instrument. And the Mulari tribe appears to be more sophisticated in its dance music which is not unlike that heard in the large Congo towns and has some similarities to our own popular music. The instruments that might be used could include the guitar, clarinet, flute and double bass, as well as the African hand piano, the *likembe*.

When Africans were sold into slavery, their forced journeys to the west resulted in a rich blend of music and dance. In each different country, there was a fusion of musical ideas with those of the other races. Thus in Brazil, the African fused with the Portugese, in Martinique and Louisiana with the French, in the United States with the Anglo-Saxon, and in so many other countries with the Spanish and Indian. The fusion was so widespread that it isn't easy to find a spot where it didn't occur.

One exception is said to be Puerto Rico, where the Spanish established their own culture which gave rise, not only to use of their own sixteenth-century dance, the *seis*, but to instruments patterned after instruments of their homeland, so the *seis* continued its tradition without outside influence. The nineteenth century in Puerto Rico produced the romantic *danza*, again without direct African influence, but thought to have been introduced from Cuba, where African influences are acknowledged. The more modern *plena* has a rhythm used by dance bands in Puerto Rico, not without a resemblance to African music. The statement that Puerto Rican music is not influenced by the Negro is open to question in some areas.

Before proceeding to the various other types of Negro dance music in the western hemisphere, I would like to say that those of us who enjoy travelogues and who have endured the same old limbo dances from island to island in the Caribbean will be delighted to know that this is not the only dance done by Negroes. A good deal of variety in movements and formations were discovered by Zora Neale Hurston on a tour of the area. It was Miss Hurston, incidentally, who antedated most of the people who presented Caribbean music and dance to North American audiences. She gave a West Indian folkloric program in New York City around 1932, which came before the success of *Run Little Chilun*, and of Katherine Dunham.

Miss Hurston discovered a dance descended from Equatorial Africa in the Congo area, in most places where Negroes were to be found. In Jamaica it was danced to a Voodoo chant called *Hand d' bowl*. This is a circular dance wherein one person follows the other with left arm held forward, elbow bent close to the left side, hand held upright and flat, with continuous movement from side to side in rhythm. Occasionally someone breaks loose and jumps in or out of the circle, doing a spontaneous, individual step. There are many jumps or jumping dances in which the dancers move forward, holding their arms akimbo. Arms and knees move out and in rhythm, with one knee lifted on the last half of the second beat. Here, too, individuals leave the group, jump into the ring and make an individual contribution. Ring plays are also circular dances with soloists who are joined by the spectators as they wish. The men go around the circle, selecting their partners by pirouetting in front of them, then their partners join them in the center. Each couple develops its own movements, some of which are quite spectacular, and these are only a few of the variants in the dance movements.

In Curaçao, Aruba and Bonaire, the music and dance reflect the many different people who live there, principally the Dutch and Negro. Most characteristic is the *tumba*, rapid with a unique, broken rhythm. It is always sung in Papiamento, a dialect which blends the Dutch, Spanish, Portuguese, French and English, and is most typical when performed in the rural areas. It is danced vigorously, more or less like a free-style ballroom dance, with its form and steps varying from individual to individual.

Haiti has a distinctive ballroom dance called the *meringue* which is somewhat musically similar to the national music and dance of the Dominican Republic, the *merengue*, spelled with a change of only one letter. This also has several forms: the original, uninhibited folky expression, danced by the country people, and a more sophisticated version danced in ballrooms to the music of good dance orchestras. There are no strenuous movements in the latter version, as there are in some African dances. It flows along using an exaggerated limp as its distinguishing step. Haiti's *meringue* has an unusual rhythmic combination. It is written in 2/4 time, and the melody is generally conservatively within that boundry, but the accompaniment is divided into five. In his opera, *Ouanga*, Clarence Cameron White makes use of this dance. Besides the Haitian *meringue*, the country people on this island seem to have preserved forms of music and dance more purely African than in any other locale. Take for example the Haitian Ibo dance song for female voices, chorus and drums, the famous Haitian drums. This music is associated with religious cults actually existing in Africa, taking its name from a tribe in southern Nigeria.

The *beguine* is a dance created on French islands in the Western hemissphere, Guadeloupe and Martinique in particular. Its basic rhythm is reminiscent of African percussion effects, while the melodies are more Parisian. Cole Porter's well-known song, *Begin the beguine*, is not a real *beguine* at all.

Trinidad's most characteristic dance is the "jump up," observed by Miss Hurston on several islands. It was originally danced to the rhythm of African drums alone, but the steel band calypso rhythms are now its usual accompaniment.

Slaves were brought, not only to the islands of the West Indies, but to the South American continent, and there the fusion followed the same pattern, excepting that this was in the main a fusion of the Spanish with the Negro. For instance, typical of Venezuela is the *joropo*, thought to be a blend of African with Spanish and Andalusian melodies brought to Venezuela by the Spanish conquerors. The *joropo*, is a name whose origin and meaning are now lost, but applies to a rhythmic form characteristic of this dance. Thus many songs, each with its own individual title, may be *joropos*. The dance always has several sections, one of which is the *zapateado*, a typically Spanish expression with rhythmic stamping of the feet. It is found in folk dances in nearly all areas settled by Spaniards. The musical instruments for the *joropo* are adapted from those originally brought from Spain: a home-made harp to carry the melody, a four-stringed guitar called the cuatro, a pair of maracas, and a singer. The *joropo* is also danced in Colombia, but there they call it the *paseo*, a shortened waltz movement.

Uruguay has an entirely different form of dance accompaniment for special occasions. It is called the *tamboril*, and consists of four drums in different sizes, each with a pitch and name of its own, the chico, the repique, the piano, and the bajo or bomba. These are accompanied by dance steps only; no song, or melody or other instrument. They are used principally during carnival season and are termed the Afro-Uruguayan *tamboril*.

Colombia and Panama share a native dance of Negro origin, a wooing dance called the *cumbia*. In this, the women hold themselves rigidly as they dance, holding lighted candles in their upraised hands. The men dance around them, each man around his own partner, in individual circles, inviting them to love. In the *Cumbia y Congo* from the *Danzas de Panamá*, my husband has simulated percussive sounds by having the musicians beat on their instruments. In Panamá, the *tamborito* is a dance of Negro origin also. Colombia has still another dance of African ancestry, a *currulao*, in which two files of men and women dance face to face in a semi-circle. They usually have seven drums of different tones, a wooden marimba, a gourd, and two harmonizing singers.

Slavery was introduced to Cuba in 1514. About half a century later, Teodora Gines, in the city of Santiago de Cuba, invented the *son*, a musical form which was adapted to fit the movements of a native dance of African origin. It spread all over the tropics. The *son* music possesses the greatest variety of all Afro-Cuban dance music with an abundance of rhythmic counterpoint (sometimes five or six different simultaneous rhythms), with any one of its usually half a dozen instrumentalists bursting into song while playing.

It is interesting to know that the tango rhythm, similar to the *habañera* (which came to Spain from Africa), is evident in all countries where Negroes live, even though it goes by different names. Sometimes, by the addition or omission of a single notes, it appears to have changed its character. W. C. Handy has shown that this rhythm is the basis for the North American Charleston. William Grant Still has noted its similarity to the most widely used rhythmic figure for the North American cakewalk. Perhaps we're not so familiar with the dance music performed in the Cuban countryside. There is an Arara cult song with female voices and rattles, with sounds that often seem to have come straight out of Africa; years and generations between have made very little difference. This music exists today in Cuba's Jovellanos province, as it did yesterday in Africa.

When one thinks of dances of Negro derivation in Brazil, probably the first one to come to mind is the *samba*, and yet that word is only a designating term for music of the Brazilian people since just before the First World War. It probably is a corruption of the last two syllables of *macumba*, an important secret Negro religious ceremony reserved for initiates with its big celebration on St. Anne's Day. One of the oldest Brazilian forms of music and dance is the *embolada*, from the northern part of the country. This was originally no more than dance tunes in which the Negro influence dominated: precipitate rhythms, syncopation, flatted intervals, and such. *Embolada*, incidentally, was Villa-Lobos' subtitle for his *Bachianas brasileiras no. 1*, inspired by dances of that name. Also from the north of Brazil comes the song *taieras*, a dance of the Mulatresses in the state of Bahia. Elsie Houston ascribes a religious aspect to this song and claims that it is a fusion of Christian and pagan elements, as well as of Negro and Portuguese. One of Brazil's most important types of songs, according to Miss Houston, is an African dance of simple structure called the *batuque*, from which word was derived *batucada*, meaning a Brazilian hot manner of playing. It is in the style of a *batuque* with an ostinato bass that mounts to a frenzy. Some of Brazil's finest composers have idealized the *batuque*, such as Villa-Lobos in his *Suite brasileira* for piano, and Oscar Lorenzo Fernández in his opera *Malazarte*. Villa-Lobos composed another work in this vein, much admired by his biographers: three *Danzas africanas*, written for piano in 1914 and expanded in 1916 for orchestra, using indigenous Brazilian instruments as well as rhythmic traditions of the Negro *macumba*, combined with those of tribes native to the Matto Grosso. I once heard someone venture the opinion that Villa-Lobos had some Negro blood. I inquired of Miss Houston. She said this was not true, though he was interested in Negro music, but that his first wife was what we would call a Colored woman in that she had a strain of Negro blood.

In the state of Michoacán in Mexico, in Tzinzuntzan, there exists a Negro dance that is really not a Negro dance, as far as I can see. It is called *Dansa de los Negritos*, but it is of colonial origin and is a parody of the ceremony in which the Indians rendered tribute to their Spanish masters. The melody is in 6/8 meter, so typical of many Mexican folk tunes. To me, there's nothing about it excepting the name which would suggest Negroes. However, there is a Mexican *bamba* which one traveler thought was a Negro corruption of the Spanish *banda*, meaning sash. He described it as an old dance of Afro-Cuban inspiration and said its music revealed the most notable contributions made by Negroes: the free, melodic improvisation, as in the vocal part, and the unrelenting syncopation which constantly alters and displaces the rhythmic values. Such intricate rhythmical play can be found whenever the Negro has intervened in American folk music. He also claimed that the famous *huapango* from Veracruz has some Negro influence, and this is quite possible, for the states of Veracruz, Guerrero and Chiapas did have Negro settlements.

Different sections of the United States were settled by people from different parts of Europe, so the Negro dances and music in each section differed in a similar manner. Perhaps the most famous were those in Louisiana, where Frenchmen and Spaniards lived. The slaves, who answered the call of African drums and other musical instruments of the Place Congo in New Orleans whenever they had a rest period, danced most of the dances then known in the New World, many of them identical to those of the West Indies. The *bamboula*, deriving its name from the *bula* (the African drum used to accompany it), was one of the best known. At least two very well-known composers idealized the *bamboula*, both of them using the authentic musical theme: Gottschalk and Coleridge-Taylor. The *calinda* was another widely known Negro dance in New Orleans. It was not only danced by the multitudes in Place Congo, but also in more formal surroundings at the Quadroon Balls in the city. The watchword here was "Dancez calinda, badoum, badoum." The contemporary composer Ulysses Kay has written a ballet titled *Calinda*, while none other than Frederick Delius, who was first inspired to become a composer while listening to Negroes sing on his Florida plantation, wrote a *calinda* in the second act of his opera *Koanga*. This was his third opera, and was said to have a Negro-Spanish background. The *calinda* in it was originally part of his *Florida Suite*. The first movement was composed in 1888, when he was twenty-six years old. The third movement of the suite is also said to be reminiscent of the Negro dance after its quiet opening. The Delius *calinda* melody seems rather conventional, but underneath we find the same rhythmic figure so typical of music written in the Negro dance idiom.

Away from Louisiana and masters of Latin origin, different types of music were developed on the southern plantations. The *plantation shout* was a rhythmic song always accompanied by some sort of physical movement, usually a circular march, according to Krehbiel. Work songs, rhythmic spirituals, sometimes accompanied by ring shouts, and secular music all followed in the course of time. The *juba* was a dance for hands and feet, named after an old African ghost. It was done to the melody of a single fiddle plus a combination of rhythmic stamps and percussive hand claps. Dr. Dett idealized this in his stirring *Juba Dance* from the piano suite *In the Bottoms*, and by Florence Price in her *Dances from the Canebrakes*.

The *cakewalk* became one of the most popular American dances of all time, and it was a Negro creation. One elderly lady told me that White folks danced the *quadrille*, but not the *cakewalk*. And yet this same *cakewalk*, later taken up by White society, found its origin in the Grand March which so often concluded the balls given by White people. Colored people simply added a variety of interesting action and the characteristic grace to the same idea, with the added incentive of walking for their cake in couples. Paul Lawrence Dunbar, the poet, and the composer Will Marion Cook collaborated on a sketch called *Clorindy, the Origin of the Cakewalk*, and when stage stars like Williams and Walker presented the *cakewalk* in their stage appearances, the dance's popularity began to spread all over the country. As it did, it inspired a great deal of *cakewalk* music, just as the later *shimmy* brought forth so many *shimmy* songs. W. C. Handy recognized dances such as *truckin'*, the *Susie-Q*, the *Big apple*, *Black bottom*, *Charleston*, and the *Lindy hop* as being evolutions of Negro folk dances, and spoke of the fact that out of all these dances came special songs to fit them. When he was a boy, there was the *Jenny cooler* and the *African pas*. The latter was accompanied by a song which went, "First you do this, then you do that," and so on, very much like the song *Ballin' the Jack*.

Before proceeding to the dance and dancers who made theatrical history, it might be interesting to take a look at the European scene as regards the Negro dance, first, at one particular composer who was himself Colored, but whose music displayed no racial characteristics as we know them. This was the flamboyant Chevalier de Saint-Georges, born in 1745 of a native mother and a Frenchman on the island of Guadeloupe. He was educated in France, became a gifted violinist, fencer and composer. He composed in the style of the period and the place, hence his music is far removed from the African. Much later, and not long before his death, we find none other than Johannes Brahms confessing to a friend that he would like to do something with the interesting rhythms of ragtime, but that he feared he was too old (this is reported in Schauffler's book, *The Unknown Brahms*). Debussy was also interested in the idiom, as shown in the final movement (Golliwogg's cakewalk) of his piano suite, *Le coin des enfants*. Cyril Scott was another composer who was enough intrigued to write a brilliant *Danse nègre* for the piano, but not enough to put into that composition elements usually recognizable as being Negroid.

We must bear in mind that in America, Negro music and dance spread from place to place while still an exclusively folk expression, but did not become known until presented on the stage to "regular" audiences. The plantation owners used to have their gifted slaves perform for visiting tobacco buyers on the long front porches. This entertainment developed into minstrel shows done by Colored performers. White people later took over that field and promptly made a caricature of the Negro. Later came successful Negro shows and successful Negro individual artists, and it was through these that the native product swept all over the world.

Tap dancing is undoubtedly a descendant of the early hoe-down, a cotton field dance. This gave way to "buck" or tap dancing, and "winging," a dance with flying steps. Minstrel shows combined these and made them into the "buck 'n' wing," done to the popular music of the period. Soft shoe dancing, done to music of the schottische type and tempo, was also a tap dance, but a more graceful one. It envolved from the dancing of the roustabouts along the banks of the Mississippi and was called the "Virginia essence." It was danced on the stage by the very first Negro minstrels, but credit for introducing it has usually been given to Billy Kersands. Remembering that Africans didn't wear shoes, and therefore had no way of indicating intricate rhythms with their feet (outside of the usual foot stamping and the sound of jungling anklets), I have often wondered whether tap dancing couldn't have been at least partly inspired by the Latin *zapateado* or heel tapping, which was adopted into so many Negro dances in the Western Hemisphere. If that is true, in whole or in part, the Negro certainly did with it as he had done with so many other matters: made it peculiarly his own. By far the most publicized tap dancer of our generation was Bill Robinson, nicknamed "Bojangles."

Credit for being the greatest Negro *cakewalk* attraction on the stage was given to the team of Johnson and Dean. They danced the *cakewalk* first in 1891 and continued to feature it in their act until they were well into their seventies. Williams and Walker, of course, were more widely-publicized artists so when, in 1896, they recognized the value of the *cakewalk*, they used in it shows in American and abroad, making it fashionable on two continents. They didn't change the dance itself. They simply improved it by giving it more style.

We must not pass this period in the American theater without paying tribute to Bob Cole, whom James Weldon Johnson called "the greatest single force in the middle period of the Negro in the American theater." The widely popular Cole and Johnson shows have now become legendary. Cole himself was a singer, dancer, instrumentalist, producer, writer, composer and actor—a bewildering array of talents for a single individual, and he was said to have done everything well.

Shuffle Along, a Negro show that made theatrical history, was a far cry from
the plantation presentation. The dances, staged by Lawrence Deas, were after-
ward used as models by other show directors. Their charm, according to W.
C. Handy, was that each dancer gave an individual expression to the set routines. Flournoy Miller, incidentally, has been the generous source of much of
my information on Negro theatrical dancing. Out of *Shuffle Along* came
many famous artists, among them the beloved Florence Mills.

Miss Mills was an instinctive dancer. She never took a dancing lesson until
she arrived at the theater and began to rehearse her new numbers. She started
dancing when she was five years old, dancing then in *Sons o' Ham*. Then
there was the fabulous Josephine Baker, who is still alive and active. She was
born Josephine Carson, in St. Louis, of a Spanish father and a Colored mother.
She was only twelve when she joined the Bob Russell Dixie Steppers as a
chorus girl. About three years later, she was in the second line of the *Shuffle
Along* chorus when one of the chorines in the first line fell ill. She substituted
for her and used the opportunity to cross her eyes, make grotesque gestures
and thus attract everyone's attention to herself. The rest is history. Josephine
Baker went to Europe, again taking every opportunity to attract attention, and
succeeding to an outstanding degree. As one writer put it, "She exaggerates
everything she does and is a great example of what can be done with a minimum of talent and a maximum of hard work." She learned to sing French
songs in an authentic style and, although she long ago abandoned the banana
skirt for the tutu, she still danced as in a music hall, with high kicks and back
bends. The French people thought of her as a savage, whereas they said of
Florence Mills that she was "no longer the tigress who stands before us, but
the marquise who has rubbed a little burnt cork on her cheeks instead of her
customary rouge, dancing a court charleston."

Eddie Anderson, Jack Benny's Rochester, began his career singing and
dancing in San Francisco hotel lobbies for servicemen of World War I. He
went on to a notable career as a comedian.

Several dancers have been instrumental in bringing native Negro dances to
the New York stage. One of these was Asadata Dafora, who was born in Sierra
Leone. He attended an Italian music school and then served as a sergeant major in the British army during the First World War, using an English name,
Austin Norton. Gradually be became interested in acquainting people with
the true customs of the African people, their manner of dressing, songs, and
a little of their mode of life. This interest resulted in the play, *Kykunkor*,

which he presented in New York in the thirties. After Dafora there were several similar presentations, some by people formerly associated with him.

Later came Pearl Primus, born in Trinidad but an expatriate to New York where she turned to expressing the Negro heritage in the dance. She went to Africa in search of usable material and, after that, specialized in tribal dancing. Her concerts took her all over, even to London for a command performance.

Forerunners of the Negro dancers engaged today on the concert stage are seldom remembered nowadays. The three most notable were Edna Guy, a Denishawn dancer who founded the New York Concert Dance Group and gave inspiration to aspiring Negro dancers; Wilson Williams, organizer of several Negro dance companies; and Hemsley Winfield, who founded the New Negro Art Theater in New York in 1931. He had the intellect and personal magnetism so necessary to climb to the heights. He gave recitals and radio lectures on the dance, and created and danced the solo ballet sequences for Louis Gruenberg's opera, *Emperor Jones*, at the Metropolitan Opera House. The composer David Guion wrote an African ballet, *Shingandi*, especially for him. Mr. Winfield fell ill during a period of worry over the fate of his dancers and of his family, and died in a New York hospital in 1934, not quite 27 years of age, a time when most careers are beginning, not ending.

Then along came Katherine Dunham, perhaps the best publicized of any Colored concert dancer. Miss Dunham was little more than a child when she organized a dance group from among the neighborhood children in Joliet, Illinois, and later studied at the University of Chicago. In the early thirties she and Mark Turby Fill, a ballet dancer of the Chicago Civic Opera Company, conceived the idea of a Negro ballet school along strict ballet lines, to be located in Chicago's art colony on Fifty-seventh Street. In 1931, she presented her group at the Chicago Beaux Arts Ball. She then formed a modern dance group in Chicago, appeared in stage productions and had leading roles in William Grant Still's ballet, *La Guiablesse*, in its two productions by the Chicago Civic Opera Company. She acquired a degree in anthropology from the University of Chicago, and then received both Rosenwald and Rockefeller awards. She was a gifted writer as well as a choreographer.

One of Miss Dunham's co-workers in later years was Syvilla Fort, an artist in her own right. Miss Fort hails from the Pacific Northwest, the University of Washington, and the Cornish School.

Currently, there are several successful Negro dancers on the American concert stage. In the Martha Graham Company, there are Clive Thompson and

Mary Hinkson. Carmen de Lavallade and her husband, Geoffrey Holder, appear frequently in concert. Miss de Lavallade and her sister, Yvonne, were products of the old Lester Horton Dance Company in Los Angeles, while Mr. Holder is a native of Trinidad. He came to New York in 1953 and became a leading male dancer at the Metropolitan Opera House. In addition, he is a gifted artist and a recipient of a Guggenheim Fellowship.

Others who started their training with Lester Horton and went on to win acclaim on their own were Alvin Ailey and Norman de Joie. The latter's specialty is the Nijinsky role in Debussy's *Afternoon of a Faun*. He is soloist with the Ballet Moderne de Paris where he went after a period of study with Syvilla Fort. Until 1950, Alvin Ailey was studying romance languages at the University of California, with a view to eventual teaching. Lester Horton remembered him, however, from a brief visit to his classes before he entered college, phoned him, and managed to interest him in a full-time dancing career. He returned to the classes and took over the Horton Company when Mr. Horton died in 1953. He then danced in films, on television and in the Broadway musical *House of flowers*. Several years later he formed his own group, The American Dance Theater, which is still functioning in a significant way. Mr. Ailey is a dancer as well as a choreographer, and includes a blues on almost every program.

A great deal of the music for modern dancing is composed to fit the dance in collaboration with the choreographer. William Grant Still's four ballets, however, were composed first and choreographed later. Each one of these represents a different type of Negro music. The African ballet, *Sahdji*, is based on a scenario by Alain Locke and Richard Bruce. It concerns the faithless wife of the chieftain of an African tribe who is forced to join her husband in death after he is killed in the hunt, when his nephew (her lover) is about to suceed him as chief. At the time this ballet was written, during the depression, there was very little authentic African folk material available for study. Books and recordings were so scarce as to be almost non-existent, so the composer had to create his own musical speech in the style of an African idiom. Like the ancient Greeks, he used a chorus as well as the orchestra. The work was dedicated to Howard Hanson of the Eastman School of Music. It was first produced in Rochester as part of the American Composers' Concerts, and was so successful that Dr. Hanson decided to devote one evening in every forthcoming festival of American music to ballets.

The second of Mr. Still's ballets was *La Guiablesse*, the name being patois for she-devil, and the setting being the island of Martinique. The scenario was adapted by Ruth Page from a story of Lafcadio Hearn and it was, you will recall, in the Chicago Opera production of this that Katherine Dunham made one of her most auspicious appearances. Here again, material on the music of Martinique was not available at the time this ballet was composed, so Mr. Still had to devise his own musical idiom to fit the purpose.

In a strikingly different mood and style is Mr. Still's ballet of the old South, *Miss Sally's Party*. This is a period piece which ends with a cakewalk, not a pure cakewalk, however, because the little boys have put a frog down the back of the smart city visitor, and the music reflects his resultant gyrations as he tries, but fails, to win the cake.

Lenox Avenue was originally written for a CBS commission, and was later converted into a ballet. As its title would imply, the subject matter and musical idiom are typical of the big city Negro. The finale combines chorus and orchestra in a scene with voices of the church choir mingling with the sound of a cabaret orchestra and a jazz pianist at a house rent party.

● At the 1970 meeting of the National Music Educators Conference, I had the pleasure of being on a program with Professor Harry Morgan of the Bank Street College of Education in New York. Professor Morgan showed a video tape of dances improvised at a special program for school drop-outs. The next month I was at a symposium on Black music developed by Professor Nicholas D'Angelo for Hobart and William Smith Colleges in Geneva, New York. Here I saw a second video tape, this one prepared by Dr. James Standifer of Temple University. Both of these experiences reminded me of ideas Mrs. Still had brought forth at our 1969 seminar, and suggested the importance within the curriculum (especially in pre-college work) of providing students with the opportunity to experience their music through dance. It might be easier for us to consider the minuets of Mozart symphonies without being overly concerned with dance steps and the interrelationships of movement to sound but, as she points out, in Black music we are dealing with a cultural manifestation which has long been more than music, and more than dance. To consider African dances in terms only of music may be as short-sighted as knowing the overture to *Rienzi* only from a band transcription, or never having heard *Carmen* in French. And, although I would hate to see Afro dances incorporated in the gym schedules along with baseball and tennis, and taught by the same staff, one cannot help but remark on the fact that these dances would contribute greatly to the development of physical fitness, and that African drumming can produce the same type of discipline toward which Hindemith's educational techniques aim.

8. *A Composer's Viewpoint*

● Hale Smith has already related how he has expressed his appreciation to Dr. Still for all of the things this distinguished gentleman did to
pave the way for the following generations of Black Americans. There
are probably very few firsts which are not a part of the William Grant
Still biography.

As Dr. Still mildly suggests, these seventy-four years were not easy
ones for him. Had he not been determined (and gifted), resolute (and
militant), the pain of these struggles would have fallen on the shoulders
of another man.

But he merits respect not because he was the first, nor because he is
Black. He is a composer who has contributed a lifetime of dedication to
music.

I would like to preface my remarks by stating what will soon be an obvious
fact to all of you, namely that I am a composer, and not an orator. You may
well decide that composers such as I ought to devote themselves to composing,
not talking. However, I have been asked to speak in public so often in recent
years that I have tried to accustom myself to what is expected, and I ask you
to bear with me now through my ordeal.

Furthermore, although we are committed to an extensive discussion of
Black music, I would like to emphasize that I speak not only as a Negro, but
also as an American. For a long time we Afro-Americans needed something
like the fact that Black can be beautiful to give us identity and pride in our
racial heritage. Now that has been accomplished. Most of us come to realize
that Black is indeed beautiful, but only as White, Brown, or Yellow are beautiful: when we make it so. The term has served its purpose, so I hope from this
time forward we will all want to emphasize our American ties, as well as
our African heritage. Our parents and grandparents, I think, wanted us above
all else to be good Americans and to get a substantial education, so that we
could compete on an equal basis with all other Americans. And speaking about
parents and grandparents, let's recapitulate for a few minutes and recall what
it was like to be a Negro musician then, and how far we have progressed.
Looking at the past may shed some light on the future.

To begin with, my father was one of those who endured all sorts of sacrifices in order to get an education and to become, on the side, a musician. Long before the turn of the century, he worked hard toward this end. He taught mathematics, had a half interest in a store, sang solos in church, and learned to play the cornet the hard way. Each lesson cost him a seventy-five mile trip from Woodville, Mississippi, to Baton Rouge, Louisiana, where the only competent teacher for miles around could be found. When he had absorbed enough of this training, he formed the only brass band in Woodville. People who knew him in those days said that he was admired by both Negroes and Whites. I can well believe it, for many Southern people have a feeling of genuine affection for Negro musicians—not enough, of course, to make them acceptable as equals, but enough to make them the objects of a certain amount of indulgence. W. C. Handy once elaborated on this by saying that if he needed money, he could get it if he pretended he wanted it to buy liquor or to gamble, but not if he said he wanted it to buy books for his children. I think this affection for Negro musicians has extended to the present day, when so many Southerners are truly interested in culture, and so many take pride in those Negro artists who have succeeded and who had their roots in the South.

My father may have been, as they said, the idol of the town, but he surely would have found it difficult to transform that worship into cash at that time and in that area. In fact, I wonder whether he ever was paid at all for his musical activities. Had he lived beyond his twenty-fourth year, he might have had enough drive to earn his living in music if he chose to do so, for he was an ambitious young man. But he didn't live, so we'll never know.

The earning capacity of Negro musicians was indeed limited in those days, and continued to be so for quite a while. I recall the serenaders, small groups of Negro musicians who, when I was a boy, would go from house to house at night, playing stringed instruments and singing. Residents would throw them coins. Yesterday that was a fitting reward. Today it would be less than a mere pittance.

When I was along in my school years, my mother engaged a teacher to give me violin lessons, and encouraged me to study music. However, I didn't want to be a performer. I wanted to compose, and no sooner did I learn to read music than I wanted to write it. This was fine, as far as my mother was concerned, until she learned that I wanted to make music my life's work. Then she opposed me. This seemed strange to me at the time, because my mother was herself a person of more than ordinary artistic ability. She taught English in the secondary school, wrote and directed plays, painted, and played the piano a little.

Her own goals were high. She constantly urged me to make something of myself, and not to follow the path of least resistance. However, a career in music was outside the bounds of consideration for her and, as she persisted in her efforts to discourage me, I began to understand why. The Negro musicians of her day were not socially accepted into the better Negro homes. In fact, many Colored people considered them immoral. They disapproved of their drinking, and they certainly looked down on their earning capacity! My mother was very explicit on the latter count. She pictured me as wearing threadbare clothes, starving, and unable to provide the bare necessities of life. Her ridicule was fairly constant and unwavering. She wanted me to become a doctor so I could make enough money to live on. Today I can see that she did what she did for my benefit, yet even today it is hard for me to realize that the structure of Negro society at that time was such that even a woman of her vision could not understand that the kind of composer I meant to be was far different from her concept, nor would she or others of that period have envisioned an Afro-American attaining a position of prominence in the symphonic or operatic fields! You can understand that when I tell you that not until I got to Oberlin and had reached my majority did I ever hear a symphony orchestra! That would explain it. I wonder what the people of that day would say today, when so many American Negroes are seeking to reach such goals, with a reasonable number actually making the grade.

After I left college, economic and racial factors did indeed influence my way of life—to my ultimate advantage, however. I was determined to make a living in music, and the popular field was the only commercial field open to me and others like me. I went into it with one thought uppermost in my mind: I intended to learn all I could from American popular music in order to put the knowledge to good use in my later career. In other words, I wanted to learn, but not to make the popular field an end in itself. I still feel that this was a wise course of action, for what I learned there was not available anywhere else. It later balanced my conservatory training to give more facets to my musical personality.

When I went to work with W. C. Handy in Memphis in 1916, playing in his orchestra and arranging, I gained a first-hand contact with Negro folk music that was not available to me at home. I learned, for example, to appreciate the beauty of the blues, and to consider this the musical expression of the yearnings of a lowly people, instead of accepting it superficially as being immoral and sexy, as so many other people did.

Most of you are no doubt aware that there came a time in our musical history when American Negroes even looked down on spirituals, because they associated them with the days of slavery. Knowing this, you can well imagine the prejudice that existed against the blues which stemmed, supposedly, from the big city dives. I recall when I was a boy in Little Rock asking a pianist to play the *Memphis Blues* for me. She was afraid, because of the bad reputation of the music. Fortunately, both spirituals and blues have emerged from the period of ill repute, and are now generally recognized as very important contributions of the Negro to our American life.

Other aspects of my association with Handy will shed light on the social conditions of the Negro musician of that period. At home I had been sheltered, and had moved in what I would consider enlightened social circles, but on the road with Handy and his orchestra, I found that the indulgence many people felt for Negro musicians did not extend to giving them much consideration for their ordinary needs. Handy's orchestra played the length and breadth of the South. Larger cities had accommodations for us (segregated, of course) but in some of the smaller communities there were no places for Negroes to stay. I remember once in winter, in the mountainous section not far from Bristol, Tennessee (where we were playing) we stayed in a mountain home where the flooring consisted of rough pieces of wood and the openings were almost a half an inch apart. The wind blew through these openings, just as if we were outdoors. It was cold even in bed! And we had to eat grits and sow belly. I'll never forget that experience.

At another time, we were playing in a little town in Arkansas. It was very interesting there. A White man came and sat by me. He liked the cello, and he stayed right there and listened. He didn't get far away at all until it came time for us to quit playing. Handy went to collect his pay, which was given without question, but we discovered that no one had thought to make arrangements for our housing. There simply was no place to stay, so we walked back to the station. It was locked, and we were out in the cold. Handy took his cornet case, broke a window, and unlatched the door. We sat inside the station for the rest of the night, and Handy later paid for the broken window.

Our traveling was done in Jim Crow cars, which were usually only half cars. They offered very little that was comfortable or desirable: cinders, smoke, unpleasant odors, and the feeling of humiliation, being compelled to pay first-class fare for third-rate accommodations. One time in Alabama, a Negro prisoner was placed in our car. His captors relieved themselves of responsibility by locking him in the toilet which, by the way, was the only one on the train

Negro passengers could use. Under these circumstances, we naturally could not use it, but the prisoner solved our problem by breaking the window and escaping.

Early one morning, our train made a short stop in Rome, Georgia. We had gone all night without food, and we were all hungry. Again there was no place for us to eat. We were told at one restaurant that if we went to the back, we would be served. We didn't want to do that, partly because of the humiliation, and partly because we were afraid of missing the train, so we got back on and rode until past noon without food.

My last incident has a brighter ending. One day in a Kentucky town, we went to the Negro restaurant, but it smelled like a privy. None of us wanted to eat there, so we went to a White restaurant right in town, across from the court house. We described our predicament to the owner and he promptly invited us in, sat us by the front window, and served us a delicious meal. With our thoughts geared to the reality of segregation, we had expected him to put up a screen in front of us, but he didn't. He treated us just like his other customers.

In relating this, I've had another purpose in mind besides telling you about Negro musicians and their world over a half-century ago. I have heard reports of Negroes today who are trying to turn the clock back, and bring separation and segregation again into our lives. I say they can't know what they are talking about. They have certainly never experienced segregation and its inconveniences as some of us have. Even if they do understand what it is, and are willing to endure its humiliations for themselves, it is not fair to advocate it for the rest of us and for our children. Instead of all this big separatist talk, they should get down on their knees and thank God that the present laws in the United States have made segregation illegal.

One prominent White California educator, on reviewing the current separatist efforts, recently wrote: "Shades of the Ku Klux Klan! What ever happened to the wonderful idea of America as one united people, the great melting pot of all nations, all colors, and all races? Has it gone forever down the drain of history? All of us had better hope not." Make no mistake about it, segregation today is illegal because those of us who came before fought a legal battle against it, and struggled against it in our rights as American citizens. And this was during a period when our opportunities were so far less than those of today. We didn't waste time and energy in returning hatred for hatred. Instead, we continued moving toward our goal, never forgetting that our progress was being hastened because of the help given us by many fine White

Americans. We won the battle with their help. Now let's take a brief look at some of the conditions that existed before the battle was won.

Today there are several capable Negro orchestral conductors active in various parts of the world. But who remembers Alli Ross? He was a capable conductor in New York, not too long ago, who worked daily to prepare himself. Every morning he would have his coffee and toast, and then start reading scores. He couldn't get a real chance because of his color, and he died a frustrated man.

And when we look at the Negro players in some of our contemporary symphony orchestras, let's not forget the colored instrumentalists who tried so hard in the old days but were always rebuffed, and finally had to adopt different professions in order to make a living. By the time there came conductors and opportunities that would have given them a chance, they had grown rusty and could not qualify. But it was they, the seemingly unsuccessful, who by knocking at the doors so persistently, helped to open them for the Negro musicians who followed. We all owe them a great debt.[1]

Many of the pioneers of Negro music were contemporaries and close friends of mine. Each took a step toward the development of our racial culture and toward its integration into American culture. I never knew Samuel Coleridge-Taylor personally, but the very fact of his success as a serious composer served as an inspiration. In college, I even tried to make my hair grow like his. That was something of a task, because his hair was bushy, and mine was fairly straight.

I did know Harry T. Burleigh. He was such a gentleman; he had beautiful manners, courtly. I knew Nathaniel Dett, and Edmund Jenkins. Jenkins was a very talented young man, who died early. He had done some symphonic writing, and was working on a symphony when he died. Had he finished it, he would have been the first. Clarence Cameron White, John Work, Florence Price—all of these are mentioned in Maud Cuney Hare's compentently researched book, *Negro Musicians and Their Music.*

I also knew bandsmen like Frank Drye, instrumentalists like Joe Douglas, Louia Von Jones, and Hazel Harrison, singers like Sissieretta Jones (who was

---

[1] James Baldwin, in *The Fire Next Time* (Middlesex: Penquin Books, 1965, p.85) states: "I have great respect for that unsung army of black men and women who trudged down back lanes and entered back doors, saying 'Yes, sir' and 'No, ma'am' in order to acquire a new roof for the schoolhouse, new books, a new chemistry lab, more beds for the dormitories, more dormitories."

also known as the Black Patti), Roland Hayes and, later, Marian Anderson, as well as orchestrators like Will Vodery. All these and many others had individual contributions to make, and for none of them was the path unfailingly easy.

Credit has been given me for being the first Negro to conduct a major symphony orchestra in the United States, and the first to do the same in the Deep South, for being the first to write a symphony which was performed, the first to have an opera produced by a major American company, and first to conduct a White radio orchestra in New York. I would like to say here that none of these accomplishments would have been possible if it had not been for the work done before by so many of our pioneers—those who were successful in their respective fields, and those who were unsuccessful too. They made tremendous efforts in their lifetime, and thus made it easier for me and for the others who came after me. I cannot conceive of any possible way in which I or anyone else could have come up absolutely alone, without any predecessors, and could have made the grade, because I believe every accomplishment has to be built on foundations established long before.

I am so well aware of these past accomplishments that when I came across the book entitled *Black Music*, published in 1967 by a reputable New York firm, I was affronted when I glanced inside and found mention of only a few contemporary jazz artists, with not one acknowledgement of progress in any other field of Negro music. I ascribe this in some measure to a bias on the part of the writer, and in some measure to ignorance and bad taste, for although no one holds authentic jazz in higher esteem than I, I still refuse to concede that it is the only or even the most important form of Negro musical expression. True, it has spread all over the world, but so have Negro spirituals, and so, I venture to guess, would a certain amount of Negro symphonic music if it had behind it the same commercial drive that has long activated jazz.

I am equally affronted by what I have been told of the new courses in our universities, purporting to be courses in Negro music but actually no more than courses in jazz. If they are solely jazz courses, let them be so labelled. If they intend to be courses in Negro music, then let them encompass the whole panorama of Negro music: the study of the development of Negro music from the songs of the African natives, on to the classic period when Negro music was represented by men like Bridgetower (who was the first to perform Beethoven's *Kreutzer* sonata) and the Chevalier de Saint-Georges (an esteemed composer), even Beethoven (who some observers believe had Negro blood).

From there the course could move on through the folk music of Latin America, the West Indies, the United States, and up to its individual creators and performers of today. What a facinating area for research! It can't be dismissed lightly, but its true value can be assessed only in its relation to music as a whole and not a separate entity.

One of my friends, Theodore Phillips, who inaugurated and taught a course in Afro-American music at one of the southern California colleges, now stresses the need for a formal study in depth, and insists that courses in Negro music should be a necessary part of the over-all study of music. Further, they should be made attractive to White as well as Colored students, for only in this way, he says, can Negro music be recognized for what it has already contributed to our culture, and I agree with this completely. It's my view that such a procedure would add a new dimension to our music, in that it would contribute to good public relations for the Negro, as it has so often in the past. Incidentally, in his initial days in the class, my friend was staggered to discover that only a few of his students had ever heard of a Negro spiritual, that none knew of the shouts or work songs! None were even aware of the advances in "serious" music!

Some of the students set themselves to challenging his every statement, no matter how simple or how obvious. Through the ages, students have been expected to inquire and to question. All of us have done it when we were forming our thoughts and planning our future actions. None of us accepted everything blindly. At the same time, it has generally been accepted that students are supposed to learn from their teachers, not to teach the teachers. It seems to me that our future might well depend on our willingness to receive instruction and to respect qualified instructors. No doubt some members of my friend's class shared the attitude of a seventeen-year-old Black Student Union member who was interviewed by the *Los Angeles Times* on March 14, 1969. He said that racist training involved teaching about Johann Sebastian Bach, whom he described as "that old, dead punk." He added that he wanted to learn about Ray Charles, The Supremes, and about Black composers. From one of my personal experiences which I plan to recount later, I'm wondering if he really meant that, or if he only wanted to know about those who fitted neatly into his concepts.

In the first place, I would suggest that students who want to learn about Negro music should undertake it in all sincerity, not with the idea that they will be taking a snap course, or that they will be permitted to sit and listen to jazz recordings during every class period. This may be enjoyable, but it is not genuine study. The latter in my opinion should be historical, analytical, comparative, and should be undertaken above all with an open mind. It should be studied and explored in all seriousness, not merely as a means of getting credits without working for them. Along with this, the Negro student of music should learn about Bach, "that old, dead punk," and all the other composers who have made valuable contributions to music. He should prepare himself from all angles.

Now that the doors are opening to us, it would be tragic to have them shut in our faces again because those who enter are not yet truly prepared. You see, I'm all for studying our racial heritage. Most people are. But I'm also with Roy Wilkins, Thurgood Marshall and Bayard Rustin when they advise young Negro students to learn what the White students are learning *in addition*, or else they will be left out in the mad scramble for jobs. Justice Marshall declared that you're not going to compete in the world until you have training, just like everybody else, and hopefully better, because when you're a Negro, you've got to be better. Bayard Rustin even went so far as to question the advantages of the so-called soul courses in college, saying that in the real world they want to know if you can do mathematics and write a correct sentence. I know that if I were an employer, I would hesitate to hire anyone who could not or would not do the work he was hired to do. Moreover, as more and more Negroes do qualify, the day will soon be past when we can blame our failures on our color. In other words, racial studies can certainly be advocated, but they should neither supersede nor supplant the regular studies, and they should be open to all who are interested. I wouldn't want anyone, Colored or White, to study music unless he feels he cannot resist it as I felt, for the competition is intensely keen. One who adopts it as a profession should feel much like a potential minister when he gets his call to service. When the musical call comes, and the individual decides that he really does want to make music his ministry, I would suggest an exhaustive review of every respect: harmony, harmonic analysis, form, counterpoint, fugue, musical history (including the history of Negro music), and so on.

Some years ago, one of my colleagues of the early jazz days came to me with a story of a Colored musician who had been engaged as an arranger because he was Colored and, therefore, was assumed to have an original slant on the music. He did very well at it for several years, despite his limited training. One day he happened to get into a discussion with someone who was quite able to talk about music in technical terms. He became quite enthusiastic during the conversation and exclaimed, "Say, this is great! I think I'll go and study harmony!" A little late in my opinion, but commendable, nonetheless.

One of my Negro friends who plays professionally in symphonic groups on the West Coast recently came to me with another problem. He had been trying to organize a Colored chamber music group, but had difficulty finding members willing to rehearse. Some wanted only to show up at the concert, sight-read the music, and collect the pay. Now this is something that not even the most famous and experienced artists dare to do; they all know the value of rehearsals. Jazz players often do it, of course, since improvisation has been one of their obligations, but in "serious" music one must stick to what is written, and the people who are so good they don't need to practice are rare indeed. In the end, my friend was forced to get an interracial group, which incidentally worked very well.

I am very pleased that I have become acquainted with the works of gifted younger composers like Hale Smith, Ulysses Kay, and others, but unfortunately for me and for the purposes of this discussion, I am not as yet familiar with the work being done by all of our young Negro composers. (So many composers never answer their mail!) Despite this, I have seen some scores and have heard some of their music, and much of this has been very encouraging, indeed! Several of the composers handle their material expertly from the viewpoint of craftsmanship and, creatively speaking, I think we can look forward to a bright future. In some instances, the younger men remind me of myself when I was their age, experimenting, learning from everything possible, and trying to develop an individual form of expression.

Some of you possibly know that, for me, the so-called avant garde is now the rear guard, for I studied with its high priest, Edgar Varèse, in the 20's, and I was a devoted disciple. Some of my early compositions in that idiom were performed auspiciously in New York. I was amused recently when a writer heard one of my works and was upset because it was not in the avant-garde idiom. The writer said, "Time has passed Mr. Still by." Well, if this writer had done his homework, he would have known that it was I who recognized the handwriting on the wall many years ago, and voluntarily left the type of time he referred to, and I'm convinced I made the right decision.

I learned a great deal from the avant-garde idiom and from Mr. Varèse but, just as with jazz, I did not bow to its complete domination. I had chosen a definite goal, namely, to elevate Negro musical idioms to a position of dignity and effectiveness in the fields of symphonic and operatic music. This would have been extremely difficult, or even impossible, had I chosen the avant-garde idiom. Through experimentation, I discovered that Negro music tends to lose its identity when subjected to the avant-garde style of treatment. I made this decision of my own free will, knowing very well that pressures would be brought to bear to make me follow the leader, and compose as others do. I have stuck to this decision, and I've not been sorry. American music is a composite of all the idioms of all the people comprising this nation, just as most of us Afro-Americans who are "officially" classed as Negroes are products of the mingling of several bloods. This makes us *individuals*, and that is how we should function, musically and otherwise. My personal feeling is that the avant-garde idiom as it stands is not the idiom of the future, no matter how its adherents try to convince me that I'm unsophisticated to think so. I've watched its deleterious effect on audiences and have noted that the general public, for whom music is supposed to be written, couldn't care less. I would urge young Afro-American composers to think of the avant garde as a phase, not an end in itself, and if not a phase, a facet of composition.

Negroes have long been known as spontaneous creators. One has only to study the wealth of artistic innovations they have given to the world. Not every Negro is a spontaneous creator naturally, nor is everything all of us do superlative. We cannot lay claim to this distinction and neither can any other group of people, but we can evaluate the past, present and future in music, and begin again to write with heart instead of brains, with love instead of disdain, and with attention to spiritual as well as scientific values. Experimentation for the sake of experimentation can only produce a poor substitute for music, and we are now in need of *real* music, not contrived sounds. We need a new contemporary goal. I suggest that this goal be beauty, and I maintain that there is no substitute for inspiration. Every composer should work toward expressing his own personality in music. I shudder to think of the consequences if all of us were to start turning out music that is like the music of all the others. Such a trend has been observed in contemporary music. It is my hope that its end is near, and that sanity will reassert itself.

Afro-American composers, incidentally, have a wonderful opportunity to influence a trend toward sanity if they will make up their minds to return to the originality for which Negroes have become famous.

I cannot close without commenting on the current riotous conditions on our college campuses. In case you think they have nothing to do with Negro music, you are wrong. If they are allowed to continue without restraint, there will be no future for any of us, in music or anywhere else. When White students riot and display their ugliness on TV, the public immediately speaks of anarchy, of communism, and the hampering of the silent majority's right to gain an education. When Negroes riot, the same thoughts are present, plus other conclusions not amicable to us as a racial group. The unfortunate result of Negro rioting is that so often those who are the most ignorant, violent and unwholesome are constantly in the forefront of our TV screen. By whose wish: theirs or the TV medium? I cannot say. One thing is certain: their images create a climate of fear and distrust among their fellow Americans, White and Colored alike. Many White Americans know they are not typical, but there are some who are positive they *are* typical, and that they represent the Negro race. Without stopping to analyze the situation, they automatically cast all of us into the same mold. Of course, it affects Negro musicians and their music just as it adversely affects all decent Afro-Americans, including the children yet unborn. In the end it will probably affect the rioters themselves. It has been said that the Negro students have been influenced by the White dissidents, but that it is the Negro students who will go to prison, while the Whites go free, and this is not an impossible theory, I think you will agree. To me, one of the most significant factors in this current trouble is that it came when there seemed to be no need for it. Negroes were already getting ahead as they qualified. The situation was not yet perfect, but it was improving, and it gave every indication of continuing to do so. There was enough of a climate of good fellowship first to make outsiders see some merit in the demands that were made by campus militants. Then, as the demand escalated and became more and more ridiculous, and as it became evident that people were coming from off-campus to incite trouble, even our friends began to lose patience. When it was noted that the ignorant were insisting upon dictating to the educated, and the inexperienced were demanding the right to direct the experienced, many formerly well disposed people were on the way to losing all their permissiveness. The picture was not an attractive one.

Only twice have I had encounters with the so-called Black militants, both times unpleasant ones. The first came during a general discussion of racial matters, when two young men found themselves in complete disagreement with me. Their displeasure came not in an orderly discussion, but in a rather belligerent verbal warfare. As I am now 74 years of age, and have been a Negro for all of the 74 years, I did not need people fifty years younger than I to tell me what it is, or what it should be, to be a Negro. The second encounter came when it was least suspected, in a college music class. I don't expect complete agreement with my views, though I do look for some respect. This I have received in every other student aggregation I have addressed, from elementary schools, even in deprived areas, to university audiences. Moreover, in this class there were only two belligerents. The rest were studious and appreciative. They did not seem to be in agreement with the militants on any count, although the militants seemed as if they were ready to do battle.

Those two should have known that they could do nothing to make me talk or compose differently, but perhaps they hoped to alter the good opinion of their classmates. Basically, they told me my music was not Negro music which, in their opinion, was the jungle-type sounds heard over a particular radio station in that city. All else was what they termed "Eur"-American music, rather than Afro-American music. They also seemed disturbed because the clarinets in the orchestras that played my music (one of them was the Royal Philharmonic of London) didn't play like Duke Ellington's clarinetist. Indeed, they seemed astonished that my compositions didn't sound like the Duke's! They were even a little sad when I told them they were not intended to sound that way. One of them prattled about the bourgeois and White man's music, while the other made it a point to let me know that he did not "identify" with my music, no doubt expecting me to be crushed by this verdict. He then made the separatist statement that we have grown up in America with only two different cultures, White and Black. This is a fallacious statement for, as you know, here in America, the melting pot, a large number of cultures may be found, gradually influencing each other. The Negro culture has definitely been influenced by Whites, just as White culture has been influenced by Negroes. In my opinion, we have both gained by the fusion, and who can define the exact line of demarcation?

The day after this second encounter, the Black Student Union asked for the resignation of their Negro instructor, despite the fact that students were then signing up for his next term course, and the enrollment had nearly doubled. The interesting angle was that the Black students themselves had requested the course with specifically a Negro instructor. The college had been fortunate enough to find a retired head of a music department from an eastern university, with a degree from the Oberlin Conservatory and almost forty years of teaching experience. The college and most of his students were pleased with his work. Only the two militants, they alone, wanted to drag his ideals down to their level, and thus limit the development of Negro music in general. This occurence cast serious doubt on the sincerity, at least, of those militants. If they made a reasonable demand which was met by the college in good faith, shouldn't they have been properly receptive? Why should they, obviously the most unprepared in class, have assumed the task of dictating to their classmates? What actually were their motives? What were they trying to accompplish? Remembering that the two militants had almost succeeded in taking over the full discussion period, I wondered why they were so insistent on freedom of expression for themselves, while denying it to all the others. They did not hesitate to insult others, but made it appear that a crime had been committed when their ideas were questioned. I confess that in one short class period, I lost whatever sympathy I might have had for militants.

Noting that this one little experience has multiplied and expanded to the level of violence on so many college campuses, I cannot blame the public in general for being impatient with such hypocrisy. It is good to take pride in one's race, but is *this* pride? When these people begin to appreciate the good things that are available within America, to respect the rights of others, to develop a sense of true values and to talk about civil responsibility along with civil rights, then everyone will be willing to listen. Our forebears were willing to assume a share of the burden, along with the blessings. Why can't we? If it is clear that our attitude is changing in a constructive way, then perhaps the violent backlash which Billy Graham has predicted will never appear. At the very least, we might say that the idea of letting unprepared students choose their studies, choose their teachers, and even indicate what they want to be taught within a given subject is certainly open to question.

To all those who talk of separation, I would say again that I am now and forever against it. I am for integration. We're all Americans in our hearts, in our music, in our very being. At this point in our history we should begin to weigh, to analyze and to evaluate, all with a view to deciding whether or not we want to jump on bandwagons indiscriminately and to making up our minds as to what we actually do want. Of course many of us are frustrated! All of us are to some extent, and all of us probably will continue to be in some degree as long as we live. But, as Thurgood Marshall has so aptly remarked, we are not going to settle anything with guns, fire bombs or rocks. It appears now that many American Negroes feel that they are frustrated specifically because of White people and their attitude, so it seems to me that we should take a long look at White people in general to see whether this is entirely correct.

In my opinion, there are three broad categories into which White people will fit. The first type has not been given enough credit, and yet it is they who have done the most to help us up the ladder to full citizenship and success. They are the sympathetic ones who try just as hard as we do to make brotherhood a reality. I know that I shall always be greateful to the many White friends who helped me. I could not have made it in a community solely of Negroes for the simple reason that Negroes did not have the facilities of the large orchestras, publishing houses and so on, which I needed in order to advance. White people made these facilities available to me in nearly every instance.

The second class of White persons is known to all of us as the uncompromising bigot. He is a difficult person to deal with, so he is best ignored.

He is still easier to take, however, than the third sort of person, the one who talks loudly about his commitment to brotherhood, enthusiastically welcomes you until you begin to measure arms with him. Then he surreptitiously opposes you while continuing to shout his love for his less fortunate brethren. He is the most frustrating, and least approachable of all. *Sneaky* would be the best word to describe him.

I've always found it wise to go my own way, doing the best that I can, and trusting that God will eventually show such people the errors of their ways, for I am convinced that we must all work together harmoniously. Only in this way can America's greatness reach its zenith. Make no mistake about it: The future of our music is tied immutably to that of the individual musician, and the future of the race as a whole is bound up in the future of America. What is good for our nation is good for the race. We must never let ourselves think otherwise, nor allow ourselves to be duped into a separatist philosophy, no matter how frustrated we may feel. We and our fellow Americans are in this together. As Americans with Negro blood, we are willing and able to contribute something of value to America. Those of us in the field of music know that our music has already proved to be a distinctive contribution. Our forebearers contributed their sweat and their blood. Our sons have fought in foreign shores for the ideal of democracy. We have an investment in this nation. We own a share of it. Now is the time to decide: shall we protect that investment, or shall we destroy it?

● He has said that he has been living the Black experience for three-quarters of a century. He has already been down the path. He was not so concerned about how many Blacks were in a major symphony orchestra, he has been concerned about where he would sleep while on tour. There's a big difference here. One can say, "Oh yes, we've come a long way" only to calm the turmoil and quiet the agitations, but he can say it because he has lived through it and, like a person of true nobility, he is the better for it. He has been nourished by the problems, because he faced them wisely *in order to win.*

His ideas are not always those of the younger generation. Youth now has the impatience he once had. As it ages, today's youth will find a distance between its ideas and those of the young men of the twenty-first century. Beethoven would doubtless have found Bach far apart from him, had they known each other, but Beethoven—the real radical that he was not withsanding—never doubted the fact that he was standing on Bach's shoulders, albeit on his own feet.

Dr. Still urges the gentle approach to integration and acceptance, which one might expect in view of his experiences and the years when these were most dynamically lived. Let no one call him an "Uncle Tom" just because he is not twenty years old now, and living in the ghetto. We must look back instead, and see those doors which Hale Smith has seen, and hear that music which William Grant Still has written. He has invested his life for ours.

9. *Problems Relative to the Publication and Recording of Music*

John Hammond

Leonard Feist

Hale Smith

Russell Sanjek

● It is of little value to attempt course offerings in an area of music if the music is not heard. Without attempting to consider program structures at this time, we need to regard questions related to the music publishing and recording industries, and we must acknowledge the very important relationship—the mutual relationship—which exists between these industries and the teacher.

Instruction in any aspect of music was certainly far different a hundred years ago. At this time, the teachers and students had to be more self-sufficient once scores were located. Perhaps, as a result, the music was known better. There is very much to be said for the student who has to copy music, who has to contemplate the score in his imagination, who can only hear the sounds from the score if he creates them himself, who can come to know the music only by means such as these.

Today we tend to be too passive unless we are provoked or stimulated. We can illustrate our lectures with the phonograph, for example, and there is little we can do or need do for the broadcasting of the music; we can listen or not listen. Were we forced to play the music from the score at the piano, we would have to concentrate.

Even so, there are probably few classrooms which do not have phonographs, and certainly no schools which lack a library of recent editions of scores. Our teaching program is based on these. What, then, do we do if we are going to include mention and illustration of the important works by the major Black composers? We know that many of the scores are no longer in print, but your librarian can be aggressive and perhaps acquire photocopies or interlibrary loan of those which are essential. What about the recordings? Do you realize that there is not a single work by William Grant Still currently available? Edward Boatner, Harry Burleigh, Coleridge-Taylor, Robert Nathaniel Dett, W. C. Handy, Clarence Cameron White—these people have been commercially recorded in the past, but the records are not on sale now. It seems to me that our programs will be very seriously handicapped without this literature.

But a defeatist attitude is akin to the passive record listener who merely puts on, say, Howard Swanson's *Night Music* and plays no part as a reactor or student. We can too easily say that we can't find a recording of William Grant Still's *Afro-American Symphony* so, therefore, we will not include it in our teaching.

Right now we have the advantage of ideas from four major figures from the industries. John Hammond, whose remarkable background in talent discovery was evidenced in the modest but important comments already presented, is from Columbia Records. The National Music Publishers' Association is represented by its distinguished executive, Leonard Feist, who has had a rich experience in music publication. Russell Sanjek is Vice-President of Broadcast Music, Inc., a performance rights organization of utmost importance in jazz and non-jazz areas. Hale Smith, already identified as a composer, is a highly respected music editor with a wide variety of contacts with music publishers. Let us secure some insight on this topic from them.

DE LERMA: Within your own areas of activity, how do you locate a work for publication or recording? Does a composer come to you and say, "I have a wonderful work for you," and you say, "Yes, it is wonderful," or does a performer bring new titles to your attention?

HAMMOND: In the popular field, I must get something like forty or forty-five tapes a week of songs people want me to listen to, but we very rarely pick up any material this way. The performer usually brings his own material, or publishers have things which are tailored for certain artists. Very often, composers come around with a track record. Although a lot of material is submitted by mail, it rarely comes up to standards. In "classical" music it's quite a different thing, which we can get to later.

FEIST: There are immense amounts of concert music coming in by mail, but it is rare that anything is actually published from this. And yet, since all manuscripts are reviewed very carefully by some companies, you do make editorial records of what you've examined. But more likely you get a sense of a composer by having read reviews, by having heard his music, and you usually decide on your own which composers you would like to publish, without mailed scores.

It was always my idea that it is preferable to publish all the works of one composer under an exclusive arrangement so you could devote all your energies, or a share of them, to the promotion and exploitation of his music rather than take single pieces by a number of composers. While I was with Associated Music Publishers, we published no more than eleven American composers. When we took a single score from a composer, rather than take everything, we made an exploratory gesture to see what would happen, but we always had an idea that we might go on with him.

DE LERMA: You mentioned concerts and reviews. This puts a lot of responsibility on the critics to be more than glib or charming, doesn't it?

FEIST: Yes, but I don't want to over-emphasize reviews. You don't necessarily believe what the critic says, but the composer's name stays in your mind. And I should have added that word of mouth plays a very important role. If people start talking respectfully about a composer, you are alerted.

DE LERMA: I'm thinking now of the young Black composer who is unpublished. His music has never been heard outside of his own community, but his work merits publication. He has no important reviews or concerts, and he does not know anyone in the game who can speak well of his work. Probably any young composer may think of himself in this rut. But there is a long step for him from the time he writes something which might be worthy of publication until the act actually takes place, no matter what his color. Performances mean quite a bit then, obviously. Now, what about your production schedules? Are they crowded?

SMITH: I'll speak on this, although I'm clearly involved in a conflict of interests: I'm editor for one company, consultant for another, and published by a third, and I do free-lace editorial work for others. Anyway, I think every publisher may be behind in his schedules. Part of this relates to the question of how much the market can absorb at any given time, and another relates to the shortage of adequate editorial personnel. There are very few people going into this area so it's not uncommon for one or two individuals to be stuck with an entire production job.

If we can go back to what John Hammond was saying, I think he's an exception in that he actually listens to works sent by mail. For the most part, publishers and recording companies ignore unsolicited manuscripts and recordings of popular music simply because it is so easily plagiarized. It's a statistical inevitability that things will cross when the basic materials of music are so simple. This is a less immediate question in the matter of complex or advanced music. Where concert or educational music is involved, however, the work may be viewed seriously, but the reasons for rejections or acceptance aren't always related to the quality of the music. Quite often, when you get a nicely phrased letter of rejection stating that the publisher is sorry that your work just does not fit his production schedule or projected plans, he may very well be telling you the truth. Publishers do work within very clearly defined guidelines, some very restrictive, some very broad, but he has to work within these guidelines in order to meet his production schedule as best he can.

HAMMOND: May I add something to what I said before? Part of my job at Columbia Records is to discover new talent. If I'm not listening to the composer, at least I'm listening to a performance, but it is company policy not to consider unsolicited manuscripts.

SMITH: However if a person comes into the office with his manuscript, that's a different animal.

FEIST: I'd like to make another addition to the additions, specifically on what Hale said about editing. As he said, there are few skilled editors, and the problem becomes increasingly difficult as the music become increasingly complex, and certain composers are hitting the absolute barrier: the end of traditional notation. Most composers really don't know how to write music, in terms of its grammar, its spelling, and its punctuation. In my experience, I remember only three composers whose works did not have to be edited to a considerable degree. Would you agree with me on that, Hale?

SMITH: Most emphatically! Most of my time is spent trying to filter the composer's intent through his notation. One of the great failings in music education is that serious attention is rarely given to the question of musical calligraphy. It is a disgrace. Considering the problems composers have in getting their works published in the first place, the fact that they do not receive training in putting musical symbols on a page is criminal. As for the composers who experiment with newer graphic means, they are not all really fully aware of what they can achieve with standard notations. The inconsistencies that one finds, even in the work of very prominent composers, is appalling.

DE LERMA: What is the market really like? How much of the material goes to the music lover, how much to the educational institutions, to radio stations?

Who uses the music that is being published and recorded? I'm sure these things will have something to do with the policies.

HAMMOND: Columbia sends out something like 3,330 copies of singles to disc jockeys and radio music librarians. That's a service in itself. Those are not net sales because no royalties are paid. A pop hit that sells anywhere over a half million has a tremendous proportion going to the general buying public. Few schools have a budget for popular single records. The juke box business is considerable, but they've got to hit the top twenty before they're sold in any volume for the juke boxes. The bulk of the sales is to rack-jobbers and the more traditional retail stores. The rack-jobber only stocks hits. He doesn't stock unknowns until they're well up on the charts of the various amusement weeklies. The essential thing, of course, is air play.

SMITH: To what extent does this relate to the production and distribution of concert music recordings?

HAMMOND: There's a very strange thing happening in concert music these days. I suspect that Columbia is the largest record company in the world. Classical recordings make up only a very small proportion of its business. Recently, the Masterworks Department first rejected, and then finally reluctantly issued, a work called "Switched-on Bach," a completely electronic recording on the Moog synthesizer of things like the third Brandenburg concerto. Now you know, if we sell 20,000 copies at retail of, say, a Mahler symphony conducted by Bernstein, we think we're doing pretty well, even though 20,000 sales doesn't pay a quarter of the cost. Thanks to disc jockeys and a very alert public, "Switched-on Bach" has gone well over 300,000 sales in this country alone.

DE LERMA: It's too bad Bach isn't getting royalties on that, but we all know that Bach is beautiful.

SANJEK: Mention of air play brings up another source of income and another tremendous market for music, and that's public performance, the business we at BMI are in. We don't publish music, and we don't record it. Public performance income for all of the performing rights licensing organizations last year was about $75,000,000. Ninety percent of that came from radio and television, the rest came from night clubs, bowling alleys, skating rinks and symphony orchestras. That is divided among something like 28,000 composers and about 13,000 publishers. When we started in business in 1940, the entire income for performing rights was about $4,500,000. Then there were 137 publishers and 1,100 writers who shared that money.

FEIST: The retail market for printed music is probably just a little bit more than that for performing rights. Last year it was about $45,000,000, which indicates that the printed page is not the major part of a composer's or publisher's income. I should mention that popular music supports to a great extent the concert music field.

DE LERMA: Do these industries accept more readily a work whose publication is subsidized?

HAMMOND: At Columbia we rarely accept subsidized recordings; however, many of the more avant-garde works have been supported by foundations, otherwise it would be economically impossible to put them out. Once in a while Columbia will undertake something like the recording of all of Webern's works. This may have sold three or four thousand copies, and the company may have lost up to $30,000 on the venture, yet they make up for it with the popular hits that come out.

SMITH: There are fewer cases of subsidized publications of music than one would imagine, the exceptions being quite notable, nonetheless. I'm thinking of the Cleveland Composer's Guild, whose works are published by Galaxy, and the work of the Fromm Foundation and the National Institute of Arts and Letters. But the royalty pattern can get so confusing, it can end up being a vanity venture for the composer. The actual sales can't help but be minimal and if the composers use copyrighted texts, as far as royalties go, it's a waste of time.

FEIST: I don't recall ever having accepted a subsidy to publish a work I wouldn't have published anyhow, and I don't recall having accepted subsidy for very many works I published over a period of more than twenty-five years. But once in a while you come to something like Ives' fourth symphony, which was absolutely and completely beyond the resources of any publisher in his right mind. We, at Associated Music Publishers, published it. To some extent, the preparation of the score was indirectly subsidized, and so was the recording which was issued by Columbia. Is that right, John?

HAMMOND: Yes.

FEIST: It was simply an unbelievable job. You know what Ives' manuscripts look like!

SMITH: He didn't take calligraphy at school.

HAMMOND: There have been a few other recordings which were subsidized. Vanguard, a very fine and progressive independent record company, has had subsidy on a few ventures with the Utah Symphony Orchestra and the Hartford Symphony, and Minneapolis was subsidized for years with Mercury. They made one of the biggest selling classical records in the history of the business, by the way, when they came out with the Tschaikovsky *1812* featuring the West Point cannon.

SMITH: With plugs for Vanguard and Mercury, let me jump in and say something about CRI, Composers Recordings Incorporated. This is a subsidiary of the American Composers' Alliance, indirectly subsidized in part by BMI, and at times by the National Institute of Arts and Letters and other organizations. CRI has a non-deletion policy; you can buy the first record and every record they have ever distributed.

HAMMOND: That's also true with Vanguard for its stereo recordings, but Vanguard and Columbia also have re-issue policies. Usually, though, if a record doesn't make a thousand sales in one year, it is deleted. Alas, a lot of good records have been lost this way, and it's hard to get them back once dropped.

DE LERMA: We should remember this point and keep our eyes on the Schwann catalog to see what happens to recordings of Black music. I might mention that CRI has at least two works of Ulysses Kay, one of Hale Smith, and one of Julia Perry. Let's check now on the ordinary arrangements for publishing and recording contracts.

HAMMOND: In recording there is a so-called statutory rate on popular recordings of two cents per single. This may be raised in the future. For unpublished works, the most reputable companies will pay a penny and a half. If there are, let's say, eight works on an LP from one publisher, the record company will try to get the statutory rate lowered, but ordinarily I think you'll find that on published material it's two cents per side.

FEIST: On concert music the rate is two cents on the first three minutes, or a quarter of a cent per minute, whichever is larger. The copyright act of 1909 is the law which sets this rate. It is one of my most dedicated activities to persuade Congress to increase that rate in keeping with current economic conditions, hopefully to eight percent.

HAMMOND: There are other inequities in the copyright law. An arrangement cannot be copyrighted unless it is written down. If the arrangement isn't, a second company with a bigger artist can copy the original freely, and the original company has no protection.

FEIST: With respect to publishers' contractual arrangements, it is ten percent for printed editions, and fifty-fifty on income from mechanicals and recordings. Public performance customarily is paid to the composer and publisher separately.

HAMMOND: This is why most artists form their own publishing companies. When there was sheet music in large numbers, there was good reason for this kind of split, but nowadays the artist wants to keep that for himself or his company, which is why there are 13,000 publishers.

DE LERMA: I'd like to direct a question now at Mr. Sanjek, acknowledging the great help BMI has been to us of the Black Music Committee in our research. If I might mention the acronyms of your competitors, what is the difference between ASCAP, BMI and SESAC?

SANJEK: One difference is age, another is income. ASCAP was founded in 1914. SESAC, the Society of European Stage Authors and Composers, has no composer-members; it's strictly an organization that licenses the performing rights of publishers, dating from the mid-thirties. We started in 1940. The majority of the publishers and writers I mentioned earlier are affiliated with BMI. Our income is about $27,000,000 out of that $75,000,000.

DE LERMA: Are there any firms in publishing or recording which are specifically seeking Black music for their catalogs?

SMITH: I'd say there are two, Marks and Sam Fox. In both cases, they tend toward emphasis on educational music because it and pop music are the two largest money-makers for the industry right now. More esoteric music might be published at times, but the odds are overwhelming that these works will sit on the shelves for years and make no money for anyone. Yet there is recognition that through out the country there is rising pressure, especially in the school systems, for music relating to the Black experience.

HAMMOND: And there are record companies, Columbia, RCA, Motown, Chess, Atlantic, Savoy and others—a lot of labels which do reach the market of the Black people. I think a lot of these companies are tremendously interested in the output of the Black jazz and popular composer. Less so, I'm afraid, in the more formal compositions of the Blacks, although this will come.

SMITH: Perhaps.

FEIST: It will come.

SMITH: O.K.

DE LERMA: Marks Corporation has been kind enough to send Don Malin, its educational director, to our seminar. Do all major publishers and record companies have educational directors?

FEIST: All major publishers do. Only a few record companies do. The educational director attends exhibits, visits universities and colleges, high schools and such. He usually has an important voice in the choice of educational material which gets published because he gets out where the need is felt. Have I left anything out, Don?

MALIN: Not really. He's supposed to be a good will ambassador between the publishers and the educational community, and I include the churches in that category too.

DE LERMA: What about the establishment of a central reference library for loans dubbings, photocopies of out-of-print materials and things of that nature? I expect there may be more of a problem when it comes to recordings, but we need something like a counterpart of University Microfilms. I know this is an idea you have heard before from David Hall. Would the industries cooperate through donation for the establishment of a research center for Black music if one single national site were funded?

FEIST: I think this is a very, very practical way of accomplishing something. There will be complications, but call them challenges, if you will. Unless there is a center where people know they can go and procure material, things are rather ineffective. Although there may not be too many scores of concert music published (not only by Black composers, but all composers), there are many which could be deposited with parts in a Black counterpart to the American Music Center. Copies of out-of-print materials could be located and certainly should be deposited there. If they are unique copies, certainly permission could be obtained for a Xerox score. I envision a depository of this kind, with chamber music, solo works, where people who wanted to build programs could visit. And it would be a shame is there were a program in a university which wasn't taped! And a shame if that tape weren't deposited in this center. Certainly, foundation money should be available. It is certainly something, however, which requires a dedicated zealot to run, because it will be a tough job. Just the correspondence would be endless. Nevertheless, it seems to me that this is almost an essential, in the lines Dominique laid down the other morning of the directions to go. I think it's a practical and effective way to do it, and I think it would work. It has *got* to work. I think you could actually publish facsimile editions. Sell them on behalf of the composers. I can't see how it wouldn't work, given the money.

SMITH: Without consideration from the American Federation of Musicians, some aspects of this would be practically hopeless.

HAMMOND: There are remarkably progressive men in the AFM. If the Black community came with reasonable requests, you might find that the Federation would be very willing to bend. May I add one thing more? We have overlooked the many great Black concert artists on records, André Watts, Reri Grist, George Shirley, Leontyne Price. I think some pressure from these artists to record works of the good Black composers would be important. With the tenor of the times nowadays, the companies would listen to these artists. And I think you have a function here, to write the presidents of the record companies and ask for more pertinent music by formal Black composers.

SMITH: This relates directly to the involvement of Afro-Americans in the music industries. There are several Black men in responsible positions in several recording companies, but the publishing industry is somewhat different. To my knowledge, I'm the only Black man who functions at this level. My connection came through Ulysses Kay, while he was with BMI. He told me that Marks was looking for an editor or, originally, a proofreader. They wanted someone who was a composer, and an arranger, with professional copying experience and work as an autographer. He had to have experience as a draftsman, experience in the graphic arts. He had to know type design and page layout. And they wanted a Black, preferably a Black woman. I didn't qualify for the latter, but I applied. My father was an architect and a printer, and he insisted I understand anything he could teach me, from working a linotype machine to running the business. I had not been able to pay a copyist, so I learned professional copying and autography. Since 1939 I have been in jazz, as arranger and composer. I was able to get the job. Now the qualifications which were imposed on me were a bit unrealistic. If there is someone who is interested in this kind of work, I'd suggest he should have a through knowledge of musical structure and of the various notational practices. In addition to a good knowledge of English, he may also have to know German, French, Italian and Spanish, which he might be working with frequently. I recently had to work with Provençal. He must be able to visualize from a rather sloppy manuscript what the final printed form will look like. He should be able to work with type faces and know the various elements which go to make up a publication.

FEIST: And if such a person exists, he'd be snapped up tomorrow morning.

SMITH: Right, but this is one of the few areas where apprenticeship is still practiced. Excellent editors have been developed this way.

QUESTION: I'd like to know what ideas you have about publishing and recording companies developing an audience of young people for Black concert music, perhaps with foundation support.

SANJEK: It seems to be that a completely planned project, perhaps twelve LP records which represented a history of Black music in the United States, is the sort of thing which might be managed, perhaps jointly by Columbia Records (or the CBS Foundation) and the Record Industry Association of America. The publishers could follow the same package approach.

QUESTION: What about a closer contact of the classroom teacher and the publisher?

SMITH: One practical way, in addition to the feed-back through the educational director we mentioned earlier, is for the teacher to speak to the publisher's representative at meetings, such as those of MENC. The only problem is that we've found there is a general lack of imagination on the part of the teachers as far as the over-all picture is concerned, and the publisher cannot afford to think in terms of the individual teacher's classroom problems. He needs something that works for Polkville, Mississippi, and Saginaw, Michigan.

MALIN: I suggest that the music dealer is an important element also. The dealer is closer, for a longer period of time, to the teacher. It's not always possible for the publisher to have a representative at the smaller meetings, but the aggressive and imaginative dealer may be there and he should be a good point of contact.

QUESTION: I think it would be a good idea to encourage a change in the curriculum content in music education courses. When the teachers are brought up
to date and acquainted with the new materials, we'll all be in a better situation.

● It is obviously not as easy as some composers would like to have
music accepted for publication or recording, and the problems are not
always related to the quality of the music. Certainly a composer may
elect to publish the music himself (via photocopy, for example) or he
might find one of the smaller companies which would issue the music,
subject to their policies, but this does not always help us. Distribution
and publicity is of greatest importance to all concerned, certainly to the
prospective client. There is a great wealth of material hidden within the
stock of a minor publisher who has not the means of announcing its
availability through those channels with which we normally come in contact. Perhaps the composer should consider this only as a first step. He
must then find people who will perform the music, and begin to work
up toward some level of national publicity so that his music will be
played more than once, and so that more people will begin to discuss it.
I'm sure this is not an easy path to follow, and it is not one which can
be traveled quickly, but if the music is really worth it, this process should
be followed seriously and constantly.

Those of us who have heard a work which, we feel, merits greater distribution (including representation in our curricula) should play our
part. If we perform it at our schools, the performance should be recorded
and we should bring the recording to the attention of people higher up
in the business. When a representative from a publishing company pays
his periodic visit, let him know about it. If your dean or music supervisor is interested (and your librarian can help), engage his active support.
Talk to your most alert music dealer about it, so that he might be stimulated to carry the message through his channels of communication.

Somewhat the same techniques can be employed if the recording or
score is no longer in print but was once available. Of course, if the publication or recording is still around and we don't buy it, we stand a
chance of having it discontinued on the mistaken evidence of disinter-
est. Those of us who belong to such groups as the Society of Black Composers, the National Association of Negro Musicians, or the Afro-American Music Opportunities Association might suggest that one of these
societies would lend its power as a pressure group, urging a particular
publication or a re-release.

There are a few things which the schools can do, also. As Hale Smith
indicated, the publishing business needs qualified editors, as well as composers versed in the techniques of calligraphy. This is certainly a curricular challenge. Graduating composers who cannot express themselves prop-

erly on paper is a parallel no English department would permit. And perhaps we have thought too long in terms of the traditional music departments (history, theory, education and applied music) to notice the colleges are not properly serving the needs of the music merchants. Is there a school which has course work in music editing? If so, how many Black students are enrolled for this? Don't let me suggest I'm discouraging music education as a major field for the Blacks, but the evidence is mounting that the world of music is destitute of Blacks in such highly responsible positions as critics and aestheticians, as editors and publishers, as musicologists and theorists. All of these areas require quite a bit more investment in time and money than a bachelor's degree in music education, but the educator is quickly finding himself in a position of not having enough Black spokesmen in these areas, and these lacunae cannot be quickly filled.

Then finally, there is a challenge of Black performers to perform Black music—maybe not exclusively Black music, but I don't think an accomplished Black singer can really justify a recital program that runs through Schubert, Schumann, Brahms, Wolf, Duparc, Respighi, Ives and Stravinsky, for example, and saves *Go Down, Moses* for an encore, and forgets Swanson, Still and Cunningham en route. We can't bend over backwards and have a Black choir which knows nothing of Schütz, Bach, Monteverdi or Webern, but I would be a bit suspicious of a Spanish chorus that knew no Victoria or Morales.

There is not any evidence to suggest direct discrimination against Black music from the publishing and recording companies in general. These people are in a business which has to be alert to the needs and interests of its clients. If these customers are apathetic or not vocal, the industries simply are forced to continue their productions along lines which they feel are correct. If they err once in a while, their income suffers and their policies are restructured, but the same thing will happen if they make a decision which is to our advantage and we ignore it.

10. Faculty Viewpoints

Eileen Southern

William Cole

Portia Maultsby

Nicholas d'Angelo

● Because numerous educators in the country came to know rather early of the work of the Black Music Committee, we have received many letters from persons who claimed they knew next to nothing about Black music, could find no sources to help them, and were due to initiate a course in a matter of weeks. There are doubtless many more than those we learned of, and many of these courses were quite likely taught rather poorly at first.

On short notice, a panel was developed of persons who have faced this problem. William Cole, from the University of Pittsburgh, proved himself throughout the conference as a distinctly alert and serious young man with a great deal to offer. Dr. Eileen J. Southern, of CUNY's York College, is a most distinguished musicologist who is well known in musical circles. As chairman of CUNY's Committee on Afro-American Music, her contribution to this panel offers a contrasting and particularly stimulating approach. Nicholas D'Angelo, from Hobart and William Smith Colleges in Geneva (New York), describes how his interest in Black music changed the curricular structure of his predominately all-White schools. Portia Maultsby, one of the intellectual student finds of our gathering, explains her relationship to the doctoral ethnomusicology program at the University of Wisconsin.

COLE: I laid out from teaching for two years, because I felt I had a tremendous gap of knowledge concerning Black music. During this time I compiled a bibliography and read as much as I could. Last September I started teaching a course to high school students. The first semester was very much of a survey. The students got their grades on the basis of research papers, and these were a great help to me. One student prepared a bibliography, which I added to the work I had already done. I think you should use your students as much as possible. First of all, it's a very helpful thing for them to be involved in the work, and secondly, it certainly helps the teacher. We had a listening test at the end of the semester, but I don't think I'll do this again. My approach, by the way, was purely from the standpoint of jazz.

We have fifteen-week trimesters at the University of Pittsburgh. The first seven weeks, I talked about history of jazz up to 1945. I went from there to the "new thing" during the last eight weeks, including Ornette Coleman, Cecil Taylor, Archie Shepp, Pharoah Sanders, John Coltrane, and so on. In the fall, Charles Bell will be with us doing a graduate class in jazz. He and I will be working together with the Black Studies Program, trying to develop some research in the area. The material which has been written is so unscholarly, you know! I feel a personal obligation to do as much as I can, as well as I can do it.

SOUTHERN: The City University of New York is possibly the largest municipal system of colleges in the United States. As of today, it consists of eighteen colleges, but there may be more by the time I get back. The system includes senior colleges, junior colleges, and a graduate program. At the senior colleges are offered undergraduate courses and first-year courses toward the master's degree. The graduate center programs offer Ph.D. degrees in seventeen areas, including musicology. Each of the colleges is independent, but we felt there was a need for communication, so we have organized the City University Music Council this past year, which is composed of the chairman of each of the music departments of the various colleges and meets every month or so. The council has set up two committees. One concerns curriculum coordination, and the other is on Afro-American and African music. I was appointed chairman of the latter. This committee includes departmental chairmen, but also special consultants with whom we consult for information in particular areas.

In June, we presented our results to the Music Council, including recommendations in five areas. Most of the City University Colleges offer a basic course in music appreciation, which is required for most of the colleges. Some are now allowing their students to take anything they wish, but we all shared concern about what should be done in the basic required music course. We decided to broaden it and include music of the Black composers, as well as consideration for the special needs of the Puerto Rican children.

Our second concern was with the music education courses, required for

prospective teachers. The students here are required to take Spanish and Afro-
American history, and know enough Black music so it can be used in their
teaching.

The third area of our concern was the matter of music electives. Following
the suggestion of Dr. Nketia of the University of Ghana, who was passing
through New York at the time, we are now offering work in African drumming, taught by African musicians. Of course, we also have jazz workshops and
training in arranging.

Our fifth concern was with the graduate program. Hunter College is presently the only college of the City University which offers a master's degree
special electives so that he would be qualified to teach on the Black experience
in music.

Our fifth concern was with the graduate program. Hunter College is presently the only college of the City University which offers a master's degree
in music with an emphasis on African music. Our committee recommended
that each of the senior colleges might think about offering a master's degree in
music. Presently, we think the degree should be in musicology, with emphasis on African music, rather than in ethnomusicology. We have plans for a
Ph.D. with the same emphasis.

I have been working with New York University, a private school, as a guest
lecturer. We are planning something here which is quite exciting, and has
been funded: an urban precentorship. There is little expert, well-documented
research in Black music, as we all know. Perhaps nowhere in the country are
there such extensive opportunities to study this field as in New York City. We
have chosen two areas of special significance: religious music, and theater
music.

The second oldest independent Negro church was founded in New York in
1796, the African Methodist Episcopal Zion Church, still in existence today.
The first Negro theater in New York was established in 1821, and I think this
was the first in the United States. It was not a continuing thing, but it did last
about ten years.

From ten to fifteen students will participate in this very special project, an
honors course. They will interview some of the pioneering musicians who
are still living, such as Hall Johnson, and W. C. Handy's brother. They will
compile a dictionary of Black musicians in New York. There will be field
trips to theaters, night clubs, and churches so they can have first-hand experience. There will be several lecture concerts, featuring jazz and African music.

We hope this will contribute to the documentary evidence from the past, helping to fill in some of the missing links in our knowledge, and place on record a variety of otherwise unrecoverable living history.

MAULTSBY: I'm not a teacher. I'm a student at the University of Wisconsin. My approach is as an ethnomusicologist, not a musicologist. My emphasis is Black music in America, with an African minor. In our Ph.D. program in ethnomusicology, musicology is a required background. There are no courses in my particular area. The only thing that is being taught presently is jazz and African music. I don't intend to deal extensively with jazz outside of its role, because much has been written already. My interest is historical: the evolution and developments of the music, not one form in itself. I spent about two months trying to develop an outline which would be the basis of my study. My first idea was to break the history into periods. First was up to 1830, with plantation music coming after that, but then I ran into problems. Too many things overlapped, and I was trying to talk about too many things at one time. Religious music existed during plantation times, but it also existed in Africa, and after the Civil War. The same goes for secular music.

The program in ethnomusicology has been going on only about a year and a half, and I'm the only student they have in it, so the program is quite flexible, and that's good. I only take three courses so I can have enough time for my own study. My research is climaxed with a paper, which is supposed to show my advisor that I know almost everything, and she is sharp. Even though she doesn't know too much in this particular area, she is steadily looking. After I turned in one paper, I went to see her. She had checked out at least fifty books from my bibliography, and she had them there, wide open, checking my footnotes. So, even if you don't know everything that's going on, writing term papers is a very important thing, as Bill said. My teacher is learning with me.

In reading these materials and sources, you've got to be very careful. You'll have to look at the author and find out who he is, where he came from, what authority he has for his remarks. First of all, many of the books are written by anthropologists and sociologists. They don't know exactly how to express what they mean. And, in describing African music, the western-trained musicologist just as bad as the anthropologist because he lacks the terminology and psychological approach. It took me months to acquire a new vocabulary and to develop a new way of listening.

After all of this, my final outline starts with origins in Africa. Then comes religious music. Secular music is my third category, then comes minstrels and, in a category by itself, musical comedy. After that I'm dealing with the blues. Next you could put down jazz but, as I said, this is not my primary interest. Then I'm going to consider rhythm and blues, or soul, and my last section will be on the music of Black composers.

D'ANGELO: Probably I represent the majority of the colleges in this country. As we know, there are over 2,300 of these, most of which are smaller institutions. My school is basically WASP, with a minimum of Black students, very high tuition, upper middle class student body which is very bright. We now have a Black studies program. We're in the area of minority group education, which means we are soliciting minority groups. Ours is an integrated program. It took me three or four years before I could get the administration to approve a course in "American music" (so I couched it), but this has now been going on for six years. The first time I offered the course, twenty-five students enrolled. This is rather large for a private liberal arts college of about 1,600 students (20 of which are Black). The second year I had 120, and since then there have been up to 135. In five years, I've had only one Black student in the class, but the White student has to know this material. He's completely ignorant of the subject, even though he comes to us with a high level of sophistication in the sciences and other areas, and was in the top 15 to 20 percent of his class. When it comes to the arts, though, he tilts. Well, in my class, I fly in jazz artists from the city (we have a grant from the Xerox Corporation which helps). My course is structured to give the students the concept that American music cannot even be thought of without acknowledgment of the major contribution from the Black people, so I implement my lectures with artists who are brought in. Having live, active people to talk about the issues makes things much more real for the students.

DE LERMA: The panelists have indicated that there is an importance in having a super-structure for a Black music program—a general Black studies program. To some extent, having course work in Black music without this overall foundation is something like teaching without a library. Sometimes, however, it is necessary to start without such a foundation. For example, we are teaching Black music despite the fact that we may have to rely on term papers, less scholarly books, and maybe rather poor library holdings. If a university lacks a Black studies program, crippled though it may be, the school or department of music should go ahead anyway with course work. Perhaps with assistance for someone in, say, the art department or another field, the need for such a foundation will eventually be inevitable and have to be acknowledged. "One little candle," you know. One other challenge which has been raised is with respect to musicology and ethnomusicology. I referred to the fact that in examining Black music, the educational institutions will have to reevaluate everything it has assumed in the past. It will have to make the techniques more vital, more useful, more socially oriented. This is a challenge to musicology not to be content only with the traditionally taught subjects, traditionally taught composers, traditionally conceived ideas, but to consider *music*—and ethnomusicology is certainly a part of this. There has also been expressed an interest in having scholarship in Black studies and less poetry, something with real, honest-to-goodness information. These three elements we are unable to care for this morning. We cannot establish a Black studies program at a university, we can only challenge the musicologists to address themselves to the world of *all* music, and we can only say that we will buy a good book on Black music when it appears. Our reason for being here, however, is to learn the techniques which these experienced people have used in developing their own programs.

D'ANGELO: Our Black studies program results from our work in the music department. We were the first to start a course which gave real attention to the area. The art department joined us then. I suggest to you that you go back to your institutions and simply start, no matter what you lack.

SOUTHERN: In conjunction with our work, our committee has collected a number of sample course descriptions and outlines for various aspects of Black music. We would be happy to share these with you.[1]

LA BREW: You speak of a need for a source book. Alan Lomax, in a lecture in Detroit, said that it's not a source book you need, but dissemination. Even if you have such a book, how could you get it printed?

DE LERMA: Excuse me, but I'm not sure if Mr. Lomax might have meant the dissemination of the information or dissemination of the music itself. If the latter is the case, I certainly agree that this is important.

LA BREW: Say that you have prepared a historical, factual book. How do you

---

[1] Dr. Southern and her colleagues at the City University of New York have joined with professors from other schools in allowing drafts of course outlines to be included in Appendix 6.

get it published? The major publishing houses are very difficult to get to, and the musicological sources want to do it for free.

DE LERMA: With respect to our source book, Kent State University Press heard about this only because they were engaged in publishing a bibliographic study of mine on Ives, which is due in the first half of 1970 by the way. They jumped at the chance to issue a contract, being an alert, young press with a real interest in such matters. But since that time, without my solicitation, I have received telephone calls from several publishers asking for the rights. Few journals pay for articles, especially the scholarly ones (which seems very strange, I know), but locating a publisher for a book of value on Black music seems not to be much of a problem these days.

LA BREW: I'm doing a history on Detroit musicians, going back to factual data, using only Negro sources which White scholars can't reach—things like the biography of Clarence Cameron White, the writings of Azalia Hackley, and so on. What sources are you going to use, Miss Maultsby?

MAULTSBY: In my research thus far, I've come across only two sources by Black people. I'm interested also in publication, by the way, but I'm at a university, so I just use their press. I really think a university press would publish valuable studies which were given to them.

LA BREW: I'm doing mine as an independent study for the National Association of Negro Musicians. Working independently, I don't have access to the publishers or the research of other scholars. I find this is happening all over the country. You have others who are doing what I'm doing, but they will not share their work.

DE LERMA: I'm sure no university press has a policy of publishing material only by a professor. As for sharing, until our book is out, Indiana University's Black Music Committee is eager to cooperate mutually with any interested individual or any society. When the book is out, if there are other ways we can help, we sure will.

COLE: Can I say something about getting information from the composers? We have been making assumptions about what is Black music in respect to the composer, running up to him and saying, "What about that is Black?" That was a question someone asked after Brother Olly Wilson played his thing here. And then people run up and say, "That's not really Black, is it?", like they didn't listen to what he had already told them. He said, "Of course it's Black, because it's me, and I'm Black!" You'd have to be blind not to see he's Black, you know! I think that's very important. I think what is more important is that no one really sat down and talked to Brother Wilson about what it is that he's doing. We had a discussion last night, late last night. It's not his position to say what about his music is Black; he's a composer. Why should he be concerned about that? He is involved with writing music. As musicologists, it is our job to find out. By talking to him last night, I understand him better, and I see how he might have been influenced by Miles Davis in his space relationship and the consumption of time. These are things *we* have to do. It has always been our position as Black people to make assumptions about our music, but by starting from a negative position, running up to people and saying, "What about that is Black?" This really amounts to running away from our heritage. We had better get into our thing, but like scholars. Black music is anything written by a Black person, because his experiences are Black. That's the foundation. After that we need to find out something about the man and his music.

MAULTSBY: Bill is suggesting an interesting point. Are you going to include style characteristics in your book?

DE LERMA: Certainly this is quite important. Users of the book will want to know what kind of a composer is this he has found. To some extent you can tell by his titles or his instrumentation. You could certainly tell if he is engaged in spiritual arrangements. Past that, it would be very functional if we could classify him as a serialist or neo-classicist, but I'm not interested for a minute in fine-line definitions.

SMITH: When I was interviewed by Dave, I was asked questions related to my style. My own feeling is that style is something quite apart from devices. Style is habit. It grows out of those things that make up a composer's individual characteristics. Any verbalization of these characteristics can't help but be misleading. I can understand the reader of the book may want to have some conception of what this composer's music is like, but he won't really know anything until he has heard the music.

DE LERMA: We are not making any stylistic analysis. This has yet to be done. But a basic, liberal terminology will not mean that the composer has a predilection for minor sub-dominants, for example, whereas it might mean that if you want tonal music, you'd better stay away from Olly Wilson.

COLE: I told Brother Wilson I wasn't going to say this, but I've been doing this kind of research all my life, as many of you have. Maybe it's because I know these people, because I've worked with them, but I have yet to be refused or find anyone reluctant to discuss his music if he thinks I am interested in it. I just told Olly that I got a call the other day from Bill Dawson who knew that I was interested in getting in touch with someone. I kept saying to my wife that I've got to see these people before they die, but he told me this composer had died on me. That's why Dr. Southern's project at NYU excites me. But, anyway, Dawson said, "Look, my symphony is being re-issued. If you want something analytical on it, I'll give it to you." In two days he sent me a complete analysis of the four movements.

QUESTION: But how valid is what a composer has to say about his music?

DE LERMA: I was particularly impressed with the coverage of his style given me by T. J. Anderson, who is an extraordinarily articulate person anyway, but I know that some composers are not the least bit interested in talking about their style, and not too many of them can.

SOUTHERN: This may be a bit pre-mature, but W. W. Norton is going to publish a history of Afro-American music (for those of you wanting a textbook) and a bibliography. Those of you who have something to publish, send it to the *Journal of the American Musicological Society*. I've been rather guilty myself, giving a great deal of attention to renaissance music. But if you read *JAMS* in the future, you will see something on Afro-American music. You should submit your articles and don't be concerned about being paid for them. The important thing is to disseminate information in such journals as *JAMS*, the *Musical Quarterly* and *Notes*, information that is valuable to scholars.

D'ANGELO: I have a bibliography and a syllbus. I'd be more than happy to Xerox them and send them to you if you wish.

DE LERMA: There have been so many offers, so many developments, so much work in progress—may I suggest that any of you who have any information, any duplicated material, anything like that, let me know about it. I would like to let all of our registrants know what is available and what price, and if we publish a transcript of this seminar, inclusion of syllabi and such would be most helpful for those who have not been able to attend our sessions.

● Perhaps the most impressive fact coming from this session is the degree of cooperation and stimulus available from and to all levels within education. Dr. Still has expressed his distaste for irresponsible students who trust their intuition more than their professor's research. The panelists at this session showed that a creative relationship between the pupil and teacher is possible. The really exceptional student can certainly influence a sensitive teacher, and the professor can urge his administration to consider new ideas or approaches. Normally, of course, one expects the hierarchy to be constructed in the other direction. To have the student change the philosophy or techniques of his administration is an inversion of educational tradition, but when the case is presented maturely and is properly documented, a quiet revolution is possible. The potentials of a similar structure has been evidenced of late with respect even to the federal government.

We have observed the tragic results when rather reasonable requests have been stated by the students as demands. The authority of the teacher or the administration is destroyed and with it, more importantly, emotional reactions take the place of calm consideration, and the demands are rejected. The established figures then forget their ex officio dignity (*noblesse oblige*, or *sagesse oblige*), and dignity, nobility and wisdom vanish, despite the fact that an older person should have richer experience in these qualities. How much different things might be if the demands were stated as requests, or if the administration would quietly take the ideas into sober consideration, not certain beforehand that youth is always wrong (an idea which our public schools have nurtured all along).

The heart of the problem is even more disturbing. A teacher or an administrator has the duty to lead. His whole social function is damaged if the student requests have to do with *evolution*, if the follower is actually in the vanguard, and the leader cannot understand the *Zeitgeist*. The seriousness of this problem should be most evident to those persons whose studies have considered the humanities, wherein the evolution of ideas (roots, causes, manifestations, implications—the whole fabric) is the most dynamic and virile element. What is more dramatic than the realization that Bach really was the culmination of so much that had come before him, that the eighteenth-century classicists were really radicals? And of what value is an administrator's experience or a teacher's historical research if he cannot distinguish current trivia from new movements?

Anyone engaged in creative teaching cannot help but come up with new ideas or facts. Because a teacher at any level is active in communication, he should be a master of the techniques. The problem then is merely a matter of finding the time to develop all of the implications of his findings and to present the material to journals or publishing houses. There is a tremendous need for information on Black music if it is offered in a scholastically responsible manner. The number of individuals who have been engaged in research in this area for many years in quite remarkable, particularly in view of the extent to which this information has been of-fered for publication. Once it has been issued, however, those of us who lament the paucity of material should cease our wailing long enough to acquire the publication or recording and digest it. We must also give financial support to the responsible author, performer or composer, by purchasing what he has offered us.

Although he could only be with us for a short time one day, we were pleased to meet Arthur LaBrew, who came as an informal representative of the National Association for Negro Musicians. Within only a few months after his departure, Mr. LaBrew personally published his own research on *The Black Swan: Elizabeth T. Greenfield, Songstress*, issued in 1969 by him from 313 East Adams Street, Detroit, Michigan, 48226. Subsequent correspondence with this serious young scholar carries the promise of continued responsible research of substantial merit.

11. *Student Viewpoints*

Rachel Foster

Robert Morris

Frank Suggs, Jr.

● As Dr. Anderson indicates in this discussion, we had hoped to hear from a fourth student, one whose ideas would have been substantially different from our trio. Unfortunately, his viewpoints were so far distant that he did not wish to participate. I cannot help but regard this as genuinely tragic. No society should condition any of its members to the extent that even communication is thought futile.

Despite this fact, the three student participants of the panel made distinct contributions. Robert Morris, who was later appointed a member of the Black Music Committee, is a graduate student in choral music at Indiana University and a composer of considerable promise. Rachel Foster, from the Hampton Institute, is an undergraduate organist, majoring in music education. Frank Suggs, a doctoral student at Indiana University in the School of Music's multiple arts program, is destined quite soon to be a major Black figure in music education.

DE LERMA: How much Black music, or facts regarding it, have you learned frm pre-college days, from college, from books and scores, from performances, from recordings, or from conversation?

MORRIS: There's very little I learned from formal study, although I was fortunate in that my elementary school had several die-hard teachers who firmly believed in our history. We were scuttled into the library once a week for study. In school and in church, most of the music that I came across was more or less traditional arrangements of spirituals. There was nothing in college excepting that at the senior level, which was so repugnant that I'd rather forget it.

DE LERMA: And yet I am personally aware that you have a great deal of information. Where did it come from?

MORRIS: When I started teaching in the city schools, I found that the young people were strengthened by knowing something that was relevant. To go home after a day's work and busy yourself with a record book is not going to help your students, so I spent this time reading and studying. I wanted to offer my students something they could hold on to. It was perhaps not scholarly, but it was something. Then, when I began working for the Black Music Committee, I got more information because now I had to search harder.

DE LERMA: Miss Foster comes from a very distinguished school which, unlike Bob's graduate institution, is predominantly Black.

FOSTER: I don't consider my school to be a Black institution. I consider it a Negro institution. The thoughts are not Black, they are White-oriented. The majority of the people there are Negro, and the teaching of music has not been Black. We're at an institution which is really a storehouse of knowledge, but no one has used it. Now they are trying to change things. But my knowledge of Black music is almost null and void; I'm quite ignorant. I know very little about what's going on with the Black people. I'm from a Baptist church where spirituals and gospel music have been rich, but I've never had the opportunity to study the material.

DE LERMA: You are an organ student, yes? Besides Bach, what is your repertoire?

FOSTER: The baroque and romantic periods, and that's it.

SUGGS: Well, fortunately or unfortunately, I was born in Mississippi. I grew up living on somebody else's place. My folks were particularly interested in the church, and were itinerant preachers, gospel and spiritual singers. My dad and uncles sang in a quartet, and I had the opportunity of singing with them when I was quite young. My sister plays gospel piano, so this was all a part of our lives. We had the beautiful experience of watching the baptisms at the lake, at the pond, and by the river. We knew the spirituals and the spiritualized versions of the hymns, particularly the lined hymns. When the family moved to Arizona, this was quite a different experience. I assume that most sophomores and juniors in high school know what it is when it really dawns on you that you are Black, and you know that you are different. You go to the library and find out there is George Washington Carver, Booker T. Washington, Marian Anderson, and Roland Hayes, but you won't find Frederick Douglas or W. E. B. DuBois. You go the route of the general school music program, and you may learn to sing spirituals. However, when I was growing up, no one ever called them spirituals—in fact, I learned the term at school, not among the people who sang them. Realizing that there was a shortage of this type of music in Douglas—this was around 1953—we decided to get a group to come to our community to give a program. We tried to get the Wings Over Jordan, but we couldn't afford them. We looked for other groups, but we couldn't find any —not in religious music, in folk music or in work songs. I did some research on my own. With a friend of mine who was an English major, we went through the University of Arizona library and found everything we could. Then we organized a group called the Spiritual Choraliers. We made it our business to go through the state and sing. I handled the music end of it. We were fortunate in having a kid who was working on his doctorate in organ. There were about twelve members all together. Cal did the sociological part of the research and we put it in a package deal for different churches of Arizona—Black, White, whoever would have us. The group held together until I graduated. When I was getting ready for my master's thesis, I wanted to work on some project which would integrate Black and White music, but the proposal was turned down, so I had to do something else. In the meantime, I had to eat, so I learned to play jazz and rock and roll—anything which will pay. I played piano and a little sax. When I started to teach, I ran into the same problem Robert hit. I wanted specific things. I began to write to people. There's a lot of material on jazz, as we've said before, but not much on non-jazz, or religious music, folk music or the work songs. The songs I heard as a boy, growing up in Mississippi, included prison songs. The prison yard was maybe only 100 yards from our house. And then the railroad ran in front of our house. Those of you who've grown up in the South will remember the railroad songs. I couldn't find any of these songs anywhere, and I couldn't find any one who had information about them. My family had been in Mississippi for a long time, before slavery almost. I went back to talk to some of the old people before they died, and I got some information from this.

As far as college is concerned, I went through it like anyone else. There was no Black music. Twentieth-century music, yes, but no Black music. When we studied Gauguin, we had to consider some African art. Same with Picasso. But we didn't do this in music. We didn't even discuss jazz excepting to mention its influences on early Stravinsky or on Debussy, but we never got down to who was a jazz musician. I had one professor who actually went into the African dance, showing where tap-dancing came from, and about the body, which in

African dance is earthy. In ballet, it is how long you can stay in the air, or seem to. In African dance the beat is on the ground. That's about all I had.

DE LERMA: We could have anticipated these answers, I think. Now, what are your ideal ambitions? And what do you think you might have to do?

MORRIS: I've gone through a period of change. The matter of being Black (which has nothing to do with complexion, as we should know by now) means that you have to reexamine yourself constantly and find out if you're really in line or in tune. This is sometimes painful, but you have to do your best to move with that group of people which is going to make this a more human society, a better society. There was a time I thought the best I could hope for was to teach in a high school, and that was it. Lately, I've changed. That's too narrow for me. When I taught in school, the children were members of the Blackstone Rangers or the Disciples. Many of these were my best students. What they did outside of school was sometimes a different thing. But I enjoyed teaching in high school. There's no need to fool yourself; every day you go there, there's a new challenge and, somehow, you have to be equal to the task. But now I think I'm finding that I turn more and more toward working in a college situation where I can help promote the idea with the Blacks of making a more integral America, in making an American fabric, a complete and real thing. The time that the White society had to take us in has gone and passed. Now the young people have taken things into their own hands. This is the way we want to do it. You don't judge us anymore. We're looking at *you*, the White American, asking are you really ready now to do what your constitution says. Are you really ready for this?

FOSTER: My mind has been shifting, just as Robert's did. Music education is my major, and I am terribly interested in this as it relates to the youngsters. The attitude of the typical high school student is really terrible when it comes to music. They learn very little, just enough to pass the teacher's exam, but they don't know anything about music. I want to go into the inner-city public school system. This is the problem that is facing society today. But I want to be well qualified when that time comes, so I've got to think about graduate study.

SUGGS: This year at Indiana University has changed my plans. My colleagues on the panel are interested in becoming in tune with the existing culture. Right now, I'm more interested in knowing what really is music, including Western, Chinese, or Black cultures. I also want to know if there really is a Black culture.

I can't accept the definition that White music is White because a White man wrote it, or Black is Black because a Black wrote it. Anthropologists tell us that music is the result of the *culture* of a given people, not that it defines these people *racially*. Any given group of people over a period of time can develop their own culture. They don't have to belong to the same race. Each culture defines what music is to it.

For the past ten years, I've had the wonderful experience of working with the Hopi and Navajo Indians. One time I walked into a classroom of all Indian children to teach them Beethoven. We were going to do an analysis of Beethoven. It wasn't very funny then. It took me a long time to realize that, to understand an individual, you must understand the culture from which he comes. Secondly, we must understand that cultures do not conceptualize identically. In Western culture, we place high value on abstract thinking. An Indian child can't understand abstract music.

Is there, then, a Black culture? Of course, I say there is. I say I have a Black culture, but also a White one. I think this is a point that Hale Smith was bringing out. Isn't it possible for a person to be racially one color, and culturally something else, to say that an individual is racially Black but culturally European? If we say that his music is culturally Black, we are trying to equate two things that can't be mixed. Realizing these problems, I have decided to go into anthropology, and to teach.

MORRIS: How are you going to ferret out those things we claim to be part of the Black culture?

SUGGS: I wish I could jump up and say I knew, but I don't. Dr. Hans Tischler knocked me down recently when he said ours is a sub-culture, that there cannot be a bi-culture. Right now, I don't know. What I see we're doing now is having an NACCP meeting. We're primarily concerned with a Black man writing in an idiom, and we more concerned with his music being heard and played. That is a matter of discrimination and segregation, not of music.

DE LERMA: What you have said is very provocative, but I think the reason we can't speak of a Black musical culture is because it hasn't been fully or properly isolated and examined. Our work, for example, is to distinguish those works written by a Black composer so this study can be undertaken. It is of no consequence if someone goes through the list of composers and says, "Oh, that guy, he's practically White, and what does this one know about Black people, and this one's a soul brother." A definition of culture has to consider all of these. Any kind of an exploration must be, within its limits, indiscriminate. If you have enough information to make decisions in more detailed levels, you have, for example, an annotated bibliography, but if your purpose is to discriminate and segregate in terms of race, you must take all manifestations. If you are after a cultural definition, you need substantially more information, and you might well end up including Frederick Delius, Harry Gilbert or Stephen Foster, and leaving out George Bridgetower or Samuel Coleridge-Taylor. I'm glad the matter came up so articulately. This is clearly a problem which is worthy of consideration. Before the floor begins to question you on some other ideas, are there any other viewpoints the panel would wish to express?

MORRIS: It's unfortunate that Black schools in particular should wait until the students storm their gates to start courses in Black history. Rachel has already indicated that many of these schools are repositories of information which has not been utilized in the past. Perhaps they are waiting for the White schools to say Black studies are O.K. Many of the schools in the South have traditions in music. I'm wondering if you feel those traditions are relevant. Are they capturing the imagination of the students? When Dr. Dawson was active at Tuskegee, there was a certain type of tradition for the spirituals. There is also a tradition at Fisk, at Hampton, at Howard. Do you find that the students you're getting now can line up with this? Is it really meaningful to them?

FOSTER: We have a tradition at Hampton which, in the days of Nathaniel Dett, was in its glory—supreme glory. We're very proud of these accomplishments, but we don't want to rest and say, well, we did this then. We need to know what are we going to do *now*, and where are we going to go in the future. We love our tradition, but we want to do our own thing.

McCALL: I'm a teacher at Hampton. I think the question is well put, and quite necessary. One of our choral conductors at Hampton was with the choir when Dett took it to Europe. He was there when Dett used the choir as a sort of testing ground for his new arrangements, before they got published. He could have been a fine concert singer, but he stuck to the spirituals, and he's continuing the tradition. The director of the College Choir is also a Hampton product, and we have two active composers on the staff who give attention to the spiritual.

May I add something? As teachers of courses in Black music, we can use our students in research situations, as Professor Cole previously suggested. But if we can perform some of this music, it must be put on tape. Perhaps at Hampton we can work out some sort of exchange in this area. If Indiana University's center gets started, I certainly think that this library should have copies of current recordings, not only of spirituals but anything than any Negro composer has written, so that all of us could refer to them. Put them on tape, stick them in the library, and we'll begin to have things we can at least listen to.

DE LERMA: In my preliminary remarks, I stated the fact that it would be a long time before the name of Monteverdi would be mentioned in any history class if that name could only be uttered by an Italian. I'd like to ask the panel members if they feel that the writing and teaching of Black music should be done only by Blacks, and why this might be a special situation.

FOSTER: I think music should be taught and studied by all racial groups. You're going to college, you're going to learn, you're supposed to be widening your horizons as much as possible. You'll have to learn about Greek history and Roman civilization, no matter if you are Greek or not. You'll have to learn about the Black man, to know his attitudes and his interests, to know why he feels his revolt is justified. When these uprisings happen, the adults say, "Oh, they're crazy! They don't know what they're doing!" but there are definite reasons why. The Blacks know the reasons. The Whites need to learn them.

MORRIS: Some people say that the Black man has contributed the only truly American music, save that of the Indian (which has not won dissemination). If this music is the thing we've got which is American, then all Americans need it. And if only Black men perform it, we would be working against ourselves.

SUGGS: I guess I'm the only one to take exception. Within this time in history, if we accept the fact that there is a Black culture, we have to accept the fact that there are unique experiences which are Black. I wouldn't ask a Hopi Indian to conduct the Beethoven fifth, or to teach it. Knowledge is not always the same thing as experience. It is possible, furthermore, for me to move to China and bring my children up with a Chinese experience, speaking Chinese, and actually knowing more about what it is to *be* Chinese than anyone could get from a book. If there is an experience which is unique to me as a Black man, and if Hale Smith is right in saying that because of this uniqueness there is something of this within the composition, then the next logical step is that this uniqueness can be found and understood by someone with a like experience. Am I saying that the individual must be Black? No, not racially. But he must be culturally Black.

MORRIS: Frank, don't you go a bit far with the Indians and Beethoven? If you will admit the White American teacher can be somewhat in tune with the Blacks, he can make a contribution. You said that the Indians didn't know who Beethoven was a few years ago. Now they know.

SUGGS: I can teach Stravinsky, because I'm westernized. I understand Western culture: I know about the Greeks, the Romans, I've read *Beowulf* and Chaucer, and I know Monteverdi. I can't name anybody who writes Chinese opera. I couldn't possibly teach it. Would I attempt to teach Indian music to the Indians? No, I would not! I can analyze it for you, and tell you about the form, how many tritones it has or what scale it uses, how many repetitions there are, and what voice inflections there are, but the Indian defines his music quite differently.

FOSTER: The problem is for you to try to understand it the way the Indian does.

SUGGS: Exactly! That's what I mean when I say the White person must become culturally Black. It's possible. As Americans, we must understand that we have many cultures. If one is White, he must be Custer, but he must also be Sitting Bull. He must be Lincoln, but also Frederick Douglas. I'm not saying that a person who teaches Black music must be racially Black.

ANDERSON: I'd like to make a few remarks. First of all, I'm sorry that one of my students from Tennessee State University was not able to join you on the panel. We are hurting because he is not here. Without a question, he would represent a totally different viewpoint. His answer would be that since we are a part of a separate culture, this culture has its own sense of values. He would take the position that Black music could only be taught by Blacks because it's relevant only to Black people. Until Whites become ebonized, they better leave it alone. I also noticed that, in indicating your future job interests, you identified yourselves within the existing structure. I have students who in no way plan to participate in it, who in every way plan to use their energies for the destruction of the system, and who are active in the society right now, in many ways. I think this is something that should be brought to the attention of this group.

DE LERMA: I'm very sorry we don't have a representative of that viewpoint. Society needs to understand it very badly.

QUESTION: In order for a person to teach Black music, Mr. Suggs, you say he must be culturally Black. Using yourself as an example, you are culturally White. You said you could teach Stravinsky and Monteverdi. Well then, if you are a culturally White Black man, who will teach Black music?

SUGGS: Although Dr. Tischler told me it was not possible, I think I am bicultural.

QUESTION: How will you work out this biculturalism in an equitable balance so that you can teach Black music?

SUGGS: This may be the question that Dr. Anderson's student would have raised, and that's the thing I wrestle with most, and yet I know I am both. DuBois spoke about the wrestling which takes place inside of the individual, and Dr. Anderson spoke about it with reference to Tolson. You ask me how I will teach. How will any Black? I can only answer for myself. I have to know both cultures, yet see them within myself as two separate things. I must sit at the feet of as many Black people as I can—and I mean Black Black—to learn as much as I can. I need to chase down the people in Mississippi, I need to know the people in my own family, I need to talk to Black composers, all of this to make sure that I do not let the academic override the other. I can't get away from the fact that I went to those schools, just like you. I was taught that music. Somehow, I have to keep them on an equal par. One is not greater than the other.

FOSTER: People run around now in dashikis and say, "Well, I'm a Black man!" but their mind is not always oriented this way. To teach music, you must get to the core of the attitude. To study jazz, you can't use Western ideals of analysis. LeRoi Jones says it in *Black Music*. You cannot approach jazz with Western attitudes. As Frank said, you can't teach Black culture as a citizen of White culture.

QUESTION: There is a dissertation called *Jazz, 1920 to 1927* by Launcelot Pyke, written in 1962, which tries this. He had all sorts of difficulty trying to transcribe the music. Six readers read the scores, and they all ended up with something different. It's a very interesting dissertation which would bear looking at, but I think it is quite inaccurate.

QUESTION: Mr. Suggs, suppose you were teaching in an all-Black school and suddenly the Justice Department comes along and you are transferred. You become the only Black teacher on a White faculty, with all White students. What would you do then?

SUGGS: What level?

QUESTION: Elementary school.

SUGGS: I'm faced with that very problem next week. What will I do Monday morning? I don't know.

FOSTER: I'd like to ask what attitude you had taken with the Black students, if this transfer happened to you. Were you teaching them as White students?

QUESTION: I never had a different kind of lesson plan for a class because the students were White or Black. I teach the subject, but with some degree of flexibility. Of course, I include Black music. By the way, I'm a Black teacher, teaching all White students.

SUGGS: I'm sorry. I threw you off rather flippantly. I didn't really mean that. My objective with the students will not be to make them either Black or White, but the make them American. We've mentioned before that this means they must identify with many cultures. When I talk about rhythm, I can illustrate this with African drummers. When I discuss line and color, I can use Indian music. When I speak about the social function of music, I can refer to music in the Negro church.

DE LERMA: This is very frustrating, but we must stop now. I'm not sure this question can be answered readily or orally. What we evidently need, quite badly, is a series of printed lesson plans which are used by teachers in various levels which you can hold in your hands and think about. Anyone who would like to share such plans may feel free to send them to us, to the Black Music Committee here at Indiana University. I'll try to develop some method whereby these can be reproduced and made available.

● "White" schools, suddenly jumping on the bandwagon for Black studies, should not be so *nouveau riche* as to deny that the major Black schools have addressed themselves to this information for many years. Even so, other factors have provided the White schools with re-sources and approaches which might, at times, be more contemporary. It has been lamented, for example, that jazz programs do not always at-tract Black performers and that Black schools are conservative in offering jazz performance studies. I've been told that mothers of Black students have been partially responsible for this, telling their children, "Now look here, you don't go down to that school to study no jazz!" This might account for the fact that Dave Baker's jazz band, which performed for one of this seminar's evenings, had not one Black member, despite the fact that the School of Music had well over fifty Black instrumental majors.

Eventually there must also be a confession that an educational institution should be more engaged in the task of stimulating, rather than teaching. The student who majors in musicology might not learn all he should with regard to the evolution of a form or an idea, but the process of understanding and evaluating what he has learned (be it related to Josquin, Wagner or Perotin) must give him the skills and techniques which will help him in his own consideration of Dett, Rossini or Coltrane.

I feel at the same time that the student should learn not only history, but repertoire. Cannot Burleigh's *Deep river* teach the Black violinist how to treat certain problems as well as Raff's *Cavatina*? Should not the Black pianist be familiar, not only with Chopin and Prokofiev, but with Cunningham and Joplin?

There is certainly no doubt but what scholarship programs must be available for Black students in music, but there should also be funds available for the advanced Black student to travel for research. Anyone who has done work in Black music, including those who grew up in certain communities, knows that there is information of value in remote locations and that those who have these data may never have been in communication with a scholar, and may be nearing the end of life. Despite the tenacity of oral tradition, a tradition which is of particular consequence in this subject, individuals are often sources which must be tapped before a new generation or new sociological elements transform the tradition.

12. Administrative Problems of Implementation, Funding and Staffing

O. Anderson Fuller

Richard M. Turner, III

Paul Klinge

● As Professor Turner will indicate, the study of Black culture is not a curricular innovation at most Black schools. The result of desegrated education, however, does place some pressure on formerly White schools to give attention to this rather formative element in American society. Schools whose administrations have delayed this consideration find it not easy to institute the programs once they are accepted in spirit. It is not easy to find specialists, equal to the school's concept of its image, who can guide the students over the materials. The addition of new courses, which might not all be elective within certain majors, poses a difficulty for those schools whose format of requirements and prerequisites suggests inflexibility. These matters can probably best be settled by schools on an individual basis, within the latitude of their abilities and the limits of their interests in emphasis areas, but special funding may often be necessary to get the programs initiated. Funding can also help the Black school who wishes to intensify or re-orient its offerings.

There is a misconception we have often noted that the larger school has greater financial resources. With state universities, this is certainly not true. The size of an operating budget does not reflect large uncommitted areas, open to the option of the administration for capital investments. To this extent, the large school has the same funding problems for new programs which the smaller institution faces. There is, however, one advantage which might be noted in some instances. Because of the complexity in operating a large university, there may be a special department of persons who are engaged on a full-time basis on the development of grant proposals, or of some channel for securing special funds for research, teaching or related supplies. In these cases, there will be someone who can translate the wishes of a faculty member or his administration into "grantsmanese," who knows which foundations or sources might have an interest in a given program, if the proposal for that program is carefully, fully, and tersely developed on paper. We are deeply fortunate in Bloomington in having the Indiana University Foundation, which has assisted in more than one instance in helping us to secure off-campus funding for projects related to Black music.

The persons participating on this panel include Professor Richard M. Turner, Chairman of the Music Department at Fisk University and conductor of the distinguished Fisk Jubilee Singers, Dr. O. Anderson Fuller, Chairman of the Music Department at Missouri's Lincoln University in Jefferson City, and Dean Paul Klinge from the Indiana University Foundation.

TURNER: The cry for Black studies in the predominately Negro colleges and universities (particularly the private or church-related institutions) often appears absurd, especially to a not-too-recent graduate of one of the most prominent of these institutions. Black institutions have been teaching Black studies for years as integral parts of their curricula. Recent public emphasis regarding the initiation of Black studies programs at San Francisco State College, Harvard, Yale and other White institutions—approximately 23 in number—must not cause us to overlook this fact. Statements in the March 15, 1969, issue of *The New Republic* to the effect that San Francisco State pioneered in Black studies should be qualified by adding "in White universities." The fact that increased numbers of Black students have chosen to attend formerly all-White institutions, as a result of school desegregation since 1954, in lieu of the predominately Negro colleges and universities, is probably the primary cause of so much of the conflict on college and university campuses regarding Black studies programs. The White institutions, which formerly either limited their enrollment of Black students or refused admission to Black students, did not foresee (or else chose to ignore) the need to provide students with a knowledge of the African heritage and of past accomplishments of Black people in the United States.

Predominately Negro institutions, for example Fisk University, have long offered students the opportunity to know the history of the Black man—the pains and struggles of slavery and strides and successes toward freedom, as well as current problems which have resulted from experiences of the past. As early as 1910, Fisk (founded in 1866 by the American Missionary Association for the "education and training of young men and women irrespective of color") offered courses in social science which were especially relevant to deal with the problems of the Black community. The catalog for this year lists a course titled "History of the Negro in America." In the light of the scarcity of information concerning Black music and musicians today, the following statements with regard to the textbook for this course may be of interest. "There is no suitable textbook to be used for the historical part of such a course, so that assigned readings are selected from standard histories from W. E. B. DuBois' *Supression of Slave Trade*, Williams' *History of the Negro in America*, Washington's *Story of the Negro*, and Harte's *Slavery and Abolition*. In addition, each student is required to use original sources and report upon Summerside's topic and to make a digest of some current writing on the Negro problem." It is apparent that at Fisk and other Black colleges, courses not specifically labeled Negro were concerned with the problems facing the Negro community. A preface to the listing of courses in social science and the same Fisk catalog 1910 contains this statement: "The time has come for the Negro college to become closely articulated with the community in which it is located. The further aim is to bring the university into closer relation with the conditions among Colored people in Nashville and to seek the cooperation of other Negro colleges in developing this much-needed phase of education."

A race relations institute held annually during the summer session has been a joint venture of the Race Relations Department of the American Missionary Association and Fisk University. Its purpose has been to provide intensive analysis of the economic, political, and social problems confronted by teachers, social workers, and other persons engaged in any way in inter-group activities. Developed in more recent years have been an African-Caribbean Center and a Center for African-American Studies. Both of these centers have the responsibility for coordinating research in the special areas, and for helping to establish interdisciplinary courses. Problems of the Negro community are studied with the aim of providing research bases for developing public policy and informed action in the Black ghetto through a recent $300,000 grant to the Political Science Department by the Ford Foundation. An illustration of the utilization of university resources in the solution of pressing community problems is the involvement of Fisk in the recent controversy surrounding the routing of Interstate Highway 40 through the center of an important Black business and residential district.

Students on campus have met personally with the most prominent personalities, both White and Black. An example of this kind of experience which is also a part of many Black university campuses is the Annual Festival of Arts, the fortieth of which was celebrated this past spring.

From the founding of this institution the most prominent White and Black faculty have been employed and have worked together successfully. The faculties have included some of the most noted scholars of their day. The Department of Music at Fisk dates back to 1882 when the Bachelor of Arts program was begun. The reputation of the university for music had been established by the Jubilee Singers who, between 1871 and 1878, traveled through northern and eastern sections of the United States and parts of Europe to raise money for the support of the university. The Singers raised over $150,000 which was used in part for the erection of Jubilee Hall, currently a senior women's dormitory, and they introduced the Negro spiritual to the world and established it as a distinctive American contribution to musical literature and art. A course in Black music appeared in the 1923 Fisk catalog entitled "Study of Negro Music and Composition." The course description is as follows: "The work of this course will consist of the study and analysis of the works of Negro composers, the recording" (I assume what is meant here is the writing) "and setting of Negro melodies and the various musical forms. The course will be a practical one and will work toward the creation of larger forms without the loss of the Negro idiom." Another music course initiated about 1950 is entitled "Music in America" and has the following description: "A survey of music in America from 1800 to the present. Folk music and jazz as well as the music of the outstanding American composers will be studied. Social conditions which have produced music of the country will likewise be studied. The Department of Music and the Department of Social Science collaborated in offering this course."

The point of this discourse is that Black institutions such as Fisk have long regarded Black studies as a respected phase of academic pursuit and are largely responsible for having brought to public attention contributions of outstanding Black people. Because of the close relationship, both personal and professional, of outstanding Black people in past years, the predominantly Negro colleges and universities are in a position to make significant contributions to future developments of programs in Black music.

You will probably want to know what our present plans are with respect to studies in Black music. Since we are in the process of developing a renewed emphasis in this area, our plans are not fully outlined yet. I suppose I should indicate that I have just completed my first year at Fisk and as music chairman. However, I shall indicate what appears to be our probable direction. Specific details will be worked out after new faculty personnel come aboard.

The present Fisk curriculum involves three degree programs: a Bachelor of Arts in Music with emphasis on music history and literature, a Bachelor of Science in Music Education, and a Master of Arts in Music with emphasis on musicology.

Within the Bachelor of Arts curriculum there are three major components. The first component is the music, the others are general education and general electives. It is possible that a B.A. music student may take as many as 20 general elective credits from among the 21 African and Afro-American courses offered by the University in the departments of anthropology, art, education, English, history, political science, sociology and music. This broad background in the undergraduate music program should prepare a student to enter our M.A. in Music with emphasis in ethnomusicology.

Among new faculty personnel in the fall we are fortunate to have a well-qualified ethnomusicologist, Darius L. Thieme, who has a specialty in African music. I'd just like to outline his background briefly. He has an A.B. in music, an M.M. in theory and composition, a licentiate from Trinity College in London with a major in music and emphasis in double bass. He spent a year in a seminar in African music at the School of Oriental and African Studies at London University. He also has a Master of Science degree in Library Science, and a Ph.D. He has had experience as a manager of a G. Schirmer branch bookstore, and as a member of the Seventh Army Symphony Orchestra. He served several years as reference librarian in the Music Division of the Library of Congress, and as an instructor in the materials and methods of ethnomusicology and research at several noted universities. Some of his important publications have included *African Music; A Briefly Annotated Bibliography* (issued for the Library of Congress in 1964), *A Descriptive Catalogue of Yoruba Musical Instruments* (his dissertation at the Catholic University of America), "Negro folksong scholarship in the United States" (which appeared in the 1960 issue of *African Music*), *Social Organization of Yoruba Musicians* (published by Howard University in 1969), "Style in Yoruba Music" (in the June 1967 issue of *Ibadan*), and *Training and Musicianship Among the Yoruba* (published by Howard University in 1969). He has furthermore published valuable articles in such periodicals as *Musart*, and the journals of the International Folk Music Council and the Society for Ethnomusicology. In 1964 to 1966, he spent two years studying the traditional Yoruba music, and made a collection of Nigerian musical instruments for the Nigerian Museum and for the Smithsonian Institute.

I expect that the development of our music program in this direction will contribute to relieve in a small way the great demand for quality faculty to teach college and university courses in Black music.

FULLER: Lincoln University is an institution which is part of the system of higher education in the state of Missouri. It was founded, as the history reads, by the Sixty-Second and Sixty-Fifth Infantries, Black veterans of the Union Army, and was part of their project during the first twelve years. In 1878, the state assumed partial responsibility and, two years later, full responsibility for the financing and supervision of education. The institution was originally oriented toward the education of Missouri Blacks. In the service to the state and to the Midwest, and ultimately to the nation and the world, Lincoln University had partly different functions and relations from those of an entirely private institution. There have been in its growth and development both curricular and capital outlay for facilities, a service that has become perhaps peculiar to an institution of its type, particularly from 1878 to 1954.

The departments of history and sociology have curricular interests developed with regard to the various ethnic groups, particularly the Negro in this country. We have had a very staunch protagonist for the study of Negros and Blacks throughout the years in the history department, particularly in the person of Dr. Lorenzo Green who grew up in his historical studies with Carter G. Woodson and Charles Wesley. Presently at Lincoln University there is a resurgence toward the study of Black activities. A committee has been appointed by the Dean of Instruction and the Administrative Dean. The demand has come from the Student Government Association and other activists regarding the return to emphasis on Black studies. Some of them will be initiated this fall.

KLINGE: This morning I was with our University Science Advisory Committee. They were discussing some of the same problems that I have been assigned on this panel. What we're talking about is a common denominator for all of us, namely money. We might as well get down to brass tacks on that.

One of the cardinal rules in this business of raising money from outside sources for university activity is one that may not have occurred to you, but it's one that anybody in this business watches. It's very simply stated. You can go broke accepting money. When you accept a grant from whatever source that happens to be, there are usually strings to that grant, as there properly should be. The donor, whether it's a government agency, a private foundation, or an individual, wants the money to be used in a certain way. Usually the money never is enough to carry on the program indefinitely, whatever the program is. Therefore the institution in soliciting and accepting money from outside sources is by that very fact making a commitment to keep that program going under certain conditions for a specific or even indefinite period of time. Under those conditions you can easily go broke accepting money. A very prominent university east of us made a big promotion scheme in raising money from a variety of foundations and agencies, and did this in such a way that money was coming in from sources which could not then be supplanted by tuition, or giving by alumni donors, or whatever. Finally, a whistle was blown and the whole house of cards collapsed. Therefore I warn you, as a cardinal rule in the business of raising money, you must be prepared to accept the consequences of it.

Let me just go through a few points here, knowing that probably the most important thing would be my response to whatever questions you might have. I do not know offhand of any specific source of money for Black music. Most of the programs the university would want funded are really combinations of areas—in this case Black and music. Therefore you would approach foundations or agencies that have interest in one of those areas, not necessarily both. This would be a rule in all fund raising for projects of a university or a college nature. Let me list some of the possible sources of money because the solicitations from these must be done a little bit differently.

Number one would be government agencies, and under that there are two naturals. One is the National Endowment for the Arts. While its funding depends on congressional support, it is the prime government agency for funding in the area of music. If your concern is to structure a curriculum for Black students, then you would approach the U.S. Office of Education, the Office of Economic Opportunity, and so on.

The second main source of funds would be private foundations. These have specific objectives and interests, and may be national, regional, or local. One must look for these foundations, find out where they are, who are the officers and how they are funded. There is a book put out periodically by an association of foundations, *The Foundation Directory*. It lists every legal foundation in the country, the address and a general statement by the officers of the foundation. The foundations are listed by geographic location. A local or regional foundation is more important than a national foundation such as the Ford, Rockefeller, Carnegie foundations, particularly if the interests are regional.

Another source of funds would be a private individual who will make a donation through his own privately endowed foundation. Even though such a foundation may have a board of directors, there is one man who gave the money for it and that one man, if he's still alive, will be the one that expresses where he wants the money to go and under what restrictions. Local sources of information on this are most important to develop and cultivate and keep current. Sometimes this money is held in the form of trusts, and sometimes you will find that people want to make a private donation, either anonymously or in a way which your institution must figure how it can be accepted. Let us say I am 75 or 80 years old, and I think a particular program is very important. On the other hand, I don't know how long I'm going to live. Therefore, you could set up some kind of a scheme where I will give you money on an annual basis but, on the other hand I will, as the donor, be allowed to have an annual income out of the trust that is set up. This is a favorite form of giving at the present time, and every university or college must have somebody around who can deal with the legal talent that is called into play on one of these operations. You will find many evidences of such giving in this university, for example, where seldom is a check received for, let us say, $1,000,000, but checks are received for $10,000 periodically. A university can then plan on a building or a program because it knows that the income is absolutely specified for that purpose for a given number of years. This is one of the methods of solicitation that most faculty members do not know about, and far too many college administrators do not know how these can be worked out. The usual form of giving from private individuals is the straight estate. Like vultures, some college administrators felt they were waiting around for the person to die because they knew in that person's will was a considerable amount of money. The trust scheme seems a lot more civilized and more charitable since the person who is giving the money can see what it's being spent for while he's still alive.

The absolute grant to cover all expenses for a particular program is largely disappearing. You must put bits and pieces together to get enough money to operate the program the way you want. Such combinations are ones that must be worked out by careful solicitation and careful planning on your administration's part.

Here are some of the techniques in soliciting. Quite often a letter is sent, or an inquiry made. It could be initiated at a cocktail party, which is where many are started. If you know someone who could support a program and has registered an interest, you make an informal inquiry to find out if they are indeed interested. This is about as informal as you can get, and yet this is the way much of this goes. It must be followed up in case there's any interest at all by either a personal visit or a letter of inquiry, but remember that anybody who is in the foundation business or a government agency staff will be very, very polite. Do not equate politeness with enthusiasm for your request.

With the proposal you finally get down to brass tacks and make it specific as to what and under what conditions. It should not be long but it by all means and under all conditions must be specific. Proposals are not made in such a flowery way that the person to whom this proposal is sent immediately wants to know why you spent so much money on the proposal. Covers purchased from your own local bookstore are just fine.

A proposal should have a cover sheet, be followed by an abstract which puts in one paragraph what you're asking for and why (and that's the most difficult part). The introduction and rationale of why you want the money should not be elaborate. Based on my experience of reading proposals for Washington agencies, I'd say this is the chief fault. Finally you get down to the program itself. Tell what you want to do, when and under what conditions. Also say something about the staff. A proposal must have names in it, names of people who are to do the work, and what their duties will be. A short paragraph on each is most important, so that any reader can figure out this institution means business with its proposal. How do you plan to get the participants in the operation? What facilities are you going to involve? And finally, a budget. But all of this short, sweet and to the point.

The university in this country which has the greatest amount of federal money during the past fiscal year is the University of Michigan. They have over 90 people on the staff to raise money who are specialists in "grantsmanship." But a grantsman, the so-called professional, can't write your proposal. Only you know what you want, and only you know why certain things in that proposal have to be.

DE LERMA: What kind of grants have your schools secured? And what can one do about acquisitions for the library, about endowed professorial chairs, additional space or equipment? This is a particular problem I think perhaps with grants. Then tying these together, what are the schools' most important needs now which funding might solve: scholarship programs, new faculty, construction, library development, what? May we start first with the initial question, since you know now where we are going, have you secured any grants in recent years for some music project?

FULLER: Title I through Title VI of federal grants have assisted with the education of music faculty, Title III and Title VI for government subsidies in library acquisitions and other educational teaching materials. On our campus is a project known as a consortium in the arts which is a part of the division of humanities and fine arts, a project involving 14 institutions known as "evolving" or "emerging" institutions—those that have had long and distinguished service but have been destitute for a long time. These emerging institutions have brought to our campus some 48 students in the theater, speech and drama. These institutions have sent selected teaching, directing, composing and writing personnel in order that the theater may come alive this summer in a minimum of three productions, totally Black related. There will be playwrights at work for experimental theater which perhaps will not be heard or seen at all by the general theater-goer, but can provide some experience for the playwright, the challenge to the playwright.

The funds that have assisted us in this project came from Title III: $52,000 for this 8-week period for operations and faculty salaries and giving some assistance to students. The larger amount of assistance to students came from the Office of Economic Opportunity to boost the stipends for students. In order to assist them, we received $18,000. The Southern Education Foundation also came to the fore with $16,000 to provide assistance to students, the acquisition of materials, and the field trips to the Starlight Theater and Municipal Opera in Kansas City in which our students perform. They will also go to Arrow Rock, the grass roots theater for Ozarkian Missouri.

DE LERMA: Many of the foundations will not grant money for equipment, although they will for supplies. Construction probably can be taken care of some way or another, but what problems exist with respect to equipment and library materials?

KLINGE: Quite a few. Let me give a prognostication here. The titles you've mentioned, the O.E.O., the U.S. Office of Education's Educational Profession Development Act, with all of these federal programs, my guess is that in the next ten years we will see a diminution of these funds and a raising of the money available to individual students. In other words, even though we will still be in the business of soliciting funds for a specific program, the thrust of money to be available from the Washington spigot will be up considerably for individual student support. This will not be across the board, but will probably have some kind of a graduation involved with it. It just seems very obvious to me the whole scheme of the G.I. Bill will now be rephrased in such a way that all prospective students who have had some type of service in the government or in some social agency (Peace Corps being a good example here) will have a second call. There'll be quite a gradation down from other students. Programs which a college or university can launch depend on students primarily. Students you want in such a program will have to be supported in some way. Most college students in this country do not have enough money to go to school. They must get the money somewhere. Therefore, the ability of a university to attract students it wants in a program is going to be more important than the ability for that university to attract money from Washingon directly. That's my first point.

The next point is on the endowed chairs. Here one must flatly go the private route, namely, knowing somebody who is interested in either Black culture, or music, or simply in that institution for whatever reason. The government absolutely will not support such operations. They will give a faculty salary for a year, maybe two years at the most; we can't really call that an endowed chair.

In the case of library support, Dr. Fuller is completely right. Titles II and VI are the important ones under the Higher Education Act, but you must never forget that the private libraries of people who no longer need these materials, whatever they happen to be, are still the chief source.

Raising budgets for higher education beginning right now and extending for the next five years is going to be tough, especially if the university or college is state supported. Dismal words and dismal news, but one doesn't have to go too far off of anybody's campus to get the mood of the people.

Government agencies as well as private foundations now believe that when a set of colleges gets together to do something in a cooperative, joint way, whether it's called a consortium or an association, it is more palatable and more appealing than having five colleges within a given region all competing with each other to secure funding for the same type of program. Getting colleges and universities within a given region to cooperate is an art itself and probably beyond all faculty members, but it must start with faculty members of similar interests and then have enough administrative blessing and push to get it done. Indiana University for example, has an extensive and very large international program, one of which is African Studies. This was initiated by a rather massive Ford Foundation grant. The original proposal stipulated that the first effort that we must make is to get together with other large state universities in the Midwest to pool our resources and get out of the competitive business in international studies, and this has been done.

DE LERMA: Mr. Turner has told me that he has not yet secured funding during the one year he has been at Fisk. The very fact that he hired a faculty member whose qualifications he read to you, even within a five-year period, is an extraordinary accomplishment. I'm sure that anyone here would be happy to work in association with someone so qualified. May I ask you then a question which came up with the student panel. Do you as administrators feel that courses in Black music should be taught by Black professors? If so, can you locate these people easily? And if you are hiring them, is there any compromise, and I don't mean that in a condescending manner, with the standards of the university with regard to rank or salary?

TURNER: The reason we chose to seek a person in ethnomusicology is that over the years we've had some strength in musicology. Carl Parrish and John Ohl were both at Fisk, and have both contributed to the reputation in this area. We were seeking either a Black musicologist with strong interest in ethnomusiology or an ethnomusicologist regardless of his ethnic background. I began by writing to members, officers and members of the Society for Ethnomusicology. I got negative responses from several persons. The College and University Staffing Bureau for the American Musicological Society and the College Music Society named this person, and through personal contacts we got attention focused on him. I might point out that he is not a Black person.

FULLER: The project which I have described has two persons who are not Black. One of these persons is a technician in direction and theater arts. Another is one who will handle the music side of the production. I asked about the acceptability of these two persons to approximately eight faculty persons; there were no reservations.

History is filled with the experiences of the arts in assisting people to achieve their political, social and religious goals. After we have definitely established our identity, I think we can move on with the matter of music, ethnically as well as aesthetically. We as administrators must keep our fingers close to the pulse in order that we not only get funds, but have the responsibility of leadership, philosophically as well as academically.

TURNER: In addition to the academic qualifications and experiences, it's important in a predominantly Negro institution to have as many qualified Black persons on the faculty, if for no other reason than to emphasize to students the opportunities for their success in the particular area.

QUESTION: I'm concerned because I'm teaching a course in September, even though our library is weak. I would not like to think I was given this assignment purely on my Blackness, because I don't teach on that basis. It seems to me the administrators on the panel had some ideas about money before the course was offered. I think it would be a mistake for me to go back and expect my college president to take my class off since we have 64 students registered already. Maybe four of these are Black. It was the students who asked for the course. We cannot implement because we do not have the faculty. We do not have the funding from the state of Missouri, which provides the 90 per cent of our faculty budget for our salaries. We do not have the library facilities. We are waiting a little bit, to see if we can equip a series of really first-rate courses. But we have to have qualified people. This is the "curse" of a publically supported institution that has to be reviewed by a teachers' committee and a curriculum committee of the state. We are happy that the student will not ask for a minor or a major or a complete series of sequences of courses in these studies until we have had time to make the very basic preparations. I hope that we can have something of which we feel, proud or not, that we have discharged our obligations to the student.

TURNER: I think that an introductory course which covers the subject, perhaps too generally, even serves a good purpose. Such a course will at least define those areas in which you may want to offer more specified courses. This fall we are beginning with a course entitled "Afro-American Music; Cross Currents in African and Afro-American Music." We're hoping that out of this course will come the areas of student interest which will help us to decide what other specific courses we will offer in this area.

DYSON: I am aware of the necessity of getting well-qualified educators, but what allowances are you making for the individuals who could possibly assist you in inaugurating the course until you can find the qualified people you are looking for?

TURNER: We would hope that a specialist, such as we will have joining us in the fall, will be able to share his expertise with our present faculty members.

FULLER: Antioch College at Yellow Springs, Ohio is in a project similar to this, without staff. They bring in doctoral candidates from the University of Chicago. They have organized the program into a teacher-consultant relationship. They have been granted a building, I don't know the size of it or the necessity for its expansive character and nature, but this is where the students work. The teachers come, sometimes their visits overlap or they come on definite schedule, or they come on request.

LaBrew: Mr. Turner, why are there no Negroes in ethnomusicology you could have hired at your university?

Turner: We did ask for a qualified Negro to fill the position but the sources that we used did not enable us to find such a person. We would have been very happy to have found one.

LaBrew: Are you going to have a training period now so that others may learn how to do this?

de Lerma: I think that the problem I would have in answering this question is the same problem that Mr. Turner has already faced. Where is there information on who is available for a job? Maybe there are some of you here who would be interested in a new position. How can you identify yourself, aside from the statement normally made on paper, which would attract an administrator to hire you. A central placement agency is not going to ask you for race, and so if there's an administrator who wants to hire a Black ethnomusicologist, it's the same story that we had with recordings and with publishing. It's going to be by word of mouth. Frankly, I think the reason there are so few Black musicologists is a matter of sociology and economy. This man has to have a Ph.D. The dissertation is part of the qualification, and that is expensive. It's a social matter also, because music education has been regarded as the Black man's "place."

Question: I am a private teacher. We have difficulty from the outside in getting our students accepted into colleges and universities. Miss Hinderas and I spoke of that this morning. We prepare students for higher positions, and we find out that, if they go to college, we have to prepare them on a performance, not a historical basis. They must be able to perform an instrument first, and by the time they reach the level of proficiency, it's time to graduate. They have no chance to concentrate on anything else. Maybe because of the deprived areas they come from, it's the most I can do to prepare them physically to be able to enter a college. The young people in colleges are saying where are the Black teachers? Once they graduate there are going to be some Black teachers, but they still will not be accepted as a total force in the community.

Anderson: I think the two questions that were raised are very much related.

What is at issue is first the scarcity of Blacks in the society with professional skills. Now if we address ourselves to this, this is a serious problem. I'd like to recommend that you read the report of the Southern Educational Fund, which shows statistically that there are fewer than 4 per cent of Blacks in higher education now. When you consider that we constitute over 10 per cent of the population (in the Black community they say 10 per cent is a conservative figure), you can see that the increase of opportunities within the society against a decrease in the number of skilled people in the society. To say that you're going to offer a course in Black studies and say that this person has to be an ethnomusicologist, have certain types of experiences which don't even exist in the structure of the university today, is to be naïve. We have to develop a creative approach into the problem.

QUESTION: If we have a 40 hour curriculum for instruction (and now it's 40 hours of White music), why not 30 hours of White music and 10 of Black, or some other more practical ratio. This doesn't cost more money. This means a shift in your program. If you teach four semesters of Western music, why not three semesters of Western music and one semester of Black? This does not cost more money. It takes a different kind of personnel but not more money. We are not adding more hours to the curriculum, merely readjusting it, and I think that's what we can do in a White school.

QUESTION: One of the areas that we have difficulty with is financial assistance for students. I suppose with the developing program this will become more of a problem. Did I understand you to say in your proposal there would be provision for financial assistance to the students generally in Black music programs, or did you have Indiana University specifically in mind?

DE LERMA: That all depends on how our program is structured. All royalities which come from the sale of the publication of our book will go directly into a scholarship fund for Black students in music, this will be handled through the I.U. Foundation, and of course it will apply to Indiana University. If we could have a national scholarship program for Black students in music established in Bloomington, in Missouri, in Oregon, or in South Carolina, fine! But I think it would be very difficult to operate such an idea on a national level.

> ● If advice for the smaller school is desired, it seems that the most important thing for that institution is to employ every idea immediately available to develop whatever approach to Black music studies it needs.

While experience in the subject is being developed, funding sources can be located and approached in the manner Dean Klinge has indicated. We should never wait for off-campus ideals to bow to undeveloped dreams; we must not be at the mercy of super-structures (as indicated in our panel of teachers) to the extent that our plans can only be developed with some *deus ex machina* solution.

At this particular time, several months after the seminar, we have submitted our proposal for the establishment of a Black Music Center at Indiana University. It has cleared the Black Music Committee, the School of Music's excellent grant specialist, Mrs. Martha Mosier, has gone over the budget and implications carefully. Dean Wilfred C. Bain has given his blessings, followed by those of the Indiana University Foundation and other officials of the school. The proposal has been read by the foundation to which it was submitted, but final action has not yet transpired. There has, incidentally, been some polishing of our aims through preliminary negotiations, but these modifications have strengthened the concept and placed it in better focus.

Meanwhile, we have not waited for funding. Tapping every means already at its disposal, the Music Library has been engaged on an aggressive drive for the acquisition of materials related to Black music. Funding is still needed for the type of reference service and research we would like to become engaged in, and there are many sources of an important but somewhat restricted nature which we will be able to contact more securely after the establishment in name and budget of the center. Despite these handicaps, the Black Music Committee wishes to encourage correspondence from scholars active in Black music research and performance who might have specific projects or problems.

We must all understand the implications of Dean Klinge's remarks, and Dr. Fuller's program, which show the value of combination programs, programs which are cooperatively developed by schools, or those which are multi- and mixed-media.

Professor Turner did not describe the difficulties he encountered in locating an ideal faculty member for the position he filled. Had this post been in music education, the appointment could have been filled much easier.

The question of staffing did not reveal the formation of the Afro-American Music Opportunities Association (AAMOA), an organization which was just being established about the time we were meeting. Persons and institutions not knowing about this group should investigate membership possibilities and advantages by addressing AAMOA, Box 662, Minneapolis, Minnesota, 55440.

It seems quite important that schools devote serious attention to the development of personnel in those areas which traditionally are years in the making: musicologists (including serious study of ethnomusicology as well), music theorists, conductors, administrators, and music librarians. The number of Blacks in any one of these areas is minimal. One cannot even have token representation on the faculties with the personnel resources currently available.

13. *Forward*

After spending most of my youth on the East Coast, between Boston and Miami, I came to Indiana in 1956 to begin my graduate study. I soon learned that I had been provincially Eastern, despite the contrasts between Brookline and Brooklyn, South Miami and Miami Beach (although I sometimes let myself wonder what is the difference between provincialism and culture). My musical education had been totally French, my fellow musicians were largely Italian or Jewish. Soul food to me was arroz con pollo, pasta, garbanzos, bagels and boeuf bourguignon. My culture and my environs were Mediterreanean until I got to the Midwest.

Perhaps Indiana belongs more to the United States than the milieu I knew. The European flavors were gone. In fact, some locales regarded them with contempt. In a lapse from my struggles to get acclimated (but not integrated), I went to Indianapolis for such staples as ricotta and olive oil (Bloomington has since changed). I arrived in Indianapolis a few years too late. A new highway had gone through the small area that used to be the Italian district, the children had married non-Italians and moved. No one spoke Italian anymore, and ricotta could be had only around Easter. A melting of cultures may be inevitable, but I was deeply saddened by the realization that such things actually *do* happen, that whole cultures can vanish in one generation.

As Dr. Still said, Black is beautiful, just as other colors are. This is one of the major goals for teaching in the humanities: to identify a culture and to know its beauty. One who belongs to that culture should never take it so for granted that its comforts and benefits make one forget its beauty but, just like nationalism, it is not necessary to submerge one's own qualities and talents rather than enrich the definition of the larger group (herein lies the danger of doing one's own racial "thing," in place of cultivating an individual garden), nor is it essential to be against other things simply because one choice of several has been made, or because a person was born into a certain culture. There is no reason why the Christian should be anti-Jewish, why the American should be anti-Russian, why the "silent" majority should be anti-intellectual, or why the White should be anti-Black.

But the situation with the Black might beg some indulgence for, when ideas are defined and first put into practice, "first fervor" is never uncommon. Furthermore, to come into a culture after having been deprived of it in one sense or another is a rather dramatic milestone. Until the time that this is openly understood by America's Whites, we will still live in Lincoln's divided house. Until the time comes that this is realized by institutional and governmental administrations, the stigma of racism will still be a reality.

At the same time, we must know that acculturation is not always exploitation. It may seem to be exactly that when the original owners of the culture do not benefit from the financial rewards of the culture, and we should know that acculturation cannot help but result in a lessening of the potency of the original idea (I am reminded of an extreme example, which claimed "All-American pizza" was to be made with frankfurters, ketchup, canned dough, and processed cheese). All instances of acculturation, however, are not *ipso facto* premeditated. If there has been some desire to make jazz a White activity, Mrs. Still has indicated that Latin-American Blacks have not left Spanish influences untouched.

White America, adolescently proud of its technological power, would like to think that herein lies its culture. To a large extent, of course, this is true. Dr. Anderson has already indicated some manifestations of this. But does this culture have a soul of its own? What is the origin of the soul within (White) American culture? Is it European, or Indian, or Black? It may seem unintentionally like a latter-day Rousseau to mention it, but could it not be that much of the heart of American culture is a distinctly Black contribution? A racist would have fun with this: Has not the uniquely American spirit which has been developing during this century come about by subtle "subversions" from the Blacks? I've seen two books by one author, not worth citing, which regard the rock and roll movement as part of the Communist conspiracy. Had the writer known how much the Beatles owed to Blacks like Chuck Berry, he would have allied with a group which regards the very existence of the Blacks as a Communist plot.

The impact of Black culture has been at times very subtle. It has entered the lives of every White American, although he has not realized it. It has filled a hole in White America's culture which needed to be filled. Too many people are not willing to admit their debt because they have no perspective of cultural identity or cultural evolution. The largest percentage of those who see these matters in some sort of (intuitive, at times) perspective belong to America's youth, those who began to jolt consciences in the 60's, whose educational opportunities are often subject to the whims of conservative legislatures, but whose ideals portend a more spiritual and less self-righteous existence for America in the near future. The culture of the Blacks and the determination of the college youths are redefining what this country is. That fact alone makes them suspect in the eyes of the older conservatives who forgot that it was their early-adult ideas which helped to bring us to where we are.

Manifestly, there is no "Black" problem. It is the problem of the Whites, and the difficulties will become more seriously theirs the more the Blacks achieve their definition and, with it, America's.

Indiana University's Black Music Committee was charged by Dean Wilfred C. Bain to explore those areas in which the university's School of Music might be active. Our responsibility is to present such proposals to our administration for its consideration with respect to current and future teaching and research programs, as well as new functions, providing suitable funding can be secured for the initiation of an area regarded as within the pattern of the school's potential. Although our committee shows every evidence of keeping itself busy for several more years, nourished not only by our own ideas but those we secure from people not on our campus, there is an inevitable stockpile of ideas which either are not appropriate for university action, or which are of more than regional importance.

Not all gifted Blacks in performance have been able to accomplish what they would like, or what they deserve, but Black instrumentalists and singers have been an important part of our musical scene for many years. In our own century, we can point with pride to Dorothy Maynor, Carol Brice, Marian Anderson, Leontyne Price, George Shirley, William Warfield, Reri Grist, Shirley Verrett, Felicia Weathers, and many other figures of unquestioned significance. Instrumentalists outside of jazz might not be quite as easily located, but André Watts and any of the Black members of the Symphony of the New World are certainly not of minor importance. Including jazz musicians at this point, we can nevertheless note that performance is based more on individual talent than extensive training.

Many singers and players, perhaps less gifted, have fallen by the wayside for want of proper training, but it is possible to become an exceptional performer if one has unusual talent, even without the full regime of college or conservatory education. Such is not the situation for music critics and aestheticians, for theorists and musicologists, for conductors and administrators. Not denying the fact that many Blacks have superb records as music educators, few in this field have been able to secure their doctorates, yet they have still been able to accomplish things of value, but a musicologist without a Ph.D. has many personal and professional disadvantages. How can more Black doctorates in music be developed? How many Black colleges offer work on this level? It seems obvious that those schools which wish to benefit from Black spokesmen among its graduate students in these areas will have to locate potential scholars, train them, and help them to secure the positions for which they are qualified. This is expensive, and I'm sure it is money rather than talent which accounts for the scarcity of Black Ph.D.'s in music. On the average, it is seven years from the time a student enters the doctoral level program in music at Indiana University until the time comes that he defends his dissertation. In *A Survey of Black-American Doctorates*, prepared by James W. Bryant and issued by the Ford Foundation in 1970, the median period of time between the baccalaureate and the doctoral degree is reported to be thirteen years, with 21.4 percent of Black doctorates having to wait more than two decades for the terminal degree. The need for a scholarship program is manifest. The same source reports that 12.4 out of 100 doctoral degrees held by Blacks are in the area of the humanities. At best, half of these may be in music. This would mean, incidentally, that there may be no more than 60 Black scholars in the United States today with doctoral degrees in music, and there are probably fewer. It is possible that this seminar had as participants more than ten percent of all Black musicians with doctorates in this country! No wonder a university might have trouble finding a Black professor or Black dean. Proportionately, there should be more like 900 Black musicians with this degree. Knowing this, are our schools going to sit back and say, "We are happy to accept those Black doctoral candidates who meet our standards," and then rest office-cloistered for the applicant to come to the school? Even the school's football staff will recruit players and find scholarships, and that division of a university is certainly no less active in student exploitation than a music department.

The idea of a Black Music Center at Indiana University was discussed rather frequently during our seminar, and has received much attention in our committee sessions. While reading proposals related to Black music for various foundations, I became concerned about the duplication of time, money and energy which is being expended by many institutions and individuals in the United States, and that very few of the results of these labors can be shared with others. Informally commenting on this in one of my reports, a major foundation asked that we prepare a proposal for such ideas as I felt to be essential. In essence, the concept is merely for the establishment of a research and reference center which will hold virtually all of the materials essential to any scholar for the development of his research, which will encourage the use and distribution of this information, and which will make itself freely available for reference and consultation services. The idea is conceived not as a monopoly on the data, but as a convenience for the researcher or performer, whose major problem (that of locating the materials he needs) is not his final one (that of presenting his findings to the public). It is too early just now to anticipate the formal establishment of this center or to detail all of the services which funding would make possible, but the plans include acquisition of printed and recorded materials, of the issue of a printed catalog of the holdings (including journal article indexing), and techniques for the distribution of performance materials, either published or in manuscript. If this project is funded, announcements will be offered for publication in the major music journals, including the Music Library Association's *Notes* and the *Journal* of the American Musicological Society.

One idea which I suggested was the establishment of a society for Black music history, an organization which would care for those areas not within the programs of the National Association of Negro Musicians, the Society for Black Composers, or the Afro-American Music Opportunities Association. I proposed that such an organization might have affiliation with the American Council of Learned Societies, the American Musicological Society, the Music Library Association, the Society for Ethnomusicology, the National Music Council, or similar groups, even if this association might be informal. If it were so constituted, and if it had a board of directors which included the most important Black composers and civil rights leaders, it would be in a position to lobby with the music industries, the orchestras, the concert managements, pit band contractors, labor groups and universities for proper acknowledgement of Black musical culture and talents. On a more passive level, it could encourage research in Black music by providing an opportunity for papers to be read at national and regional meetings, perhaps even meeting jointly at times with one of the scholarly groups mentioned above. Student memberships would be possible and, if it published *monumenta* (e.g., anthologies of works by 19th century Black-American composers, or the *opera omnia* of such a figure as Clarence Cameron White, William Grant Still or Robert Nathaniel Dett) and had some additional revenue sources, it might even be in the position eventually of issuing scholarships and research grants to deserving individuals.

With respect to the society's pressuring for certain goals, I would refer to sentiments expressed at the end of Chapter 10. My point is not in trying to water down the potency of any requests, but in presenting a solid and strong case with a little bit more elegance than has become vogue since the citizens of the United States allowed themselves to leave moderation for one of the two extremes. Too many communications are patterned for rejection *da capo*. If a person or group wishes to win a battle it will be evident by the manner in which the case is presented. Explain the need tersely, relate the interests of the group to those of the company being addressed, don't be offensive, and carry with you the power of a unified organization. If you wish to have released, for example, new pressings of specific older recordings, list them by label number. Show that you know what the contents really are, that you have examined the question carefully and that your evaluation of the project is reliable. Let the company know what your organization will do to support the sales. Will you carry free advertisements or write an article on the release, secure that your early investigation has pre-determined the merits? Is the request coordinated so that, for example, the score will be published at the same time, perhaps as a package deal? If you assume the individuals of the company are human beings, businessmen or not, your literary style will acknowledge this. Your letter will certainly not contain such a sentence as "If serious consideration is not given to the enclosed statement, it will therefore be our duty to . . ." Play the game to win, and follow the rules you also will want honored.

Arthur LaBrew of Detroit, I have just learned, is giving consideration to the following project from his own viewpoint. Nonetheless, I present my ideas as they were expressed in informal gatherings related to the 1969 seminar: There may be real merit in the publication of a quarterly journal devoted to Black music. This periodical might be part of the activities of a society, or it may be a totally independent venture. Having it issued by a society, or being firmly assured of at least 2,000 subscribers, may be a very major financial consideration. It is also possible of course, that a foundation might underwrite a preliminary issue or two if it appears that the journal will be able to serve a large enough patronage.

Such a journal could include reviews of a scholarly nature on books and recordings. It could abstract dissertations and articles (note that many valuable studies have appeared in journals not fully dedicated to music), and it could report on grants awarded, and of funding possibilities for special projects. It would be valuable to have information on new works by Black composers (which listing can be keyed as a supplement to our forthcoming *Black Music* bibliography), on performances and commissions (although these are regularly cited now in AAMOA's *Reports*, which came into existence independently after our seminar). The periodical could include coverage of major research in progress. It could have specialized bibliographies and discographies, as well as indexed locations of earlier work in these areas (e.g., the series of discographies on major jazz figures by Jorgen Jepsen, issued from Copenhagen by Karl Emil Knudsen in 1969). Feature articles might be biographical or historical, or consist of important interviews. It could list positions open or jobs desired, without charge for a given period (possibly two issues). Advertisements by publishers and record companies would be revenue producing for the journal, and would encourage the industry to design its advertising for potential customers of Black music. The periodical could reprint major articles from the past (or, with copyright permission, recent ones as well). In the case of earlier articles, appropriate footnotes could be added. It would be possible to make arrangements for the publication of translations of such articles as Victoria Ocampo's "Vuelta a Harlem," Gustavo Pesenti's "Canti e ritmi arabici, somalici e suahili," Marius Schneider's "Ueber die Verbreitung afrikanischer Chorformen," and Caspar Höweler's "De beeldspraak van de Negrospirituals." Editorially, the periodical could focus attention on areas needing attention (including reissues of earlier books or recordings), and a letters-to-the-editor column could be a sounding board for ideas or requests for assistance in certain research areas.

Not all schools can provide its faculty with sabbaticals. In such an instance, it seems that some exchange-of-persons program could be arranged between two schools, so that a professor might have a year as a scholar-in-residence at an institution with major research resources, which would provide the scholar's school with a qualified person whose teaching experience could be accordingly enriched.

There may be some merit in having available certain lecturers and other consultants, who can bring to the attention of a group of students or faculty new information, or to their administration some outside insight on possible innovations regarding philosophy, curricular structures, research materials, and the like.

If the *Music Educators Journal* is a barometer of the changes finally taking place in pre-college education, the music teachers in the urban city schools are advanced well past their university counterparts. Even so, the following suggestions are offered. It should be possible for every school child in the nation to hear live music in school at least once a year. I'm not suggesting the program should be all woodwind quintets, or only works by Saint-Georges or Coltrane; if the repertoires were merely one notch above the present tastes of the children and were reflective of the racial makeup of the student body (never again over-looking the stronger minorities, if any must be by-passed), a real service might be given. Funding for such concerts has been available in the past and, I as-sume, is still available to union performers.

In the same area, I wonder if such projects as those of BAG or AACM indi-cate a failure on the part of the school instrumental programs, or if the school budgets and resources do not permit proper instruction. Possibly these projects are intended as supplementary to those available in the schools?

Not only for pre-college work, but for study on the undergraduate level as well, I think that some enterprising (Black?) music jobber would assemble a package deal of recordings and scores of Black music in a tasteful but inex-pensive manner. At least two series could be possible, one for college and one for high school.

There should be greater publicity for that work undertaken in certain school systems which might be of great value to teachers and students in other cities. Perhaps most educators know something of the work in Detroit by Robert Klotman (now at Indiana University), Ollie McFarland and their associates, but how much detailed information is shared by those in other communities?

It would be well if all persons in teaching would decide if education were a matter of self-discovery or technique training, if it were a matter of investiga-tion and questioning, or one of conformity.

Could we not manage to teach music less like sex education? Is it not pos-sible to develop an emotional reaction without making form and analysis the be-all and end-all? If we are to develop the potentials for emotional develop-ment, for the respect of various cultures, for the admiration of man's artistic integrity (let all teachers understand these before attempting to teach them), what does it matter which point of entry is used: soul, Chávez or Chopin?

Imaginative teachers, such as Lena McLin, know that their subjects can be moulded according to the student's need. It is not the reverse. A subject that is not flexible is not one of the arts. The obligation to know all of the facets and manifestations and exceptions is not that which must be accepted by the novice in the field, even though we must eventually move from the known to the unknown, and must know that a musically educated person should be able to react as easily to Aretha Franklin as to Bach.

In the first of a series of articles (which, because of the demise of the periodical, was never completed), "New Music for Woodwinds" (in *Woodwind World*, v.8, no 3, 1968, p. 9), I raised a question about the evolution of culture. Do changes in taste come about as an individual reacts daily to his society, or does this occur only when a new generation takes over? The answer varies, of course, from individual to individual. It is a question of whether the student does the teaching (or protesting) while the teacher platitudes his habitual ways, or whether the teacher astounds the student with ideas which may provide him with a stimulus to develop potentials which he and his society might not have suspected in those terms or in that context. Richard Strauss was certainly a splendid composer and a daring one in his youth, but was he a better teacher than Schönberg? Was not one of the problems with Mendelssohn's teaching that his *Zeitgeist* was best in tune with those years when he was a young man? Which current politicians would make the best government professors on retirement from public service? A liberal would readily answer it would be he who is most needed in public service. The point of this argument is that it would be difficult for a teacher to help stimulate an emotional reaction to the works of Olly Wilson if that teacher still found Varèse a personal problem. Far better if our teacher training institutions would provide more remedial work when needed, but the student teacher does have access to scores, recordings and concerts. A further point is that this teacher, if he be White, should understand the ramifications of the Black movement (even if it is only an intellectual understanding) and how this might relate to his students and his topics, just as he expects his students from the ghetto to have some grasp of Wagner or Mozart, who might be equally removed from these experiences.

The teacher, like most of Establishment White America, must be able to see himself in perspective. He must know to what extent he is measuring his students and his subject in terms of White concepts. If he feels that some ideas are of absolute value, not subject to reevaluation, let him admit it to his students, but he should not impose the frustration of these standards without that explanation. There is too much in our world we feel we cannot fight because the core of the problem is too removed from us or too institutionalized for an individual's questions. If the teacher feels he has been taught for all time the answer, the approach, the technique, the subject, or the material, he merits challenge.

Black music has opened the door for all of us. Attention must be given this culture but not from fear of petitions, demonstrations or riots. There is no room in the arts or in education for reactionary movements. The attention which must be given to Black music has to come from an awareness of its quality and the substance of its history, and from the knowledge that it is an important and valuable element of American culture.

Of course, there are also social reasons; any factor in our lives becomes a social matter by that fact alone, but the importance of these reasons is manifest in the contributions of our seminar participants and in the very reason why any of the humanities is worth studying. No matter what problems the United States may have in the future, there is enough evidence now to indicate this decade has to correct the myth of White cultural supremacy. William Braden, in *The Age of Aquarius* (New York: Quadrangle, 1970) expresses concern over White America's life style and soul which have been victimized by technology, indicating that instrumentalization and institutionalism have been given priority over the spirit of an individual as a person. Not surprisingly, he sees possible salvation for the country and, consequently, the world, in the influence of the Blacks—nothing other than another acknowledgement of the Black man's burden. We can see validity to his argument in the matter of music and music education. The entire point relates to humanism, whose most direct voice is found in the humanities. And, of all the arts, music seems the most potent medium for the Black expression.

This time, at long last, we have to go right on.

A Selective List of Scores

Allan, Lewis, 1903–
  Strange fruit, for voice and piano. New York: Marks, 1940 (pl. no.
  11,113).
Anderson, Thomas Jefferson, Jr., 1928–
  Chamber symphony. New York: Composers Facsimile Edition. 1969.
  In memoriam: Zach Walker, for band. New York: Composers Facsimile
  Edition, 1968.
  Portraits of two people, for piano (four hands). New York: Composers
  Facsimile Edition, 1967.
Baker, David N., 1931–
  Black America: to the memory of Martin Luther King, Jr., for narrator,
  vocal quintet, large jazz band and cello octet. Available from the com-
  poser, c/o Black Music Committee, Indiana University, Bloomington,
  Indiana, 47401.
  Concerto, violin and jazz band. Available from the composer.
  I. U. swing machine, for jazz band. Available from the composer.
  One for J. S., for jazz band. Available from the composer.
  Settings, for soprano and piano. Available from the composer.
  Sonata, violoncello and piano. Available from the composer.
Basie, Count, 1904–
  King Joe, for jazz band. New York: Bregman, Vocco & Conn, 1942.
Belafonte, Harry, 1927–
  Recognition, for voice and guitar. New York: Marks, 1968 (in *Ballad of
  Ira Hayes and other new folk songs*; pl. no. 14812).
Bell, Charles Henderson, 1933–
  Brother Malcolm, for piano, double bass, electric bass, flute, percussion
  and cello). Available from the composer (c/o Lehman College, Bronx,
  New York).
Billups, Kenneth Brownes, 1918–
  Cain and Abel, for mixed chorus and piano. New York: Sam Fox.
  Cert'ly Lord, for mixed chorus and piano. New York: Belwin, 1950
  (Octavo no. 1047).
  New born again, for mixed chorus. New York: Belwin, 1951 (Bel. Oct.
  1100-7).
  Swing low, for children's chorus. New York: G. Schrimer, 1938.

Blake, Eubie, 1883–
> *Chevy chase*, for piano. New York: Marks.
> *Gypsy blues*, for voice and piano. New York: Witmark.

Bland, James A., 1854–1911.
> *The James A. Bland album of outstanding songs.* New York: Marks,
> 1946 (pl. no. 12300).

Bledsoe, Julius C., 1898–1943.
> *Negro folksongs and spirituals.* New York: Marks.

Boatner, Edward Hammond, 1898–
> *Afro-American choral spirituals*, for mixed chorus. New York: Hammond
> Music, for the American Festival of Negro Arts, 1964.
> *He's got the whole world in his hands*, for mixed chorus and piano. New
> York: Emanuel A. Middleton, 1968.
> *Ride on, King Jesus*, for mixed chorus. New York: Columbo, 1953.

Bonds, Margaret Allison, 1913–
> *Dream portraits*, for voice and piano. New York: Ricordi, 1959.

Brooks, Harry, 1895–
> *Connie's hot chocolates*, opera. New York: Mills, 1929.

Brown, Oscar, Jr., 1926–
> *Kicks & Co.*, opera. New York: Marks (*Ernest's theme*, for piano, issued
> in 1961, pl. no. 14454; *Love is like a newborn child* issued in 1958, pl.
> no. 14456; *Worldful of gray* issued in 1961, pl. no. 14457).
> *Songs.* New York: Marks, 1962 (pl. no. 14486).

Burleigh, Harry Thacker, 1866–1949.
> *Balm in Gilead*, arr. for mixed chorus by R. Vené. New York: Columbo,
> 1954.
> *Deep river*, for mixed chorus. New York: Columbo, 1913.
> *Old songs hymnal*, for mixed chorus. New York: Columbo, 1929.
> *Plantation songs*, for voice and piano. New York: Columbo, 1902 (pl.
> no. 15894).
> *Saracen songs*, for voice and piano. New York: Ricordi, 1914 (pl. no.
> 114181).

Carter, John, 1937–
> *Cantata*, for voice and orchestra (or piano). New York: Southern Music,
> 1964.
> *Requiem seditiosam; in memoriam to Medgar Evers*, for orchestra (piano
> reduction available). New York: American Music Center, ca.1967.

Chandler, Len H., Jr.
> *The lovin' people*, for voice and guitar. New York: Marks, 1967 (pl. no.
> 15191).

Clark, Edgar Rogie, 1917–
> *Copper sun*, for voice and piano. Bryn Mawr: Presser, 1957.
> *Mango walk*, for mixed chorus. New York: Boosey & Hawkes.

Sit down servant, for mixed chorus. New York: Boosey & Hawkes.

Wade in the water, for mixed chorus. New York: Marks, 1941 (pl. no. 11383).

Coleridge-Taylor, Samuel, 1875–1912.

African romances, for voice and piano. London: Augener, 1897.

Choral ballads, for mixed chorus and orchestra. Wiesbaden: Breitkopf und Härtel, 1904.

Hiawatha's wedding feast, cantata. New York: G. Schirmer.

Petite suite de concert, arr. for violin and piano. London: Hawkes, 1916.

Quintet, clarinet & strings, op. 10, F sharp minor. Wiesbaden: Breitkopf und Härtel, after 1895.

Cook, Will Marion, 1869–1944.

In Dahomey, opera. London: Keith, Prowse & Co., 1903 (pl. no. K.P. & Co. Ltd. 1570, 1574).

My lady, for voice and piano. New York: G. Schirmer, 1914.

Cordero, Roque, 1917–

Adagio tragico, for string orchestra. New York: Peer.

Concerto, violin and orchestra. New York: Peer, 1969.

Mensajes breves, for viola and piano. New York: Peer, 1970.

Paz, paix, peace, for large chamber ensemble. Probably available from Peer (New York) in near future.

Sonatina rítmica, piano. New York: Peer, 1954 (pl. no. 5–16).

Cunningham, Arthur, 1928–

Concentrics, for orchestra. Possibly available on rental from the composer (4 North Pine, Nyack, N.Y., 10960).

el-Dabh, Halim, 1921–

Clytemnestra, ballet. New York: C. F. Peters.

Hindi-yaat, no. 1, for percussion ensemble. New York: C. F. Peters, 1965 (Edition Peters, 6197).

Sonic, no. 7, for derabucca or timpani. New York: C. F. Peters, 1965 (Edition Peters, 6186).

Davenport, Charles, 1895–1955.

The boogie-woogie blues folio. New York: C. Williams, 1940.

Dawson, William Levi, 1897–

Mary had a baby, for mixed chorus. Tuskegee: Music Press (Tuskegee choir series, T–118).

Negro folk symphony, for orchestra. Delaware Water Gap (Pa.): Shawnee Music Press, 1965.

Soon ah will be done, for men's chorus. Tuskegee: Music Press (Tuskegee choir series, T–101A).

Dett, Robert Nathaniel, 1882–1943.

In the bottoms, for piano. Chicago: Summy, 1913 (Summy edition, 61).

Magnolia suite, for piano. Chicago: Summy, 1912 (Summy edition, 83; pl. no. C.F.S. co. 1387).

The ordering of Moses, oratorio. New York: J. Fischer & Bro., 1937 (Fischer edition, 7230).

Dorsey, Thomas A., 1899–

Dorsey's songs of the kingdom. Chicago: The Composer (4154 South Ellis Avenue, Zip 60653), 1951.

Dorsey's songs with a message. Chicago: The Composer, 1951.

Duncan, John, 1911–

Atavisms, for voice, brass and percussion. Montgomery: The Composer (c/o Alabama State University).

Atavistic string quartet. Montgomery: The Composer.

Concerto, trombone. Montgomery: The Composer.

An Easter canticle, for mixed chorus and winds. Montgomery: The Composer.

Europe, Jim Reese, 1881–1919.

Blue eyed Susan, for voice and piano. New York: S. Bloom, 1904.

Fischer, William S., 1935–

Batucáda fantástica, for percussion and tape. Music may be available from the composer (1365 St. Nicholas Avenue, Apt. 135, New York, 10033).

Concerto grosso, jazz quintet and orchestra. Available from the composer.

Experience in E, for jazz quintet and orchestra. Available from the composer.

Joy of love, for women's chorus and piano (text by LeRoi Jones). Available from the composer.

Sonata, violin and piano. Available from the composer.

Fountain, Clarence.

Soul!, a collection of 17 songs by Clarence Fountain and John Bowden. New York: Marks, 1967.

Hackley, Emma Azalia (Smith).

Carola, for voice and piano. New York: Handy Bros., 1953.

Hairston, Jester, 1901–

Amen, for mixed chorus. New York: Bourne.

Angels rolled de stone away, for mixed chorus. New York: Bourne.

Dis ol' hammer, for mixed chorus. New York: Bourne.

Joshua fit de battle of Jericho, for mixed chorus. New York: Bourne.

Negro spirituals and folksongs. New York: Bourne, 1960.

Holiday, Billie, 1915–1959.

Billie's blues, or *I love my man,* for voice and piano. New York: Marks, 1962, 1956 (pl. no. 14603).

God bless the child, vocal duet with piano, co-composed with Arthur Herzog. New York: Marks, 1969 (pl. no. 15408).

    Long gone blues, for voice and piano. New York: Marks, 1962, 1960
       (pl. no. 14551).

Jackson, Calvin
    Fly, Blackbird. From this musical show are several songs published in New
       York by Marks in 1962: *Couldn't we?* (pl. no. 14525), *Ev'rything
       comes to those who wait* (pl. no. 14592), *Fly, blackbird* (pl. no.
       (14527), *Natchitoches, Louisiana* (pl. no. 14526), and *Wake up* (pl.
       no. 14528), as well as the four-part chorus with piano *Rivers to the
       south* (pl. no. 14561).

James, Willis Laurence
    Negro bell carol, for four-part chorus. New York: C. Fischer, 1952.

Jessye, Eva, 1895–
    Nobody, for four-part men's chorus and piano. New York: Marks, 1956
       (pl. no. 13419).
    When the saints go marching in, for chorus and piano. New York: Marks,
       1956 (Eva Jessye choral series; pl. no. 13416).

Johnson, Hall, 1888–
    Ain't got time to die, for four-part chorus. New York: G. Schirmer, 1955
       (pl. no. 10301).
    Cert'n'y Lord, for four-part chorus. New York: C. Fischer, 1952.
    Negro Spirituals, for voice and piano. Zürich: Musikverlag zum Pelikan,
       1965.
    Sometimes I feel like a motherless child, for four-part chorus. New York:
       Marks, 1956 (Marks choral library, 4007; pl. no. 13425).
    Walk together, chillun, for four-part chorus. New York: Marks, 1956
       (Marks choral library, 4006; pl. no. 13397).

Johnson, J. J.
    El camino real, for jazz band. New York: MJQ.
    Judy, for jazz band. New York: MJQ.
    Minor mist, for jazz band. New York: MJQ.
    Mohawk, for jazz band. New York: MJQ.
    Perceptions, for jazz band. New York: MJQ.
    Poem for brass. New York: Associated Music Publishers, 1961.
    Rondeau, for jazz quartet and orchestra. New York: MJQ.
    Scenario, for trombone and orchestra. New York: MJQ.
    Sketch, for trombone and jazz band. New York: MJQ.

Johnson, James Price, 1894–1955.
    Caprice rag, for piano. New York: Mills, 1914.
    Charleston, for voice and piano. New York: T. B. Harms & Co., 1923.
    Harlem symphony, for orchestra. New York: Robbins Music, 1932.
    Jasmine concerto, for piano and orchestra. New York: Mills, 1935.
    Yamacraw, opera. New York (Hotel Markwell, 220 W. 49th Street):
       Julius Rutin (published in 1928 by Alfred & Co.).

Johnson, James Rosamond, 1873–1954.
> *Album of Negro spirituals,* for voice and piano. New York: Marks, 1940 (pl. no. 11197).
>
> *Congo love song,* for men's chorus and piano. New York: Marks, 1956 (pl. no. 13567).
>
> *Lift every voice and sing* (various arrangements available from the publisher, Marks, in New York).

Joplin, Scott, 1868–1919.
> *Maple leaf rag,* for piano. New York: Marks, 1958 (Radio City series, 13896; pl. no. 13896).
>
> *Scott Joplin's new rag,* for piano. New York: Marks, 1940 (pl. no. 7210).
>
> *Treemonisha,* opera. Weston, Ont.: Ragtime Society.

Kay, Ulysses Simpson, 1917–
> *Brief elegy,* for oboe and strings. New York: MCA, 1964 (Leeds solo series).
>
> *Choral triptych,* for four-part chorus and strings. New York: Associated Music Publishers.
>
> *Concerto,* for orchestra. New York: Duchess.
>
> *Dances,* string orchestra. New York: Duchess, 1965 (Leeds contemporary classics for string orchestra).
>
> *Fantasy variations,* for orchestra. New York: MCA, 1966.
>
> *How stands the glass around?,* for five-part chorus. New York: Associated Music Publishers (no. A228).
>
> *Hymn-anthems on the tune "Hanover",* for mixed chorus and organ. New York: C. F. Peters, 1960.
>
> *Meditations,* for organ. New York: H. W. Gray, 1951 (Contemporary organ series, 27).
>
> *Of new horizons,* for orchestra. New York: C. F. Peters, 1961 (Peters Edition, 6253).
>
> *Quartet,* trumpets & trombones. New York: Peer International, 1958.
>
> *Serenade,* for orchestra. New York: Associated Music Publishers.
>
> *Umbrian scene,* for orchestra. New York: Duchess Music.

Lewis, John, 1920–
> *An afternoon in Paris,* for jazz ensemble. New York: MJQ.
>
> *The comedy,* for jazz ensemble. New York: MJQ, 1961.
>
> *Django,* for jazz ensemble. New York: MJQ.
>
> *England's carol,* for jazz ensemble. New York: MJQ.
>
> *Jazz ostinato,* for jazz ensemble and orchestra. New York: MJQ, 1969.
>
> *The queen's fancy,* for jazz ensemble. New York: MJQ.
>
> *Sketch for double quartet,* for jazz quartet and string quartet. New York: MJQ, 1960.

Lovingood, Penman, Sr., 1895–
> *Chaconne,* for viola and piano. Compton, Calif.: Lovingood.

Nocturne, piano. Compton, Calif.: Lovingood.

Saturday's child, for voice and piano. Compton, Calif.: Lovingood.

McLin, Lena Johnson

    The earth is the Lord's, for four-part chorus and piano. Westbury (N.Y.): Pro Arte, 1969 (Pro Oct. 2531).

    Glory, glory, hallelujah, for four-part chorus. Park Ridge: Neil A. Kjos, 1964 (Ed. 5430).

    In this world, for chorus, electric guitar, flute, cello and electronic piano. Chicago: Neil Kjos, 1970.

    Written down my name, for four-part chorus. Park Ridge: Neil A. Kjos, 1967 (Ed. 5460).

Merrifield, Norman L., 1906–

    Down by the rivuhside, for four-part chorus. Park Ridge: Neil A. Kjos, 1953 (Kjos select choral series; Ed. 5231).

    Remember, O Lord, for four-part chorus and organ or piano. Boston: The Boston Music Co., 1964 (Boston Music Company octavo sacred music, 13205; pl. no. M.C.Co. 13205).

Miller, Edward

    Joshua commanded, for four-part chorus and piano. New York: Marks, 1953.

Moore, Undine (Smith)

    Daniel, Daniel, servant of the Lord, for eight-part chorus. New York: Witmark (Octavo no. 5-W3475).

    Hail! warrior!, for four-part chorus. New York: Witmark (Octavo no. W3544).

Morton, Jelly Roll, 1885–1941.

    Crazy chords, for piano. New York: Southern Music.

    Frog-i-more rag, for piano. Washington: Tempo Music Co., 1946.

Nelson, Oliver E., 1932–

    Blues and the abstract truth, for piano. New York: Marks, 1965, 1960 (pl. no. 14778).

    Emancipation blues, for jazz band. New York: Marks, 1963 (pl. no. 14767).

    Majorca, for band. New York: Marks, 1964 (pl. no. 15089).

Nickerson, Camille

    Gué-gué solingaié, for four-part chorus and piano. New York: Leeds, 1948 (pl. no. L–183).

Parker, Charlie, 1920–

    Billie's bounce, for jazz band. Newark: Savoy Music.

    Confirmation, for jazz band. Hollywood: Atlantic Music Corp.

    Now's the time, for jazz band. Newark: Savoy Music.

    Ornithology, for jazz band. Hollywood: Atlantic Music Corp.

    Yardbird suite, for jazz band. Hollywood: Atlantic Music Corp.

Patterson, Benjamin
  The four suits, individual and group investigations into the ontology of learning. New York: Something Else Press.
Perry, Julia
  How beautiful are the feet, for voice and piano. New York: Galaxy, 1964.
  Stabat mater, for contralto and string quartet (or string orchestra). New York: Southern, 1954 (pl. no. 213).
  Ye who seek the truth, for tenor and four-part chorus. New York: Galaxy, 1952.
Peterson, Oscar
  Soulville samba, for jazz band. Toronto: BMI Canada (Tomi Music).
Pittman, Evelyn LaRue
  Rock-a my soul, for baritone and five-part chorus. New York: Carl Fischer, 1952.
Price, Florence B., 1888–1953.
  Adoration, for organ. Dayton: Lorenz.
  The goblin and the mosquito, for piano. Chicago: Summy.
  In quiet mood, for organ. New York: Galaxy.
Roldán, Amadeo, 1900–1939.
  Motivos de son, for voice and instrumental ensemble. San Francisco: New Music, 1935 (New Music orchestra series, 16).
  Preludio cubano, for piano. New York: Southern Music, 1967.
  Rítmicas, no. 5, for 11 percussionists. New York: Southern Music, 1967.
  Rítmicas, no. 6, for 11 percussionists. New York: Southern Music, 1967.
Russell, George, 1923–
  All about Rosie, for jazz band. New York: Russ-Hix Music.
  The day John Brown was hanged, for jazz quartet. New York: Russ-Hix Music.
  Ezz-thetic, for jazz sextet. New York: Russ-Hix Music.
  Stratusphunk, for jazz sextet. New York: Russ-Hix Music.
Saint-Georges, Joseph Boulogne, Chevalier de, 1739–1799.
  Symphonie concertante, G major, op. 13, for 2 violins and orchestra. Included in *La symphonie française dans la seconde moitié du XVIIIe siècle* (v.3) by Barry Brook. Paris: Université de Paris, Institut de Musique, 1962.
Shorter, Rick
  The people had no faces, for voice and piano. New York: Marks, 1966 (pl. no. 14992).
Smith, Hale, 1925–
  Brevities, for flute. New York: Marks, 1969 (pl. no. 15411).
  Contours, for orchestra. New York: C. F. Peters, 1962.
  Evocation, for piano. New York: University Society (International library of piano music).

Expansions, for band. New York: Marks, 1967 (pl. no. 15157–FS).

Faces of jazz, for piano. New York: Marks, 1968 (pl. no. 15334).

In memoriam Beryl Rubinstein, for four-part chorus and orchestra (or piano). New York: Highgate Press, 1968 (Cleveland Composers' Guild publication series).

Somersault, for band. New York: Frank, 1964.

Smith, William Henry

Climbin' up the mountain, for four-part chorus. Park Ridge: Neil Kjos (pl. no. 1001).

Southall, Mitchell B.

Elf dance, for piano. New York: G. Schirmer, ca.1947.

Ev'ry time I feel the spirit, for four-part chorus. Glen Rocks, N.J.: J. Fischer & Bro., 1957.

Improptu militaire, for piano. New York: G. Schirmer, ca.1950.

In silent night, for four-part chorus. Cincinnati: Willis Music, 1957.

Steal away, for four-part chorus. Cincinnati: Willis Music, 1959.

Sowande, Fela, 1905–

Chorale-preludes on Yoruba sacred melodies, for organ. London: Novello.

Still, William Grant, 1895–

And they lynched him on a tree, for contralto, eight-part chorus, narrator and orchestra. Glen Rock, N.J.: J. Fischer & Bro.

Breath of a rose, for voice and piano. New York: G. Schirmer, 1928.

Danzas de Panamá, for string quartet (or string orchestra). New York: Southern Music, 1953.

Folk suite no. 4, for band. New York: Bourne, 1966 (Bourne symphonic library).

In memoriam: the Colored soldiers who died for democracy, for orchestra. New York: Delkas, 1946.

Lenox Avenue, for orchestra. Glen Rock, N.J.: J. Fischer & Bro., 1938.

Miniatures, for piano, flute and oboe. London, New York: Oxford University Press, 1963.

Sahdji, ballet. New York: C. Fischer, 1961 (American composers edition).

Symphony no. 1 (Afro-American). Glen Rock, N.J.: J. Fischer & Bro., 1935 (Fischer ed. 0318).

Swanson, Howard

A death song, for voice and piano. New York: Weintraub, 1951.

Ghosts in love, for voice and piano. New York: Weintraub, 1950.

The Negro speaks of rivers, for voice and piano. New York: Leeds, 1949.

Night music, for instrumental ensemble. New York: Weintraub, 1951.

Nocturne, for violin and piano. New York: Weintraub, 1951.

Short symphony, for orchestra. New York: Weintraub, 1951.

Sonata, for piano. New York: Weintraub, 1950.

Suite, for violoncello and piano. New York: Weintraub, 1951.

Turpin, Tom, 1873–1922.

The Bowery buck, for piano. Weston (Ont.): Ragtime Society.

Harlem rag, for piano. Weston (Ont.): Ragtime Society.

St. Louis rag, for piano. Weston (Ont.): Ragtime Society.

Waldron, Mal, 1926–

Left alone, for voice and piano. New York: Marks, 1961 (pl. no. 14441).

Sweet love, bitter: Della's dream, for piano. New York: Marks, 1967 (pl. no. 15108 of the Piedmont catalog).

Walker, George Theophilus, 1922–

Gloria; in memoriam, for four-part chorus and organ. Northampton (Mass.): New Valley Music Press.

Psalm 81, for chorus. New York: Galaxy.

Sonata, violin & piano, no. 2. New York: Associated Music Publishers, 1966.

Stars, for four-part chorus. New York: Associated Music Publishers, 1967.

Waller, Fats, 1904–1943.

Ain't misbehavin', for voice and piano. New York: Mills, 1929.

Handful of keys, for piano. New York: Southern Music, 1930.

Stealin' apples, for voice and piano. New York: Mills, 1936.

White, Clarence Cameron, 1880–1960.

Bandanna sketches, for violin and piano. New York: C. Fischer.

Cabin memories, for voice and piano. New York: C. Fischer.

Divertimento, for orchestra. New York: Sam Fox.

Hear the good news, for voice and piano. Bryn Mawr (Pa.): Presser.

Levee dance, for violin and piano. New York: C. Fischer.

March triumphal, for band. Bryn Mawr (Pa.): Presser.

Suite on Negro themes, for orchestra. New York: Sam Fox.

Williams, Bert

Nobody, for voice and piano. New York: Marks, 1933 (pl. no. 10074).

Work, John Wesley, Jr., 1901–ca.1967.

American Negro songs. Bryn Mawr (Pa.): Presser, 1960, 1940.

Appalachia, for piano. Delaware Water Gap (Pa.): Shawnee Music Press, 1945.

Go tell it on the mountain (various arrangements published by Galaxy, in New York).

I, John, saw the holy number, for chorus. New York: Galaxy, 1962.

I've known rivers, for chorus. New York: Galaxy.

Jubilee, for four-part chorus. New York: Holt, Rinehart & Winston, 1962.

Rockin' Jerusalem, for chorus. Bryn Mawr (Pa.): Presser, 1940.

Scuppernong, for piano. Delaware Water Gap (Pa.): Shawnee Music Press, 1951.

The singers, for baritone and mixed chorus. New York: Mills, 1949.

A Selective List of Recordings

This is a representative list of recordings, commercially available in the earlier part of 1970. Sources for this information include the *Schwann Long Playing Record Catalog*, brochures on individual composers issued by Broadcast Music, Inc. (to whom appreciation is expressed for their use), and references from miscellaneous sources. Particular notice should be made that this discography is not complete with respect to jazz recordings (the reader is referred to Appendix 5 for supplementary jazz discographies). As indicated in the panel discussion on the publication and recording of music, the continued availability of many of these labels is subject to annual review in terms of sales. With so few works in non-jazz available, this condition is particularly tenuous.

Abrams, Richard Muhall, 1930–
 Levels and degrees of sound.
  Delmark Records.
Anderson, Thomas Jefferson, Jr., 1928–
 Chamber symphony.
  CRI
Baker, David N., Jr., 1931–
 Le chat qui pêche.
  Silver Crest Records CBD-69-6A.
 Honesty.
  Riverside 375.
  Isis I-608.
  Clark Terry.
 I.U. swing machine.
  Silver Crest Records CBD-69-6A.
 J is for loveliness.
  Isis I-608.
 Kentucky oysters.
  Riverside 341.
 Lunacy.
  Decca DL-4183.

121 Bank Street.
  Decca DL-1920.
Le roi.
  Fermata FB-97.
  ESP Records.
  Atlantic 1428.
The screamin' meemies.
  Silver Crest Records CBD-69-6A.
Silver chalice.
  Silver Crest Records CBD-69-6A.
Soft summer rain.
  Silver Crest CBD-69-6A.
Son-mar.
  Silver Crest Records CBD-69-6A.
Stereophrenic.
  Riverside 9412.
War gewesen.
  Decca DL-4183.
Blake, Eubie, 1883–
 Eighty-six years.
  Columbia C2S-847.

Bowie, Lester, 1941–
   Numbers 1 & 2.
      Nessa Records.
Braxton, Anthony.
   N M488 44M.
      Delmark Records.
Coleman, Ornette, 1930–
   Forms and sounds.
      Victor LSC-9282.
   Saints and soldiers.
      Victor LSC-9282.
   Space flight.
      Victor LSC-9282.
Davis, Miles, 1926–
   All blues.
      Columbia CL-1355; CS-
        8163.
   L'ascenseur pour l'enchafaud.
      Columbia CL-1268.
   Blue haze.
      Columbia CL-1084.
      Kapp KL-1046.
      Prestige 7054.
   Blue in green.
      Columbia CL-1355; CS-
        8163.
      Riverside RLP-315.
      Riverside S-1162.
   Blues by five.
      Prestige 7094.
   Bluing.
      Prestige 7012.
   Boplicity.
      Capitol T-762.
      Capitol T(S)-1309.
   Budo.
      Capitol T-762.
      Columbia CL-1020.
      Savoy MG-12064.
      Verve MGV-8268.
   Compulsion.
      Prestige 7044.
   Deception.
      Capitol T-762.

Denial.
   Prestige 7012.
Dig.
   Prestige 7012.
   Prestige 7062.
Down.
   Prestige 7025.
Flamenco sketches.
   Columbia CL-1355.
   Columbia CS-8163.
Four.
   Bethlehem BCP-30.
   Contemporary CTP-3540.
   Prestige 7054.
   Prestige 7143.
   Prestige 7166.
   Prestige 7176.
   Verve MGV-8028.
   Verve 8283.
   World Pacific 1264.
Freddie freeleader.
   Columbia CL-1355.
   Columbia CS-8163.
Green haze.
   Prestige 7007.
Half Nelson.
   Bethlehem BCP-75.
   Gene Norman Presents
      GNP-20.
   Prestige 7166.
   Savoy MG-12001.
   Savoy MG-12039.
I didn't.
   Prestige 7007.
Lazy Susan.
   Blue note 1502.
The leap.
   Blue note 1502.
Little Willie leaps.
   Atlantic 1319.
   Savoy MG-12001.
Miles.
   Columbia CL-1193.
Miles ahead.

Columbia CL-1041.
Prestige 7054.
Milestones.
Jazzland 27; 927S.
Savoy MG-12000.
United Artists UAL(S)-
4034.
Nardis.
Riverside 12-269.
No line.
Prestige 7044.
Out of the blue.
Contemporary CTP-3528.
Prestige 7012.
The serpent's tooth.
Bethlehem BCP-75.
Contemporary CTP-3549.
Prestige 7044.
Sid's ahead.
Columbia CL-1193.
Sippins at bells.
Savoy MG-12009.
Smooch.
Prestige 7054.
So what?
Columbia CL-1355;
CS-8163.
Solar.
ABC-Paramount 170.
Prestige 7067.
Prestige 8024.
Riverside RLP-281.
World Pacific 1260.
Somethin' else.
Blue note 1595.
Swing spring.
Epic LN-3376.
Prestige 7150.
Take off.
Blue note 1502.
The theme.
Prestige 7166.
Tune up.
Blue note 4001.

Columbia CL-1161.
Jubilee J-1093.
Mercury MG-36140.
Prestige 7094.
Prestige 7054.
Riverside RLP-282.
Vierd blues.
Prestige 7044.
Wierdo.
Blue note 1502.
Dawson, William Levi, 1899–
Negro folk symphony.
Decca DL-10077.
Dixon, Bill, 1925–
All the king's women.
Savoy.
The dragon suite.
Savoy SMG-12190.
Elysa.
Savoy SMG-12191.
Good golly, Miss Nancy.
Savoy SMG-12189.
Marzette.
Savoy MG-12193.
Metamorphosis: 1962–1966.
Victor LPM-3844;
LPS-3844.
Nightfall pieces, nos. 1 & 2.
Victor LPM-3844;
LPS-3844.
October song.
Savoy MG-12193.
*Quartet, saxophone, trumpet,
percussion & double bass.*
Savoy MG-12178.
Trio.
Savoy MG-12178.
The twelfth December.
Savoy MG-12184.
Voices.
Victor LPM-3844;
LPS-3844.
Winter song, 1964.
Savoy MG-12184.

Jarman, Joseph, 1937–
  As if it were the seasons.
    Delmark Records.
  Song for.
    Delmark Records.
Johnson, J. J., 1924–
  Aquarius.
    Columbia CL-1606;
      CS-8406.
  Bee Jay.
    Savoy 12106.
  Bloozineff.
    Columbia CL-1737;
      CS-8537.
  Blue mode.
    Prestige 7024.
  Blues for trombones.
    Savoy 12010.
  Blues in F.
    King 4307.
  Coffee pot.
    Blue note 1505.
  Daylie double.
    Blue Note 1506.
  Eight ball.
    King 4400.
  Elora.
    Prestige 7024.
  Embryo.
    Victor 20-2892.
  Enigma.
    Blue Note 1501.
  Fatback.
    Columbia CL-1606;
      CS-8406.
  Flat back.
    Columbia CL-1737;
      CS-8537.
  Four plus four.
    Columbia CL-892.
  Foxhunt.
    Prestige 7023.
  Groovin'.
    Blue Note 1506.

  In walked Horace.
    Columbia CL-1606;
      CS-8406.
  Jay.
    Blue Note 1505.
  Jay Bird.
    Savoy 12106.
    Mercury 20442.
    Mercury 60117.
  Jay Jay.
    Savoy 12106.
  King's spinner.
    King 4299.
  Kelo.
    Blue Note 1501.
  Lament.
    Savoy 12101.
    Argo 672.
  Mad be bop.
    Savoy 12106.
  Minor mist.
    Columbia CL-1606;
      CS-8406.
  Mohawk.
    Columbia CL-1606;
      CS-8046.
  Neckbones.
    Warner Brothers 1272.
  Nickels and dimes.
    Columbia CL-1030.
  Opus V.
    Prestige 7023.
  Poem for brass.
    Columbia CL-941.
  Scamparoo.
    King 4259.
  Shutter-bug.
    Columbia CL-1606;
      CS-8406.
  Suede jacket.
    King 4242.
  Teapot.
    Prestige 7024.

Turnabout.
    Columbia CL-742.
Turnpike.
    Blue Note 1505.
Viscosity.
    Blue Note 1506.
Vista.
    Vik 1040.
We too.
    Columbia CL-742.
Wee dot.
    Savoy 9009.
    Blue Note 1522.
    Blue Note 1530.
    Epic 16020.
    Epic 17020.
    New Jazz 8249.
    United Artists 4040.
Joplin, Scott, 1868–1917.
   Treemonisha. Selections.
    Portents 3.
   Works, piano. Selections.
    Audiophile AP-71/2.
    Riverside RLP 126.
Kay, Ulysses Simpson, 1917–
   Choral triptych.
    Cambridge CRM-416.
   Dances, string orchestra.
    Round dance and polka.
    CRI-119.
   Fantasy variations, orchestra.
    CRI-CD-209; SD-209.
   How stands the glass around?
    CRI-102.
   Quartet, trumpets & trombones.
    Folkways 3651.
   Serenade, orchestra.
    LOU 545-8.
   Sinfonia, E.
    CRI-139.
   Suite, orchestra.
    LOU 545-8.
   Umbrian scene.
    LOU 651.

What's in a name?
    CRI-102.
Lewis, John, 1920–
   Morpheus.
    Prestige 7025.
   Rouge.
    Capitol T-762.
Mingus, Charlie, 1922–
   Alice's wonderland, or Diane.
    Columbia CL-1440.
    Columbia CS-8236.
    United Artists UAS-5036.
   All the things you could be now.
    Candid 8005; 9005.
   Backstage.
    MGM E-3697.
   Bas-ically speaking.
    Debut LP-3.
   Bemonable lady.
    Mercury.
   Better git it in your soul.
    Columbia CL-1370;
      CS-8171.
   Bird calls.
    Columbia CL-1370;
      CS-8171.
   Blue cee.
    Atlantic 1260.
   Boogie stop shuffle.
    Columbia CL-1370;
      CS-8171.
   Boston tea party.
    Vik.
   Celia.
    Bethlehem BCP-6019.
   Chazzanova.
    Debut LP-12; LP-126.
   The clown.
    Atlantic 1260.
   Conversation.
    Bethlehem BCP-6019.
   Cryin' blues.
    Atlantic 1305.

Mingus, Charlie *(continued)*
  Double G train.
    MGM E-3697.
  Duke's choice.
    Bethlehem BCP-6026.
  E's flat, ah's flat too.
    Atlantic 1305.
  East coasting.
    Bethlehem BCP-6019.
  Eclipse.
    Debut LP-198.
    Mercury.
  Eulogy for Rudy Williams.
    Savoy MG-12059.
  Extrasensory perception.
    Debut M-103; 198.
  Fables of Faubus.
    Columbia CL-1370;
      CS-8171.
  Far Wells, Mill Valley.
    Columbia CL-1440;
      CS-8236.
  Fifty-first Street blues.
    Bethlehem BCP-6019.
  Folks forms, no. 1.
    Candid 8005; 9005.
  Four hands.
    Bethlehem BCP-65.
  Getting together.
    Savoy MG-12059.
  Gregarian chant.
    Savoy MG-12059.
  Goodbye, pork pie hat.
    Columbia CL-1370;
      CS-8171.
  Gunslinging Bird.
    Columbia CL-1440;
      CS-8236.
  Haitian fight song.
    Atlantic 1260.
  Half mast inhibition.
    Mercury.

Jelly roll.
  Columbia CL-1370;
    CS-8171.
Jump, monk.
  Debut LP-123.
  MGM E-3697.
Love bird.
  Roost LP-2222.
Love chant.
  Atlantic 1237.
Midnight stroll.
  MGM E-2697.
Mingus fingers.
  Decca A-661.
  Decca 24428.
Minor intrusion.
  Bethlehem BCP-65.
Moanin'.
  Atlantic 1305.
Montage.
  Debut M-103.
My jelly roll soul.
  Atlantic 1305.
New now, know now.
  Columbia CL-1440;
    CS-8236.
New York sketchbook.
  Bethlehem BCP-6026.
No private income.
  United Artists UAL-4036.
Nostalgia on Times Square.
  United Artists UAL-4036.
Nouroog.
  Bethlehem BCP-6026.
Original Faubus fables.
  Candid 8005; 9005.
Paris in blue.
  Debut 198.
Passive resistance.
  Mercury.
Open letter to Duke.
  Columbia CL-1370;
    CS-8171.

Pithecanthropus erectus.
    Atlantic 1237.
Portrait.
    Debut M-101.
    Mercury.
Precognition.
    Debut M-101.
Profile of Jackie.
    Atlantic 1237.
Purple heart.
    Savoy MG-12059.
Pussy cat blues.
    Columbia CL-1370;
        CS-8171.
Put me in that dungeon.
    Columbia CL-1440;
        CS-8236.
Reflections.
    Savoy MG-12010.
Reincarnation of a love bird.
    Atlantic 1260.
Revelations. First movement.
    Columbia WL-127.
Scenes in the city.
    Bethlehem BCP-6026.
Self-portrait in three colors.
    Columbia CL-1370;
        CS-8171.
Slippers.
    Bethlehem BCP-6026.
Slop.
    Columbia CL-1440;
        CS-8236.
Smooch.
    Prestige 7054.
Song with organ.
    Columbia CL-1440;
        CS-8236.
The stranger.
    MGM E-3697.
Tensions.
    Atlantic 1305.

Thrice upon a theme.
    Bethlehem BCP-65.
Tia Juana table dance.
    Vik.
Wednesday night prayer meeting
    Atlantic 1305.
Wierd nightmare.
    MGM E-3697.
    Mercury.
What love.
    Candid 8005; 9005.
West coast ghost.
    Bethlehem BCP-6019.
Ysef, Isef too.
    Mercury.
Zoo-baba-dah-oo-ee.
    Decca A-661; 24431.
Mitchell, Roscoe Edward, Jr., 1940–
    Congliptious.
        Nessa Records.
    Sound.
        Delmark Records.
Monk, Thelonius, 1920–
    Ask me now.
        Blue Note LP-1511.
        Riverside LP-12-305; 1150.
        New Jazz LP-8206.
    Ba-lue bolivar ba-lues are.
        Riverside LP-12-336.
    Bemsha swing.
        Prestige LP-7159.
        Prestige LP-7150.
        Riverside LP-12-226; 1174.
        Epic LN-3376.
    Blue hawk.
        Riverside LP-13-312; 1158.
    Blue monk.
        Prestige LP-7169.
        Atlantic LP-1278.
        Riverside LP-12-262.
        Riverside LP-12-312.
        Atlantic LP-1330.

Columbia CL-1161;
 CS-8009.
Monk's dream.
 Prestige LP-7159.
Monk's mood.
 Blue Note LP-1511.
 Riverside LP-12-235.
 Riverside LP-12-300; 1138.
Nutty.
 Prestige LP-7169.
Off minor.
 Blue Note LP-1510.
 Riverside LP-12-242; 1102.
 Riverside LP-12-300; 1138.
 Prestige LP-7117.
Pannonica.
 Riverside LP-12-226; 1174.
 Riverside LP-12-321; 1158.
Played twice.
 Riverside LP-12-305; 1150.
Reflections.
 Prestige LP-7159.
 Swing 33342.
 Blue Note LP-1558.
 New Jazz LP-8206.
Rhythm-a-ning.
 Atlantic LP-1278.
 Riverside LP-12-247; 1106.
 Riverside LP-12-262.
 Jazzland 39; S-939.
 New Jazz LP-8219.
Round about midnight.
 Blue Note LP-1510.
 Swing 3342.
 Riverside LP-12-235.
 Riverside LP-12-247; 1106
 Riverside LP-12-323; 1171.
Round lights.
 Riverside LP-12-312; 1158.
Ruby, my dear.
 Blue Note LP-1510.
 Riverside LP-12-242; 1102.
 Riverside LP-12-312; 1158.

Shuffle boil.
 Savoy MG-12137.
Skippy.
 Blue Note LP-1511.
 New Jazz LP-8206.
Straight, no chaser.
 Blue Note LP-1511.
 Riverside LP-12-247; 1106.
 Riverside LP-12-305; 1150.
 Columbia CL-1193.
 Mercury 36135.
 New Jazz LP-8219.
 Prestige LP-7191.
 World Pacific 1027.
Thelonius.
 Blue Note LP-1510.
 Riverside LP-12-300; 1138.
Think of one.
 Prestige LP-7053.
Trinkle tinkle.
 Prestige LP-7159.
We see.
 Prestige LP-7053.
 Verve MGV-8387;
 VS-68387.
Well, you needn't.
 Blue Note LP-1510.
 Swing 33342.
 Riverside LP-12-242; 1102.
 Argo LP-685.
 Blue Note LP-1525.
 Epic BA-16008; 17008.
 Jazzland 39; S-939.
 Prestige LP-7117.
 Riverside LP-12-285.
Who knows?
 Blue Note LP-1511.
Work.
 Prestige LP-7169.
 Prestige LP-7125.
Worry later.
 Riverside LP-12-323; 1171.

Parker, Charlie, 1909–1955.
  Ah-leu-cha.
    Savoy MG-12000.
    Columbia ML-949.
    Emarcy MG-36080.
    World Wide 20093.
  Another hair do.
    Savoy MG-12000.
  Au private.
    Verve MGV-8002.
    Mercury MG-36127.
    Verve MGVS-6108.
    Blue Note 4002.
  Back home blues.
    Verve MGV-8010.
  Ballade.
    Verve MGV-8002.
  Barbados.
    Savoy MG-12000.
    Savoy MG-12014.
    Atlantic LP-1235.
    Columbia ML-1084.
  Billie's bounce.
    Savoy MG-12009.
    Savoy MG-12015.
    Verve MGV-8265.
    Verve MGV-8209.
    Serve MGV-8030.
    World Pacific 1240.
    Mercury MG-36127.
    Decca DL-8393.
    Metro Jazz 1011.
    Blue Note 1515.
  The bird.
    Verve MGV-8001.
  Bird gets the worm.
    Savoy MG-12000.
  Bloomdido.
    Verve MGV-8230.
  Bluebird.
    Savoy MG-12000.
    Savoy MG-12014.
    Omega 1047.

    Savoy MG-12053.
    Bethlehem BCP-75.
    Savoy MG-12111.
  Blues for Alice.
    Verve MGV-8010.
  Buzzy.   .
    Savoy MG-12000.
    Savoy MG-12138.
  Cardboard.
    Verve MGV-8009.
  Celebrity.
    Verve MGV-8002.
  Chasin' the bird.
    Savoy MG-12000.
    Savoy MG-12009.
    Columbia CL-935.
    Blue Note 1569.
  Cheryl.
    Savoy MG-12001.
  Chi chi.
    Verve MGV-8005.
    Debut LP-13.
  Confirmation.
    Verve MGV-8001.
    Contemporary 3544.
    Bethlehem BCP-36.
    Bethlehem BCP-75.
    Mercury MG-36127.
    Blue Note 4012.
  Constellation.
    Savoy MG-12000.
    Capitol T-626.
    Verve MGV-8217.
  Cosmic rays.
    Verve MGV-8005.
  Diverse.
    Verve MGV-8009.
  Donna Lee.
    Savoy MG-12009.
    Atlantic LP-1217.
    Riverside LP-12-237.
    Harmony HL-7088.
    Contemporary 3568.

K. C. blues.
    Verve MGV-8010.
Kim.
    Verve MGV-8005.
Klaunstance.
    Savoy MG-12014.
Ko ko.
    Savoy MG-12014.
    Mercury MG-36127.
Laird baird.
    Verve MGV-8002.
Marmaduke.
    Savoy MG-12000.
    Savoy MG-12001.
    World Wide 20003.
Merry-go-round.
    Savoy MG-12000.
    Savoy MG-12014.
Moose the mooche.
    Dial 201.
    Contemporary 3519.
    Blue Note 1571.
Mohawk.
    Verve MGV-8002.
My little suede shoes.
    Verve MGV-8000.
    Bethlehem BCP-125.
    Prestige 7095.
Now's the time.
    Savoy MG-12001.
    Verve MGV-8001.
    Blue Note 1522.
    Verve MGV-8183.
    Savoy MG-12080.
    Debut DBT-126.
    Columbia CL-1161.
    Savoy MG-12023.
    Atlantic LP-1313.
    Decca DL-79209.
    Verve MGV 8129.
    World Wide 20003.
    Metro Jazz 1005.

    Savoy MG-12007.
    World Pacific 1264.
Ornithology.
    Dial 201.
    Bethlehem BCP-157.
    World Pacific PJ-1241.
    Blue Note 1503.
    Coral 57239.
    Harmony HL-7088.
An Oscar for Treadwell.
    Verve MGV-8002.
Parker's mood.
    Savoy MG-12000.
    Prestige 7128.
    World Wide 20003.
    Savoy MG-12138.
    Mercury MG-36127.
Passport.
    Verve MGV-8000.
Perhaps.
    Savoy MG-12000.
    Savoy MG-12009.
Red cross.
    Savoy MG-12001.
    Decca DL-8088.
    Bethlehem BCP-55.
    Columbia CS-8187.
Relaxin' with Lee.
    Verve MGV-8006.
Segment.
    Verve MGV-8009.
Si si.
    Verve MGV-8010.
She rote.
    Verve MGV-8002.
Steeplechase.
    Savoy MG-12000.
    Contemporary 3515.
    Bethlehem BCP-41.
    Savoy MG-12138.
Swedish schnapps.
    Verve MGV-8010.

Smith, Hale, 1925–
    Contours.
        LOU-623.
    In memoriam, Beryl Rubinstein.
        CRI-182.
Swanson, Howard.
    Night music.
        Decca DL-8511.

    Night song.
        Desto 6442.
Wilson, Olly.
    Cetus.
        Turnabout 34301.

A Selective List of Out-of-Print Recordings

The recordings listed below are titles of the "non-jazz" category which have previously been available commercially but have since been discontinued. Names of principal performers are parenthetically indicated when these have been determined.

Boatner, Edward Hammond, 1898–
Oh, what a beautiful city.
London LPS-182 (Ellabelle Davis, soprano).
On ma journey.
London LPS-182 (Ellabelle Davis, soprano).
Columbia ML-2108 (Carol Brice, contralto).
Plenty good room.
London LPS-182 (Ellabelle Davis, soprano).
Brown, ?
I'm goin' to tell God all my troubles.
Period SLP-580 (Inez Matthews, mezzo-soprano).
Brown, Lawrence, 1905–
Spirituals.
Victor 2032.
Victor 20793.
Victor 1982.
Victor 101040.
Burleigh, Harry Thacker, 1866–1949.
De gospel train.
Period SLP-580 (Inez Matthews, mezzo-soprano).
I stood on the ribber ob Jerdon.
London LPS-182 (Ellabelle Davis, soprano).

Nobody knows the trouble I've seen.
London LPS-182 (Ellabelle Davis, soprano).
Spirituals.
Victor 8959.
Victor 2032.
Victor 4371.
Victor 20793.
Victor 1799.
Victor 1966.
Victor 101114.
Victor C-27.
Victor M-554.
Coleridge-Taylor, Samuel, 1875–1912.
Big lady moon.
HMV D-688 (V. Oppenshaw, contralto).
Characteristic waltzes, piano, op. 22; arr., orchestra.
RCA Victor 27225/6; B-8378/9 (New Light Symphony Orchestra).
Christmas overture, op. 74, no. 4.
Columbia 9137 (BBC Symphony Orchestra).
The death of Minnehaha.
Columbia C-2210/3 (Royal Choral Society; Sir Malcolm Sargent, conductor)
Dream dances, piano, op. 74, no. 2.

Decca M-11, M-16
  (Cameron).
Victor 27230/1 (London
  Palladium Orchestra).
Eleanore.
  Columbia DB-2083 (H.
    Wendon, tenor; Gerald
    Moore, piano).
  P-E11192 (Morel, tenor).
  HMV B-9451 (W. Booth,
    tenor).
  Decca F-1699 (R. Hender-
    son, tenor).
  HMV D-1273 (T. Davies,
    tenor).
  Gramophone D-3730
    (Oldham, tenor).
Faust. Nos. 1 & 3.
  Boosey & Hawkes 1922
    (Regent Concert
    Orchestra).
Hiawatha's wedding feast.
  HMV C-1931/4 (Royal
    Albert Hall Orchestra;
    Sir Malcolm Sargent,
    conductor).
*Intermezzo, orchestra, op. 74,
  no. 3.*
  J-B8113.
Life and death.
  HMV B-9451 (W. Booth,
    tenor).
Onaway, awake, beloved.
  HMV C-3407 (W. Booth,
    tenor).
  Decca DX-1512 (J.
    McHugh, tenor).
  HMV D-1242 (T. Davies,
    tenor).
  Decca K-543 (F. T.
    Herton, tenor).
Othello suite, orchestra.
  Brunswick 4273/4 (New

Symphony; Sir Malcolm
  Sargent).
Petite suite de concert, orchestra.
  Columbia DX-1041/2
    (Royal Marines).
  Columbia DB-2479/80
    (Queen's Hall Light
    Orchestra).
  G-C2372/3 (Sir
    Malcolm Sargent).
  Columbia ML-2180
    (Queen's Hall Light
    Orchestra).
  Victor 11283/4 (London
    Symphony Orchestra;
    Sir Malcolm Sargent,
    conductor).
  Columbia DX-651/2
    (Bournemouth Munici-
    pal Orchestra).
  Columbia DB-2205/6 (M.
    Rawicz & W. Lindauer,
    pianos).
  Columbia 9340/1
    (Ansell).
  Decca LF-1010 [*Démande
    et réponse*, only] (R.
    Crean).
  London LPB-196
    [*Démande et réponse*,
    only] (R. Crean).
  Boosey & Hawkes S-2096
    [*Démande et réponse*,
    only] (J. Wilbur String
    Ensemble).
St. Agnes Eve. Nos. 1-2.
  Boosey & Hawkes 1909
    (Regent Concert
    Orchestra).
She rested by the broken brook.
  HMV DA-1778 (John
    McCormack, tenor;
    Gerald Moore, piano).

Coleridge-Taylor, Samuel *(cont.)*
  *Sonata, violin & Piano, op. 28,
    D minor.*
      Columbia L-1396/7 (A.
        Catterall, violin).
  *Song of Hiawatha. No. 2. The
    pursuit; arr., orchestra* (A.
    Lotter).
      Boosey & Hawkes 1916
        (Regent Concert
        Orchestra).
  *Song of Hiawatha. No. 3.
    Conjurer's dance; arr.,
    orchestra* (P. Fletcher).
      Boosey & Hawkes 1922
        (Regent Concert
        Orchestra).
  *Song of Hiawatha. No. 4. The
    homecoming; arr., orchestra*
    (A. Lotter).
      Boosey & Hawkes 1916
        (Regent Concert
        Orchestra).
  *Songs of sun and shade. Thou
    art risen, my beloved.*
      Columbia FB-3031 (T.
        Layton, tenor).
      HMV E-414 (T. Davies,
        tenor).
      HMV B-8285 [contains
        two songs, only] (A.
        Reckless, tenor).
  Sons of the sea.
      HMV C-2728 (P. Dawson)
  *Sorrow songs, op. 57, No. 5.
    Unmindful of the roses.*
      HMV 9451 (W. Booth,
        tenor).
      HMV B-8285 (A. Reckless,
        tenor).
  Spring had come.
      G-D3476 (Suddaby,
        soprano).

  *Valse suite, piano, op. 71.
    Nos. 2 & 6; arr., orchestra.*
      Columbia DB-2212 (Palm
        Court Orchestra; Sandler,
        piano).
  When I am dead, my dearest.
      HMV B-572 (V.
        Oppenheim, contralto).
Dawson, William Levi, 1899–
  Mary had a baby.
      Carillon Records LP-101
        (Yale University; J.
        Somary, conductor).
  Soon ah will be done.
      Columbia AL-45 (De Paur
        Infantry Chorus).
      Monitor MP-576 (Brank
        Krsmanovich Chorus of
        Jugoslavia).
      Capitol P-8431 (Roger
        Wagner Chorale).
  Spiritual.
      Victor 4556.
Dett, Robert Nathaniel, 1882–1943.
  Adagio cantabile, piano.
      Victor 17912 (Behrend,
        piano).
  I'm a-traveling to the grave.
      London LPS-182 (Ellabelle
        Davis, soprano).
  In the bottoms suite, piano.
      Decca set A-586 (Percy
        Grainger, piano).
      Music Sound Books
        MSB-78028 (Hamburg
        Philharmonia).
      MGM E-3195 (Hamburg
        Philharmonia).
      Victor 21750 (Victor
        Orchestra).
  Listen to the lambs.
      Philips NBL-5012
        (Mormon Tabernacle
        Choir).

The ordering of Moses.
 U.S. Department of State.
Spirituals.
 Victor M-879.
Dos Santos, Ernesto, 1891–
 Works. Selections.
  Columbia (Leopold
  Stokowski, conductor).
Handy, William Christopher,
1873–1958.
 St. Louis blues.
  RCA Victor LPM-1714.
 Works. Selections.
  Heritage LPH-0052.
  Folkways FG-3540
  (Katherine Handy
  Lewis).
  Capitol SW-993 (Nat
  King Cole).
Hairston, Jester Joseph, 1901–
 In dat great gettin' up mornin'.
  Columbia AL-45 (De
  Paur Infantry Chorus).
Hayes, Roland, 1887–
 Good news.
  London LPS-182 (Ellabelle
  Davis, soprano).
 Hear de lambs a-cryin'.
  Period SPL-580 (Inez
  Matthews, soprano).
 Littl' boy.
  Period SPL-580 (Inez
  Matthews, soprano).
 Live a humble.
  Period SPL-580 (Inez
  Matthews, soprano).
 My God is so high.
  A440 Records 12-3
  (Reginald Boardman,
  piano).
 Plenty good room.
  Period SPL-580 (Inez
  Matthews, soprano).

Round about de mountain.
 Period SPL-580 (Inez
 Matthews, soprano).
*You must come in by an' thro'
de lamb.*
 Period SPL-580 (Inez
 Matthews, soprano).
Johnson, Hall, 1888–1970.
 Fix me, Jesus.
  Period SPL-580 (Inez
  Matthews, soprano).
 Hold on.
  Period SPL-580 (Inez
  Matthews, soprano).
 My Lord done been here.
  Columbia ML-2180 (Carol
  Brice, contralto).
 They led my Lord away.
  Period SPL-580 (Inez
  Matthews, soprano).
 Who built de ark?
  Columbia AL-45 (De Paur
  Infantry Chorus).
 Witness.
  Period SPL-580 (Inez
  Matthews, soprano).
  Columbia ML-2108 (Carol
  Brice, contralto).
Kay, Ulysses Simpson, 1917–
 Concerto, orchestra.
  Remington Musirama
  R-199-173 (Teatro La
  Fenice; Jonel Perlea,
  conductor).
 Of new horizons.
  University of Arizona
  Records.
 Suite, string orchestra.
  LOU 634 (Louisville
  Orchestra; Robert
  Whitney, conductor).
Lomothe, Ludovic, 1882–
 Works, piano. Selections.
  Victor.

Price, Florence, 1888–1953.
  My soul's been anchored in de Lord.
    London LPS-182 (Ellabelle Davis, soprano).
  Spiritual.
    Victor 1799.
Roldán, Amadeo, 1900–1939.
  Aye me degeson negro.
    NMR 1213 (Judith Litante, soprano; Henry Brandt, piano).
Sowande, Fela, 1905–
  African suite, orchestra.
    London LS-426 (Harvey).
  The Negro in sacred idiom.
    London LL-533 (Sowande).
Spirituals (Miscellaneous).
    RCA Victor LM-110 (Marian Anderson, contralto).
    MGM E-156 (Camilla Williams, soprano).
    Columbia AAL-32 (William Warfield, baritone).
Still, William Grant, 1895–
  From the delta. No. 1, work song.
    Columbia ML2029 (Gould).
  Here's one.
    Concert Hall Society CHS-1140 (Louis Kaufman, violin).
  Lenox Avenue. Blues.
    New Records NRLP-105 (Gordon Manley, piano)
    Concert Hall Society CHS-1140 (Louis Kaufman, violin).
  Sahdji.
    Mercury MG-50257;

SR-90257 (Eastman-Rochester Symphony Orchestra).
  Symphony, no. 1 (Afro-American).
    New Records NRLP-105 (Vienna State Opera; Karl Krueger, conductor).
    Victor 2059 [Scherzo, only] (Eastman-Rochester Symphony Orchestra).
    Columbia 11992D [Scherzo, only] (Leopold Stokowski, conductor).
  To you, America.
    ASCAP CB-177 (U.S. Military Academy Band; F. E. Resta, conductor).
  Visions.
    New Records NRLP-105 (Gordon Manley, piano)
Swanson, Howard.
  Ghosts in love.
    ARS 10 (Helen Thigpin, soprano).
    Desto 6422 (Helen Thigpin, soprano).
  Joy.
    ARS 10 (Helen Thigpin, soprano).
    Desto 6422 (Helen Thigpin, soprano).
  The junk man.
    ARS 10 (Helen Thigpin, soprano).
    Desto 6422 (Helen Thigpin, soprano).
  The Negro speaks of rivers.
    ARS 10 (Helen Thigpin, soprano).

Desto 6422 (Helen
Thigpin, soprano).
Short symphony.
Vanguard VRS-434
(Vienna State Opera;
F. Litschauer, conduc-
tor).
ARS-7; ARS-116 (ARS
Orchestra; Dean Dixon,
conductor).
Suite, violoncello & piano.
SPA-54 (Carl Stern,
cello; Abba Bogin,
piano).
The valley.
ARS 10 (Helen Thigpin,
soprano).

Desto 6422 (Helen
Thigpin, soprano).
White, Clarence Cameron,
1880–1960.
Concerto, violin, op. 63.
Stark Recordings Studio
(Zimmer, violin).
Levee dance.
[label not identified]
(Jascha Heifetz, violin).
Williams, Mary Lou, 1911–
Zodiac suite.
Asch.

SPECIAL NOTE:

Hopefully, all institutions make tape copies of works which are performed on their campuses. Because of the need of chances to hear more Black music than appears on commercial recordings, it is quite important that schools and conductors have knowledge of the existence of suitable recordings for reference.

Indiana University's Music Library has begun making an effort to acquire copies of non-commercial recordings, usually on tape. The Black Music Committee offers itself as a clearing house for information regarding similar collections elsewhere. Subject to copyright and performers' right restrictions, exchanges or loans may subsequently be developed as a part of the proposed Black Music Center. Under any circumstances, it would be valuable to issue a union list of such recordings. Individuals and institutions wishing to register recordings for possible future announcements are invited to correspond with the Black Music Committee regarding exploration of this idea.

A Selective List of Films

The films listed below are directly related to some aspect of Black music. These 16mm sound films, all black and white unless noted otherwise, are available from the Audio-Visual Center of Indiana University (Bloomington, Indiana, 47401), which can supply information regarding rental. The Center's 1970 catalog of educational motion pictures contains 8,798 titles and includes many items of peripheral interest on Black history, civil rights, Africa, acoustics, musical form, instrumental lessons, music appreciation and history, ballet, biographies, etc. The descriptions below are taken from this catalog.

African musicians.   14 minutes.   RS-615.
Pictures and describes a number of common African musical instruments. Indicates the probable origin of the instruments. Among those shown and played are the tom-tom, skin drums, horns of various types, and the xylophone.   (de Boe; Brandon)

American music: from folk to jazz and pop. 46 minutes, 2 reels. RS-689.
Introduces development of jazz and pop music from folk music origins and features original performances of prominent musicians. Shows some effects of cultural and historical developments on the courses of musical trends. Features commentary and analyses by Duke Ellington, Richard Rodgers, and Billy Taylor.   (ABC; McGraw-Hill)

Begone dull care.   8 minutes.   RSC-197 (color).
Norman McLaren uses animation to interpret a modern jazz composition performed by the Oscar Peterson Trio. The slow, quiet middle section, in black and white, is in contrast with the colorful, swift-moving opening and closing sections. *McLaren film series*.   (McLaren; NFBC)

Chronicle of America's jazz age—The golden twenties.   67 minutes.   CS-582.
Uses newsreel footage to present the highlights of the 1920's. Includes politics, Wall Street activities, religion, athletics, prohibition, military and foreign situations, the arts, and novel happenings which reflect the spirit of the times.   (MOT).

Dance: echoes of jazz.   30 minutes.   RS-660.
Traces the development of American jazz dance, from tap dancing through the stylized theatrical form of the 1900's and orchestrated jazz of the Thirties, to the cool, abstract music of the Sixties. Demonstrates the basic steps of tap dance (sand, shuffle, waltz clog, time step, buck-and wing) as performed by Honi Coles. Presents Paula Kelly, Dudley Williams, and William Luther dancing to "Storyville, New Orleans" and the music recorded by Jelly Roll Morton, and Grover Dale and

Michel Harty dancing in "Idiom 59" and to recorded music of the same title by Duke Ellington. Presents John Butler's choreography of music by Gunther Schuller (variations on a theme by John Lewis, "Django") danced by John Butler, Mary Hinkson, and Buzz Miller. (NET; Indiana U A-V Center)

Doctors all. 3 minutes. NET -147 9.

Uses dance routines and originally scored music to portray reactions to human illness. Described methods of detection, treatment, and acceptance of treatment. Compares Americans, the Ojibway Indians of Canada, and the Djuka Bush Negroes of Dutch Guiana. *People are taught to be different series.* (NET: Indiana U A-V Center)

Duro Lapido. 30 minutes. RS-700.

Introduces Duro Lapido, the founder, director, playwright, composer, and principal male actor of the Duro Lapido Traveling Theatre Company of Oshogbo, Nigeria. Explains how Lapido became interested in drama and music. Shows members of the company touring native villages. (NET; Indiana U A-V Center)

Ethnic dance—Roundtrip to Trinidad. 29 minutes. RS-530.

Explores the significance of ethnic dance in the field of formal dance. Presents a variety of West Indian dances. Explains their deviations and movements. Includes *bele,* a West Indian adaptation of the minuet; *yanvallou,* a voodoo dance; and *banda,* a Haitian dance about death. Features Geoffrey Holder and Carmen de Lavallade. *A time to dance series.* (NET; Indiana U A-V Center)

Family of Ghana. 3 minutes. GS-941.

Experiences of a family in the African nation of Ghana illustrate the culture of that country. Suggest striving for new ideas and methods in this developing nation by the younger people, while the older ones cling to tradition. Dramatizes this contest within a Ghanan family when the son wishes to acquire a motorized boat for ocean fishing. His father, however, fears departing from the "old ways." Includes sequences of Accra and of native music and dancing. (NFBC; McGraw-Hill)

The first World Festival of Negro Arts. 22 minutes (color). CSC-2044.

Discloses the purpose of the first World Festival of Negro Art held in Dakar as an attempt to create an awareness of Negro art and culture. Surveys the contributions in music, dance, textiles, poetry, sculpture, and painting. Explains the arts and its creation in terms of the religious, social and evolutionary culture of Africans. (Sahia Studios for UNESCO; McGraw-Hill)

Helen Tamiris and her Negro spirituals. 16 minutes. RS-593.

Illustrates modern dance as exemplified by Negro spirituals. Miss Tamiris creates her dances to the familiar spirituals *Swing low, sweet chariot, Go down Moses,* and *Get on board lil' children.* Muriel Rahn, soprano, and

Eugene Brice, baritone, accompany Miss Tamiris.   (Nagtam; McGraw-Hill)

Life of a primitive people (Africa).   14 minutes.   GSC-702 (color).   GS-702 (black and white)

Shows typical activities of a primitive African tribe by following the hunting, cooking, handicraft, home building, and home life of a jungle hunter and his family. Presents models of cave dwellings and neolithic huts. Depicts tribal organization, shelter and clothing, cultivation and use of cotton and rice, tools, domestic animals, control of fire, drum communication, music, and religious rituals of the primitive people.   (Cornet)

Marian Anderson.   27 minutes.   RS-363.

Presents Marian Anderson as she sings a program of songs in rehearsal as well as on concert stage. She sings *Begrüssung* by Händel, *O What a beautiful city, He's got the whole world in his hands, Crucifixion, Deep river, Comin' thro' the rye,* and Schubert's *Ave Maria.* Provides details of her life, including her birthplace, friends that have helped her, her farm home in Connecticut, and the honors bestowed upon her. *Concerts on film series.*   (WAI)

Music from oil drums.   16 minutes.   RS-438.

Describes the historical development of the steel drum on the island of Trinidad. Shows how the instrument is made by hand and kept in tune; how drums with various tonal ranges are combined by the players to form a band; how perfection of rhythmic pattern is the ideal of the players; and how the instruments are adapted for use by a school group in the United States.   (P. and T. Seeger; Folkways)

Music of Africa.   30 minutes.   RS-741.

Features Fela Sowande of Nigeria, a leading African musicologist, composer, and organist, along with other Nigerian musicians demonstrating how contemporary African music has mingled traditional African and Western idioms to create new forms. Explains that African music places a greater stress on melody rather than rhythm. The music, therefore, more closely resembles African dialects where the meaning is expressed by tonal inflection. Summarizes from this that the talking drum can be either a musical function or a transmitter of messages. (NET; Indiana U A-V Center)

Music of Williamsburg.   29 minutes (color).   RSC-575.

Depicts the regular part that music played in the everyday life of eighteenth-century Williamsburg. Shows adults and children performing vocal and instrumental music that ranges from the simplest folk songs to that performed by a semi-professional ensemble and a professional opera company. Selections included are the sailor's chantey *Johnny Todd,* Negro folk music, *Psalm 150, Sonata in D major* by D. Scarlatti, Handel's *Concerto in B flat major, Symphony no. 4* by Arne, and excerpts from Gay's *Beggar's opera.* (CW)

People of the Congo (The Mangbetu). 10 minutes. GS-16.

Shows the environment, activities, and customs of the Mangbetu people in the Congo region; the sources and nature of their food and its preparation; their primitive household equipment and their division of labor; head binding, facial treatments, and styles of hairdress; the bartering of services; ivory carving, the preparation of paint, designing and painting; the construction of a stringed musical instrument; and the demonstration of a native dance. (Erpi; EBEC).

Rhythm—instruments and movements. 11 minutes. RS-220.

A visit by the Indian, Thundering Hill, arouses a primary class's interest in rhythm. Shows the children collecting rhythmic instruments from China, Cuba, South America, and Africa and comparing their music with that of the drum, rattle, and bells played by Thundering Hill. Demonstrates how the children fit out their rhythm band with self-constructed gongs, rattles, cymbals, drums, and sticks and finally invite Thundering Hill back to hear their concert. (EBF; EBEC)

Rhythm of Africa. 16 minutes. GS-298.

Depicts the culture of the Chad in French Equatorial Africa. Shows various types of transportation, villages and markets, various forms of adornment, farming, fishing, weaving, and metal working. Native music is used throughout, and the ceremonial dance of atonement is shown. (Cocteau; Film Images)

The semantics of the popular song. 30 minutes. CS-1097.

Contrasts the attitude toward love developed by the lyrics of popular songs and the blues. Uses the concept of the idealization-frustration-despair disease to illustrate the orientation of the lyrics of most popular songs. Shows that the blues present a more realistic rather than magical treatment of love. Questions whether popular songs make attainment of emotional maturity more difficult. Featured guest is Clancy Hayes, jazz singer. *Language in action series.* (NET; Indiana U A-V Center)

Slavery. 30 minutes. CS-1663.

Based on actual testimony of former slaves, tells of the tragic and sometimes humorous experiences of life in the old South. Tells of small incidents in the lives of many slaves and depcits the liberation of slaves by the Yankee troups. Uses Negro spirituals to help tell the story of slavery. *History of the Negro people series.* (NET; Indiana U A-V Center)

Suite of Berber dances. 10 minutes. RS-285.

Discusses the background and customs of the Berbers of Morocco, and shows three types of Berber dances. Shows first a dance done by men and boys as entertainment for city dwellers, then a war dance, and third, the jug dance, performed by girls for the entertainment of men. Explains

the significance of some of the dance steps and postures.   (CCM; Film
Images).

The tender game.   6 minutes.   RSC-579 (color).

Presents an interpretation using semi-abstract animation of the song
"Tenderly," as performed by Ella Fitzgerald and the Oscar Peterson
Trio. The story tells of a girl and boy falling in love.   (Hubley; Stan-
dord U).

A time to dance.   29 minutes.   RS-523.

Discusses and illustrates the three major froms of dance—ethnic, ballet,
and modern. Introduces the series *A time to dance* with paintings, sculpture, and film clips showing ethnic dances throughout history and the
world. Follows two performances of European ethnic dances. Concludes
with examples of a seventeenth-century court dance, classical ballet,
and dance satire to introduce forms of modern dance. Features Melissa
Hayden and Jacques D'Ambroise, Daniel Negrin, and members of the
Ximenez-Vargas Company. *A time to dance series.*   (NET; Indiana U
A-V Center)

To hear your banjo play.   17 minutes.   RS-155.

Pictures the American folk singers in various parts of the country and
discusses briefly the development of folk music here. Pete Seeger is shown
singing and playing his banjo in a city setting, and then other singers,
including mountaineers, sharecroppers, migratory workers, Negroes, and
railroad builders are shown.   (Creative Age; Brandon)

When boys encounter puberty. 30 minutes.   NET-1473.

Uses dance routines and originally scored music to portray male adoles-
cent rituals as a means of passing boys to manhood. Emphasizes differences in methods of promotion and resulting personality types. Compares Americans, the Pokot of Kenya, and the Nupe of northern Nigeria.
People are taught to be different series.   (NET; Indiana U A-V Center)

A Selective List of Books and Articles

The materials listed below are primarily items which should be currently available. This small bibliography was selected from preliminary drafts for the third edition of *The Black-American Musical Heritage* which may be submitted for publication late in 1971.

Although it is commercially important to support the authors and publishing companies which are active in issuing these materials, potential researchers should be reminded that loan service between cooperating libraries is possible if the desired title is not available. Such arrangements can be made by the Interlibrary Loan Office or the reference desk of almost any local public or university library. This service is generally restricted to those patrons engaged in research above the undergraduate level, and loans are made from one participating library to another, who then loans it out to the individual.

Afro-American Music Opportunities Association, Inc. *AAMOA reports.* Maurice W. Britts, ed. Minneapolis: v.1 (1969)– .

Alberts, Arthur S. *Tribal, folk and café music of West Africa, recorded and edited.* Texts and commentaries by Melville Herskovits, Duncan Emrich, Richard Waterman and Marshall Stearns. New York: Field Recordings, 1950.

Alen, William Francis, 1830–1889, comp. *Slave songs of the United States; the complete original collection (136 songs).* Collected and compiled by William Francis Allen, Charles Pickard Ware and Lucy McKim Garrison in 1867. New York: Dover Publications, 1970.

Allison, Roland Lewis, 1923– *Classification of the vocal works of Harry T. Burleigh (1866–1949) and some suggestions for their use in teaching diction in singing.* Ann Arbor: University Microfilms (66-14,791), 1966. 394p. Dissertation, Indiana University.

Anderson, Marian. *My Lord, what a morning; an autobiography.* New York: Viking Press, 1956. Library of Congress card 56-10402.

Aning, B.A. *An annotated bibliography of music and dance in English-speaking Africa.* Legon: University of Ghana, Institute of African Studies, 1967.

Ankermann, Bernhard. *Die afrikanischen Musikinstrumente.* xii, 132p. Dissertation, Leipzig, 1901.

Aretz de Ramón y Rivera, Isabel. *Resumen de un estudio sobre las expresiones negras en el folklore musical y coreografico de Venezuela.* Caracas: Instituto de Antropología y Historia y de Filología "Andres Bell," Facultad

de Humanidades y Educación, Universidad Central de Venezuela, 19—.
Library of Congress card 63-4238rev/MN.

Armstrong, Louis Daniel, 1800– . *Satchmo; my life in New Orleans.* New
York: Prentice-Hall, 1956.

Arvey, Verna, 1910– . "Negro music in the Americas" by Verna Arvey
and William Grant Still, in *Revue internationale de musique* (Bruxelles)
v.1 (1938) p.280–288.

———. *William Grant Still.* New York: J. Fischer & Bro., 1939.

Austin, William W. *Music in the 20th century, from Debussy to Stravinsky.*
New York: W. W. Norton, 1966. xvii, 708p. Library of Congress card
65-18776/MN.

Bailey, Pearl. *The raw Pearl.* New York: Harcourt, 1968. 206p.

Baines, Jimmy Dalton. *Samuel S. Sanford and Negro minstrelsy.* Ann Arbor:
University Microfilms (68-2890) 1967. 290p. Dissertation, George Pea-
body College for Teachers.

Baker, David N., Jr., 1931– . "The string player in jazz" in *Downbeat*
(Chicago) v. 37, no.5 (March 5, 1970) p.37–38, and following issues.

Ballanta, Nicholas George Julius. *St. Helena Island spirituals.* New York: G.
Schirmer, 1925.

Balliett, Whitney. *Dinosaurs in the morning; 41 pieces on jazz.* Philadelphia,
New York: J. B. Lippincott, 1962. 224p.

Bamboté, Makombo. "Traditional music alive in Central Africa" in *Afrika*
(Bonn) v.8, no.3 (1966) p.48.

Barony, Lawrence. "Introduction à la musique africaine" in *Musique de
tous les temps* (Paris) v.44, no.45 (April 1967) p.8–22.

Baskerville, David Ross. *Jazz influence on art music to mid-century.* Ann
Arbor: University Microfilms (65-15,175), 1965. 535p. Dissertation,
University of California, Los Angeles. Library of Congress card Mic65-
15,175.

*The baton; an informative monthly publication on viewing and listening en-
tertainment.* Philadelphia: Joseph V. Baker Associates, v.1-3, no. 10,
1950–1953.

Bechet, Sidney, 1891–1959. *Treat it gentle.* New York: Hill & Wang; London:
Cassell, 1960.

Belton, Geneva R. *The contributions of Negro music and musicians in World
War II.* Thesis (M.M.), Northwestern University, 1946.

Beltz, Carl. *The story of rock.* New York: Oxford University Press, 1969.
256p.

Berendt, Joachim Ernst. *Blues [English-Deutsch].* München: Nymphenberger
Verlag, 1962. (Schwarzer Gesang, 2).

———. *The new jazz book; a history and guide.* Transl. from the German
by Dan Morgenstern (from *Das Jazz Buch; Entwicklung und Bedeutung
der Jazz Musik*). New York: Hill & Wang, 1962. 314p.

———. *Spirituals; geistliche Lieder der Neger Amerikas.* München: Nymphenberger Verlag, 1961, 1955. Library of Congress card 63-38350/M.

"Bibliography of Negro folk songs" in *Journal of the American Folklore Society* (New York) v.24 (1911) p.393-394.

Billups, Kenneth Brown, 1918– . *The inclusion of Negro music as a course of study in the school curriculum.* Thesis (M.M.), Northwestern University, 1947.

Bims, Hamilton. "Felicia Weathers: dauntless diva" in *Ebony* (Chicago) v.25, no.7 (May 1970) p.52–56, 58.

Blackring, John A. R. *The role of music amongst the Venda of the northern Transvaal.* Johannesburg: International Library of African Music, 1957.

Blackstone, Orin, comp. *Index to jazz: part 1 (A-E).* New Orleans: The compiler, 1950. 312p.

Blesh, Rudi, 1899– . *Shining trumpets; a history of jazz.* London: Cassell, 1954. xvi, 392p.

———. *They all played ragtime.* Rev., with new additional material, including scores to 13 never before published compositions. New York: Oak Publications, 1966. xxiv, 347p.

Bontemps, Arna. *Chariot in the sky; a study of the Jubilee Singers.* Illustrations by Cyrus Leroy Baldridge. Philadelphia, Toronto: John C. Winston, 1951.

Bradford, Perry. *Born with the blues; Perry Bradford's own story: the true story of the pioneering blues singers and musicians in the early days of jazz.* New York: Oak Publications, 1965. 175p.

Braithwaite, Coleridge A. *The achievements and contributions to the history of music by Samuel Coleridge-Taylor, colored English musician.* Thesis (A.B.), Harvard University, 1939.

Brandel, Rose. *The music of central Africa; an ethnomusicological study.* New York: William S. Heinman; Den Haag: Martinus Nijhoff, 1961. xii, 272p.

Brawley, Benjamin Griffith, 1882– . *The Negro genius; a new appraisal of the achievement of the American Negro in literature and the fine arts.* New York: Biblo & Tannen, 1966, 1937. xii, 366p.

Broonzy, William, d.1958. *Big Bill blues; William Broonzy's story as told to Yannick Bruynoghe.* Illus. by Paul Oliver. Foreword by Charles Ed. Smith. New York: Oak Publications, 1964. 176p.

Burlin, Natalie (Curtis), 1875–1921. *Negro folk-songs.* New York: G. Schirmer, 1918–1919. 4 vols. (Hampton series, 6716, 6726, 2576, 6766).

———. "A plea for our native art" in *Musical quarterly* (New York) v.6 (1920) p.175–178.

Burns, Jim. "Miles Davis: the early years" in *Jazz journal* (London) v.23, no.1 (Jan. 1970) p.2–4.

Butcher, Margaret (Just). *The Negro in American culture.* Based on materials left by Alain Locke. New York: Alfred A. Knopf, 1956.

Cable, George Washington. "Creole slave songs" in *Century magazine* (New York) v.31, no.6 (April 1886) p.807–828.

Carámbula, Rubén. *Negro y tambor; poemas, pregones, danzas y leyendas sobre motivos del folklore afrorioplatense.* Melodias y anotaciones ritmicas del autor. Ensayo literario sobre el candombe; estudio sobre el lenguaje afro-criollo de los negros rioplatenses. Ilus. de Guillermo E. Clulow. Buenos Aires [?]: Editorial Folklórica Americana, 1952. 234p.

Carawan, Guy, 1928– *Freedom is a constant struggle; songs of the freedom movement with documentary photographs.* By Guy and Candie Carawan. New York: Oak Publications, 1968. Library of Congress card 67-27261/M.

———. *We shall overcome!, songs of the Southern freedom movement.* Compiled for the Student Non-Violent Coordinating Committee. New York: Oak Publications, 1963. 112p. Library of Congress card 63-23278/M.

Carrington, John F. *Talking drums of Africa.* New York: Negro Universities Press, 1969, 1949. 96p.

Caswell, Austin B. "What is Black music?" in *Music journal* (New York) v.27, no.8 (October 1969) p.31.

Charters, Ann, ed. *The ragtime songbook; songs of the ragtime era by Scott Joplin, Hughie Cannon, Ben Harney, Will Marion Cook, Alex Rogers and others.* Compiled and ed. with historical notes concerning the songs and times. New York: Oak Publications, 1965. 112p.

Charters, Samuel Barclay. *The bluesmen; the story and the music of the men who made the blues.* New York: Oak Publications, 1967. 223p.

———. *Jazz: New Orleans, 1885–1963; an index to the Negro musicians of New Orleans.* Rev. ed. New York: Oak Publications, 1963. 173p.

———. *The poetry of the blues.* Photographs by Ann Charters. New York: Oak Publications, 1963. 111p.

Christensen, Abigail M. Holmes. "Spirituals and shouts of southern Negroes" in *Journal of the American Folklore Society* (New York) v.7 (1894) p.154–155.

Clark, Edgar Rogie, 1917– "Music education in the Negro school and college" in *Journal of Negro education* (Washington) v.9 (1940) p.580–590.

———. "Negro folk music in America" in *Journal of the American Folklore Society* (New York) v.64 (1951) p.281-287.

Cohn, Nik. *Rock from the beginning.* New York: Stein and Day, 1969. 256p.

Cook, Will Marion, 1869–1944. "Cloundy, the origin of the cakewalk: how the first all-Negro show landed on Broadway in 1898" in *Theatre arts,* v.31 (September 1947) p.61–65.

Cooke, Peter R. "A music course in Uganda" in *Notes on education and research in African music* (Legon) no.1 (July 1967) p.32–37.

Corrêa de Azevedo, Luís Heitor. "L'héritage africain dans la musique du nouveau monde" in *Revue musicale* (Paris) no. spécial 242 (1958) p.109–112.

Courlander, Harold, 1908– *The drum and the hoe; life and lore of the Haitian people.* Berkeley, Los Angeles: University of California Press, 1960. xv, 371p.

————. *Negro folk music, U.S.A.* New York: Columbia University Press, 1970.

————. *Negro songs from Alabama.* Music transcribed by John Benson Brooks. New York: Oak Publications, 1963. Library of Congress card 63-23691.

Cox, John Harrington, ed. *Folk-songs of the South.* Collected under the auspices of the West Virginia Folklore Society. New York: Dover, 1967. xxxii, 545p. (Dover books on folklore, popular culture, folk art, T1804).

Crawford, Lucille Hayes. *The musical activities of James Weldon Johnson.* Thesis (M.A.), Fisk University, 1941.

Creed, Ruth. *African influences on Latin-American music.* Thesis (M.M.), Northwestern University, 1947.

Cusack, Thomas. *Jelly Roll Morton; an essay in discography.* London: Cassell, 1952. vii, 9, 40p.

Daly, John. *Song in his heart; the life and times of James A. Bland.* Introd. by Harry F. Byrd, illus. by Marian L. Larer. Philadelphia: John C. Winston, 1951. ix, 102p.

Dance, Stanley. *Jazz era; the 'forties.* London: MacGibbon & Kee, 1961. 253p.

Daniel, Vattel Elbert. "Ritual and stratification in Chicago Negro churches" in *American sociological review,* v.7 (1942) p.352–361.

Dankworth, Avril. *Jazz: an introduction to its musical basis.* London, New York: Oxford University Press, 1968. xi, 91p.

Daughtry, Willia Estelle. *Sissieretta Jones: a study of the Negro's contribution to nineteenth century American concert and theatrical life.* Ann Arbor: University Microfilms (68-13,823), 1968. x, 241p. Dissertation, Syracuse University, 1968.

Davis, Sammy, Jr. *Yes, I can.* New York: Farrar, Straus & Giroux, 1965.

de Lerma, Dominique-René, 1928–   . "Black-American music viewed from Europe" in *Your musical cue* (Bloomington) v.6, no.3 (December 1969/ January 1970) p.22–24.

————. *The Black-American musical heritage; a preliminary and selective bibliography.* Kent (Ohio): Kent State University, School of Library Science, for the Midwest Chapter of the Music Library Association, 1969. 45p. (Explorations in music librarianship, 3).

————, ed. *Black music; a preliminary register of the composers and their works.* Kent (Ohio): Kent State University Press. Expected date of publication: 1971.

————. "Bridgetower: Beethoven's Black violinist" in *Your musical cue* (Bloomington) v.5, no.3 (December 1968/January 1969) p.7–9.

Demeusy, Bertrand, comp. *Discography of Lionel Hampton, 1954–1958.* By Bertrand Demeusy & Otto Flückiger. Basel: Jazz-Publications, 1962. 29p.

Dennison, Tim. *The American Negro and his amazing music.* New York: Vantage Press, 1963. 76p.

Dett, Robert Nathaniel, 1882–1943. *The development of the Negro spiritual.* Mineapolis: Schmitt, Hall & McCreary, 1936.

————. *Religious folk-songs of the Negro as sung at Hampton Institute.* Hampton (Va.): Hampton Institute Press, 1927. Library of Congress card 27-10635.

Dexter, Dave. *The jazz story, from the 90's to the 60's.* With a foreword by Woody Herman. Englewood Cliffs (N.J.): Prentice-Hall, 1964. xiii, 176p.

Dietz, Betty Warner. *Musical instruments of Africa; their nature, use and place in the life of a deeply musical people.* By Betty Warner Dietz and Michaek Babatunde Olatunji. New York: John Day, 1965. 115p., phonodisc.

Dixon, Christa. *Wesen und Wandel geistlicher Volkslieder: Negro Spirituals.* Wuppertal: Jugenddienst, 1967. 333p.

Dixon, Robert M. *Blues and gospel records, 1902–1942.* By Robert M. Dixon and John Godrich. Swansea [?]: 1963. 765p. Library of Congress card 64-6615/MN.

Dorigné, Michel. *Jazz I; les origines du jazz, le style Nouvelle Orléans et ses prolongements.* Paris: L'École des Loisirs, 1968. 160p.

DuBois, William Edward Burghardt. *The souls of Black folk.* New York: Avon Books, 1969.

Duncan, John. *Afro-American music; a guide for students [in] Music 444–445, 544–545.* Montgomery: Alabama State University, 1969. 58p.

Durham, Frank. *DuBose Heyward; the man who wrote "Porgy."* Columbia: University of South Carolina Press, 1954. xiii, 152p.

Echezona, William W. C. *Ibo musical instruments in Ibo culture,* Ann Arbor: University Microfilms, 1963. Dissertation, Michigan State University. Library of Congress card Mic64-4950.

Edet, Edna M. "Music education in Nigeria" in *Notes on education and research in African music* (Legon) no.1 (July 1967) p.38–42.

Eisen, Jonathan, comp. *The age of rock, sound of the American cultural revolution; a reader.* New York: Random House, 1969. 388p.

Elmenhorst, Gernot W. *Die Jazz-Diskothek.* Von Gernot W. Elmenhorst & Walter von Bebenburg. Reinbeck bei Hamburg: Rowohlt, 1961. 362p. (Rowohlt's Monographies, 55/56).

Epstein, Dena J. "Slave music in the United States before 1860" in *Notes*

(Ann Arbor) v.20, no.2 (Spring 1963) p.195–212; v.20, no.3 (Summer 1963) p.377–390.

Europe, Jim. "A Negro explains jazz" in *Literary digest*, v.61 (April 26, 1919) p.28–29.

Feather, Leonard. *The encyclopedia of jazz in the sixties*. Foreword by John Lewis. New York: Horizon Press, 1966.

Fisher, Miles Mark, 1899–   . *Negro slave songs in the United States*. New York: Russell & Russell, 1968. 223p.

Fletcher, Tom, 1873–1954. *100 years of the Negro in show business; the Tom Fletcher story*. New York: Burdge, 1954. x, 337p. Library of Congress card 55-1843.

Fox, Charles. *Jazz in perspective*. London: British Broadcasting Corporation, 1969.

————. *Jazz on record; a critical guide*. By Charles Fox [and others]. London: Hutchinson, 1960. 352p.

Francis, André. *Jazz*. New York: Grove Press, 1960.

Gabree, John. *The world of rock*. Greenwich (Conn.): Fawcett Publications, 1968. 176p.

Gammond, Peter, ed. *Duke Ellington; his life and music*. London: Phoenix House, 1958.

Garland, Phyl. *The sound of soul*. Chicago: Henry Regnery, 1969.

Gaskin, L. J. P., comp. *A select bibliography of music in Africa*. New York: International Publications Service, 1965.

George, Zelma Watson, 1903–   . *A guide to Negro music: an annotated bibliography of Negro folk music, and art music by Negro composers, or based on Negro thematic material*. Ann Arbor: University Microfilms (8021), 1954. 302p. Dissertation (Ed.D.), New York University, 1953. Library of Congress card Mic55-3378.

Gillis, Frank. *Ethnomusicology and folk music: an international bibliography of dissertations and theses*, by Frank Gillis and Alan P. Merriam. Middletown (Conn.); Wesleyan University Press for the Society for Ethnomusicology, 1966. vii. 183p.

Gitler, Ira. *Jazz masters of the forties*. New York: Macmillan; London: Collier-Macmillan, 1966. 290p.

Glazer, Irving William. *Negro music in early America from 1619 to the Civil War*. Thesis (M.A.), New York University, 1945.

Götze, Werner. *Dizzy Gillespie; ein Porträt*. Wetzlar: Pegasus, 1960. 48p. (Jazz Bücherei, 7).

Goines, Leonard. *Music and music education in predominately Negro colleges and universities offering a four-year program of music study terminating in a degree*. Ann Arbor: University Microfilms, 1963. 292p. Dissertation, Columbia University. Library of Congress card 64-1476.

Gold, Robert S. *A jazz lexicon*. New York: A. A. Knopf, 1964. xxvi, 363p.

Goldberg, Joe. *Jazz masters of the fifties.* New York: Macmillan, 1965. 246p.

Gombosi, Otto. "The pedigree of the blues" in *Proceedings of the Music Teachers National Association* (1946) p.382–389.

Gorer, Geoffrey. *Africa dances.* New York: W. W. Norton, 1962.

Graham, Philip. *Showboats; the history of an American institution.* Austin: University of Texas Press, 1951. x, 224p.

Graham, Shirley. *Paul Robeson; citizen of the world.* New York: Julian Messner, 1946.

Greenway, John. *American folksongs of protest.* Gloucester: Peter Smith, 1962. x, 348p.

Grissom, Mary Allen. *The Negro sings a new heaven.* Chapel Hill: University of North Carolina Press, 1930. 101p. (University of North Carolina social study series).

Günther, Robert. *Musik in Rwanda; ein Beitrag zur Musikethnologie Zentralafrikas, avec un résumé en français.* Tervuren: Musée Royal de l'Afrique Central, 1964. 128p. (its Annales, série in-8°, sciences humaines, 50).

Hadlock, Richard. *Jazz masters of the twenties.* New York: Macmillan, 1965. 255p.

Handy, William Christopher, 1873–1958. *Father of the blues.* New York: Collier-Macmillan, 1970. 320p.

————. *Negro authors and composers of the United States.* New York: Handy Brothers, 1941.

Hannerz, Ulf. *Soulside; inquiries into ghetto culture and community.* New York: Columbia University Press, 1969.

Hare, Maud (Cuney), 1874–1936. *Negro musicians and their music.* Washington: The Associated Publishers, 1936.

Harrison, Max. *Charlie Parker.* New York: Barnes, 1961, 1960. 84p. (Perpetua book, P-4034).

Hartwig, Charlotte Mae. *An intercultural approach to music education in underdeveloped areas.* Thesis (M.M.E.), Indiana University, 1967.

Haywood, Charles, 1904– . *A bibliography of North American folklore and folksongs.* 2d rev. ed. New York: Dover, 1961. xxxii, 748; xii, 749–1301p.

Hentoff, Nat. *The jazz life.* London: Hamilton, 1964, 1961. 221p.

Herskovits, Melville Jean, 1895– . "Drums and drummers in Afro-Brazilian cult life" in *Musical quarterly* (New York) v.30, no.4 (1944) p.447–492.

Herzog, George. *Research in primitive and folk music in the United States.* Washington: American Council of Learned Societies, 1936. (its Bulletin, no. 24).

Hodeir, André. *Jazz: its evolution and essence.* New York: Grove Press, 1956.

————. *Toward jazz.* Transl. by Noel Burch. New York: Grove Press, 1962. 224p.

Hornbostel, Erich Moritz von. *African Negro music.* London: Oxford University Press, 1928.

Horne, Lena. *Lena.* By Lena Horne and Richard Schickel. London: Deutsch; Garden City (N.Y.): Doubleday, 1966. 300p.

Howard, John Tasker. *Our American music; a comprehensive history from 1620 to the present.* 4th ed. New York: Thomas Y. Crowell, 1965. xxii, 944p.

Hoyt, Edwin Palmer. *Paul Robeson, the American Othello.* Cleveland: World Publishing Co., 1967. xxii, 360p.

Hughes, Allen. "The kids want rock; why don't teachers teach it?" [reprinted from the *New York times*] in *Triad* (Oxford, Ohio) v.37, no.4 (February 1970), p.6–7.

Hughes, Langston, 1902–1967. *Black magic; a pictoral history of the Negro in American entertainment.* By Langston Hughes and Milton Meltzer. Englewood Cliffs (N.J.): Prentice-Hall, 1967. 375p.

Huskisson, Yvonne. *Die Bantoe-komponiste van suider-Afrika; the Bantu composers of southern Africa.* Foreword by Douglas Fuchs. Johannesburg (S.A.): South African Broadcasting Corporation, 1970.

Hyslop, Graham. *The prospects for music in education in Kenya.* Nairobi: Government Printer, 1964. 20p.

Jackson, George Pullen, 1874– . *White and Negro spirituals; their life span and kinship, tracing 200 years of untrammeled song making and singing among our country folk, with 116 songs as sung by both races.* New York: J. J. Augustin, 1943. Library of Congress card 44-3923. [A paperback reprint was reportedly issued in 1965].

Jackson, Mahalia. *Movin' on up.* By Mahalia Jackson with Even McLeod Wylie. New York: Hawthorne Books, 1966. 212p.

Jahn, Janheinz. *Blues and work songs.* Frankfurt am Main, Hamburg: Fischer-Bücherei, 1964. (Fischer-Bücherei, 597).

———. *Negro Spirituals.* Ed. & trans. Frankfurt am Main: Fischer-Bücherei, 1962. Library of Congress card 63-45493/M.

James, Sydney Michael. *Miles Davis.* London: Cassell, 1961. 90p. (Kings of jazz series, 9).

Jazz catalogue; a complete discography of all jazz releases issued in Great Britain. London: Jazz Journal, 1965. 321p.

Jørgensen, John. *Mosaik Jazzlexikon.* Hrsg. von John Jörgensen, Erik Wiedemann. Ins Deutsche übertragen und bearbeitet von Hans-Georg Ehmke from *Jazzens hvem-hvand-hvor*, by Jørgensen. Hamburg: Mosaik Verlag, 1966. 399p.

Johns, Altona (Trent). *Play songs of the deep South.* Washington: Associated Publishers, 1944. Library of Congress card 45-18263.

Johnson, Guy Benton, 1901– . *Folk culture on St. Helena Island, South*

Carolina. Foreword by Don Yoder. Hatboro (Pa.): Folklore Associates, 1968. xxi, 183p.

Johnson, James Weldon, 1871–1938. *The books of American Negro spirituals, including The book of American Negro spirituals and The second book of Negro spirituals,* by J. W. Johnson and J. Rosamond Johnson. New York: Viking Press, 1964.

Jones, Arthur Morris. *Studies in African music.* New York: Oxford University Press, 1959. 2 vols.

Jones, Charles Colcock, 1831–1893. *Negro myths from the Georgia coast, told in the vernacular.* Detroit: Singing Tree Press, 1969, 1888. Library of Congress card 68-21779.

Jones, LeRoi. *Black music.* Unabridged republication of the first edition published in 1963. New York: William Morrow, 1968. 221p.

———. *Blues people; Negro music in white America.* New York: Apollo, 1965. 244p.

Katz, Bernard, ed. *The social implications of early Negro music in the United States, with over 150 of the songs, many of them with their music.* New York: Arno Press, 1969. 146p.

Katz, Frederic M. *Rock: the history, criticism and discography of rock-and-roll music.* Clifton (N.J.): William Morrow, 1968.

Keepnews, Orrin, comp. *A pictoral history of jazz; people and places from New Orleans to modern jazz.* New ed. rev. by Orrin Keepnews, with Bill Grauer, Jr. New York: Crown Publishers, 1966. 297p.

Keil, Charles. *Urban blues.* Chicago: University of Chicago Press, 1968, 1966. 231p. Library of Congress card 66-13876/M.

King, Anthony. *Yoruba sacred music from Ekiti.* Ibadan (Nigeria): Idaban University Press, 1961. 45p.

Kirby, Percival Robson. *The musical instruments of the native races of South Africa.* 2d ed. Johannesburg: Witwatersrand University Press, 1965. 293p.

Kirkeby, W. T. *Ain't misbehavin': the story of Fats Waller.* By the author in collaboration with Duncan P. Schiedt and Sinclair Traill. London: Davies; New York: Dodd, Mead, 1966. 575p.

Klotman, Robert H. "The supervisor must know the city score" in *Music educators journal* (Washington) v.56, no.5 (January 1970) p.58–59, 125–130.

Kmen, Henry A. *Music in New Orleans: the formative years, 1791–1841.* Baton Rouge: Louisiana State University Press, 1966. vii, 314p.

Krehbiel, Henry Edward. *Afro-American folksongs; a study in racial and national music.* New York: G. Schirmer, Frederick Unger, 1962.

Kubik, Gerhard. *Mehrstimmigkeit und Tonsysteme in Zentral- und Ostofrika; Bemerkungen zu den eigenen, in Phonogrammarchiv der Österr. Akad. der Wissenschaft archivierten Expeditionsaufnahmen.* Wien: Hermann

Böhlaus, 1968. 65p. (Österreichische Akademie der Wissenchaft, Philosophische-Historische Klasse, Sitzungsberichte 254, Band 4, Abhandlung, Mitteilungen der Phonogrammarchivs-Kommission, 83).

Lambert, George E. *Duke Ellington.* New York: Barnes, 1961, 1959. 88p. (Perpetua book, P-4029).

Landeck, Beatrice, ed. *Echoes of Africa in folk songs of the Americas.* Instrumental arrangements by Milton Kaye. English version of foreign lyrics by Margaret Marks. New York: McKay, 1961. viii, 184p. Library of Congress card M61-1013.

Lange, Horst Heinz. *Die deutsche "78er"; Discographie der Jazz und Hot-Dance-Musik 1903–1958.* Berlin: Colloguium Verlag, 1966.

———. *Jazz in Deutschland; die deutsche Jazz-Chronique 1900–1960.* Berlin: Colloquium Verlag, 1966. 210p.

Larkin, Philip. *All what jazz; a record diary, 1961–8.* London: Faber & Faber, 1970.

Laubenstein, Paul Fritz. "Race values in Afroamerican music" in *Musical quarterly* (New York) v.16 (1930) p.378–403.

Laurenty, Jean S. *Les cordophones du Congo belge et du Ruanda-Urundi.* Tervuren: Musée Royal du Congo Belge, 1960. 230p.; 38p. (its Annales, nouvelle série, science de l'homme).

Lawrenz, Marguerite Martha. *Bibliography and index of Negro music.* Detroit: Detroit Public Schools, Department of Music Education, 1968.

Leadbetter, Huddie, 1885?–1949. *Leadbelly; a collection of world-famous songs,* edited by John A. Lomax and Alan Lomax. New York: Folkways Music Publishers, 1959. 80p. Library of Congress card M59-1604.

———. *The leadbelly legend.* New York: TRO Folkways Music, 1965. Library of Congress card 65-80113/M.

Leadbitter, Mike. *Blue records, January 1943 to December 1966.* By Mike Leadbitter and Neil Slaven. London: Hanover Books; distributed in U.S.A. and Canada by Oak Publications (New York), 1968. 381p.

Lee, Robert Charles. "The Afro-American foundation of the jazz idiom and its cultural heritage" in *Jazz forum* (Warsaw) nos. 9–13 (September 1970–September 1971).

———. "The social dilemma and aesthetic quandry over jazz" in *Ruch muzyczny* (Warsaw) nos. 15-16 (August 1969).

Lehmann, Theo. *Blues and trouble* [in German]. Berlin: Henschel, 1966. 190p. Library of Congress card 67-76077/MN.

———. *Negro Spirituals; Geschichte und Theologie.* Witten, Berlin: Eskart Verlag, 1965. 415p. Library of Congress 67-82778/MN.

Locke, Alain LeRoy, 1886– . *The Negro and his music. Negro art: past and present.* New York: Arno Press, 1969. 142, 122p.

Lomax, Alan. *Black musical style.* New York: Cantometrics Project, 1969.

Lomax, Ruby Terrill. "Negro baptizing" in *Texas Folklore Society Publications* (Dallas & Austin) no.10 (1944) p.1–8.

Longstreet, Stephen. *The real jazz, old and new.* Baton Rouge: Louisiana State University Press, 1956.

————. *Sportin' house; a history of the New Orleans sinners and the birth of jazz.* Los Angeles: Sherbourne Press, 1965. 293p.

Lucas, John Samuel. *Rhythm of Negro music and Negro poetry.* Thesis (M.A.), University of Missouri, 1945.

Lyric. Los Angeles, v.1–, 1958– .

McBrier, Vivian Flagg. *The life and works of Robert Nathaniel Dett.* Ann Arbor: University Microfilms (67-17,142), 1967. 217p. (Studies in music, 32). Dissertation, Catholic University of America.

McCarthy, Albert J. *Coleman Hawkins.* London: Cassell, 1963. 90p. (Kings of jazz series, 12).

————. *Jazz on records; a critical guide to the first fifty years, 1917–1967.* By A. McCarthy, Alun Morgan, Paul Oliver and Max Harrison. London: Hanover Books; distributed in U.S.A. by Oak Publications (New York), 1968. 416p.

————. *Louis Armstrong.* New York: Barnes, 1961, 1959. 85p. (Perpetua book, P-4033).

McCray, Norma. *Teaching units on Afro-American composers*: 1. Harry T. Burleigh; 2. Robert Nathaniel Dett; 3. Edward Kennedy (Duke) Ellington; 4. William Grant Still. Washington: Howard University, Project in African Music, [n.d.?].

McRae, Barry. *The jazz cataclysm.* South Brunswick (N.Y.): A. S. Barnes; London: Dent, 1967. 184p.

Makeba, Miriam. *The world of African song.* Introd. and notes by Solomon Mbabi-Katana. [n.p.?]: Quadrangle, 1970. ca. 192p.

Malson, Lucien. *Les maîtres du jazz.* 5e éd. Paris: Presses Universitaires de France, 1966. 128p.

Marcus, Greil, comp. *Rock and roll will stand.* Boston: Beacon Press, 1969. 182p.

Marks, J. *Rock and other four letter words; music of the electric generation.* New York: Bantam Books, 1968.

Marsh, J. B. T. *The story of the Jubilee Singers; with their songs.* Rev. ed. New York: Negro Universities Press, 1969. viii, 243p. Library of Congress card 79-78583.

Mbabi-Katana, Solomon. *An introduction to East African music for schools.* Kampala: Milton Obote Foundation, 1967. Thesis, Washington State University.

Mecklenburg, Carl Grégor, Herzog zu. *International jazz bibliography (1919–1968).* Baden-Baden: Editions P. H. Heitz, 1970. ca. 180p.

————. *Die Theorie des Blues im modernen Jazz.* Von C. G. Herzog zu Mecklenburg & Waldemar Scheck. Baden-Baden: Librairie Heitz, 1963.

Meller, Wilfred. *Music in a new found land: themes and developments in the history of American music.* New York: Alfred A. Knopf, 1965.

Merriam, Alan P. *The anthropology of music.* Evanston: Northwestern University Press, 1964. xi, 358p.

————. *A bibliography of jazz.* By Alan P. Merriam with the assistance of Robert J. Benford. Philadelphia: American Folklore Society, 1954. xii, 145p. (Bibliographical series, v.4).

————. *Instruments and instrumental usages in the history of jazz.* Thesis (M.M.), Northwestern University, 1948.

Merritt, Nancy G. *Negro spirituals in American collections; a handbook for students studying Negro spirituals.* Thesis (M.A.), Howard University, 1940.

Mezzro, Milton. *Really the blues.* By Milton "Mezzo" Mezzro and Bernard Wolfe. London: Transworld, 1961. 381p.

Montgomery, Elizabeth Rider. *William C. Handy, father of the blues.* Illus. by David Hodges. Champaign (Ill.): Garrad Publishing Co., 1968. 95p. (Americans all series).

Nathan, Hans, 1910– . *Dan Emmett and the rise of early Negro minstrelsy.* Norman: University of Oklahoma Press, 1962. xiv, 496p. Library of Congress card 62-10769.

Negro music journal; a monthly devoted to the educational interest of the Negro in music. Washington: v.1–2, no.1–15, September 1902–November 1903.

Nettl, Bruno. *Folk and traditional music of the western continents.* Englewood Cliffs (N.J.): Prentice-Hall, 1965.

————. *An introduction to folk music in the United States.* Rev. ed. Detroit: Wayne State University Press, 1962. Library of Congress card 62-16346/MN.

————. "Die Negro-Spirituals" in *Musica* (Kassel, May/June 1950) p.197–199.

————. *Reference materials in ethnomusicology; a bibliographic essay.* 2d ed., rev. Detroit: Information Coordinators, 1967. xv, 40p. (Detroit studies in music bibliography, 1).

Nettl, Paul. "Angelo Soliman, friend of Mozart" in *Phylon* (Atlanta) v.7, no.1 (March 1946).

————. "Traces of the Negroid in the mauresques of the 16th and 17th century" in *Phylon* (Atlanta) v.8, no. 10 (January 1944).

Newman, Shirlee P. *Marian Anderson; lady from Philadelphia.* Philadelphia: Westminster Press, 1965. 175p.

Nicolausson, Harry. *Svensk jazz diskografi.* Stockholm Nordisk Musikförlag, 1953. 115p.

Nikiprowetzky, Tolia, ed. *La musique dans la vie; l'Afrique, ses prolonge-ments, ses voisins.* Etude réalisée sous les auspices de l'OCORA. Paris: Office de Coopération Radiophonique, 1967. 297p.

Nketia, Joseph Hanson Kwabena. *African music in Ghana.* Evanston: North-western University Press, 1963. ix, 148p. (Northwestern University, African studies, 11).

————. *Drumming in Akan communities of Ghana.* London: Published in behalf of the University of Ghana by Thomas Nelson & Sons; Evanston: Northewestern University Press, 1963. x, 212p.

Obojski, Robert. *Prodigy at the piano; the amazing story of "Sugarchile" Robinson.* Parma (Ohio): The Author, 1962. 160p.

Odum, Howard Washington. *The Negro and his songs; a study of typical Negro songs.* By Howard Washington Odum and Guy B. Johnson. New York: Negro Universities Press, 1968, 1925. 306p.

Oliver, Paul. *Bessie Smith.* New York: Barnes, 1961, 1959. 82p. (Perpetua book, P-4031).

————. *The meaning of the blues* [originally titled *The blues fell this morn-ing*]. Foreword by Richard Wright. New York: Collier, 1963. 372p.

————. *Conversation with the blues.* New York: Horizon Press, 1965. 217p. Library of Congress card 65-10650/MN.

Ortiz Fernández, Fernando. *La africanía de la música folklórica de Cuba.* 2. ed. revisada. La Habaña: Editora Universitaria, 1965. xix, 489p.

————. *Los instrumentos de la música afrocubano.* La Habaña: Cardenas y Cia, 1952–1954. 306; 344; 472, 4 leaves; 449p. 4 vols.

Ortiz Oderigo, Néstor R., 1912– . *La música afronorteamericano.* Buenos Aires: Editorial Universitaria de Buenos Aires, 1963. 1962. 109p. (Bib-lioteca de América, libros del tiempo nuevo, 6). Library of Congress card 64-4267/MN.

Ostransky, Leroy. *The anatomy of jazz.* Seattle: University of Washington Press; Nottingham: Hall, 1960. xii, 362p.

Panassié, Hugues. *The real jazz* [transl. of *Histoire du vrai jazz*]. New York: Smith & Durrall, 1960.

Parrish, Lydia (Austin), comp. *Slave songs of the Georgia Sea Islands.* Mu-sic transcribed by Creighton Churchill and Robert MacGimsey. Introd. by Olin Downes. Foreword by Bruce Jackson. Hatboro (Pa.): Folklore Associates, 1965. xi, xxiii, 256p. Library of Congress card 65-8748/M.

Patterson, Lindsay, comp. *The Negro in music and art.* 2d ed. rev. New York: Publishers Co., 1968. xvi, 304p. (International library of Negro life and history, v.3).

Patton, Marian. *Music in Negro schools of the college level.* Thesis (M.M.), Eastman School of Music, 1940.

Phillips, Theodore De W. *The life and musical compositions of S. Coleridge-Taylor.* Thesis (M.M.), Oberlin College, 1935.

Pleasants, Henry. *Serious music and all that jazz; an adventure in music criticism.* New York: Simon and Schuster, 1969. 256p.

Powne, Michael. *Ethiopian music; and introduction: a survey of ecclesiatical and secular Ethiopian music and instruments.* London, New York: Oxford University Press, 1968, xviii, 156p.

Pyke, Launcelot Allen, II. *Jazz, 1920 to 1927; an analytical study.* Ann Arbor: University Microfilms (62-4988), 1962. 115p. Dissertation, State University of Iowa.

Ramsey, Frederic, Jr., 1915– *Been here and gone.* New Brunswick (N.J.): Rutgers University Press, 1960. 177p.

————. *A guide to longplay jazz records.* New York: Long Player Publications, 1954. xii, 263p.

Raniello, John, ed. *Prelude to the blues: an anthology of Black slave poetry.* Beverly Hills: Rainbow Press, 1969.

Rauhe, Hermann. *Musikerziehung durch Jazz.* Wolfenbüttel, Zürich: Möseler, 1962. 105p. (Beiträge zur Schulmusik, 12).

Reeder, Barbara. "Afro music: as tough as a Mozart quartet" in *Music educators journal* (Washington) v.56, no.5 (January 1970), p.88–91.

Reimer, Bennett. "General music for the black ghetto child" in *Music educators journal* (Washington) v.56, no.5 (January 1970), p.94–97, 145–152.

Reisner, Robert George. *Bird; the legend of Charlie Parker.* New York: Citadel Press, 1962. 256p.

————. *The literature of jazz; a preliminary bibliography.* With an introduction by Marshall W. Stearns. New York: New York Public Library, 1954. 53p.

Roach, Hildred. *Black music in America.* Springfield (Va.): Norvec Publishing Co., 1970.

Roxon, Lillian. *Rock encyclopedia.* New York: Grosset & Dunlap, 1969. 611p. Library of Congress card 77-75342.

Rust, Brian A., comp. *Jazz records, A–Z, 1897–1931.* Hatch End (Eng.): [n.p.?], 1961. 884p.

Sachs, Curt. *The rise of music in the ancient world.* New York: W. W. Norton, 1943.

————. *World history of the dance.* New York: W. W. Norton, 1940.

Sargent, Winthrop. *Jazz: a history.* Rev. ed. New York, London: McGraw-Hill, 1964. x, 286p.

Sayers, W. C. Berwick. *Samuel Coleridge-Taylor, musician; his life and letters.* London: Cassell, 1927.

Scarborough, Dorothy, 1878–1935. *On the trail of Negro folk-songs.* By Dorothy Scarborough and Ola Lee Gulledge. Foreword by Roger D. Abrahams. Hatboro (Pa.): Folklore Associates, 1963. ix, 295p. Library of Congress card 63-24576/MN.

Schuller, Gunther. *The history of jazz. Vol. I: Early jazz; its roots and musi-*

cal development. New York: Oxford University Press, 1968. xii, 401p. Library of Congress card 68-17610/MN.

Shapiro, Elliott. "Ragtime, U.S.A." in *Notes* (Washington) v.8, no.3 (June 1951), p.457–470.

Shapiro, Nat, comp. *Hear me talkin' to ya; the story of jazz as told by the men who made it.* New York: Dover Publications, 1966, 1955. xvi, 429p.

Shaw, Arnold J. *Belafonte; an unauthorized biography.* New York: Pyramid Books, 1961. 338p. (Pyramid R-556).

————. *The rock revolution.* New York: Crowell-Collier Press, 1969. 215p.

————. *World of soul: the black contributions to pop music.* New York: Cowles Education Corporation, 1969.

Shockett, Bernard Irwin. *A stylistic study of the blues as recorded by jazz instrumentalists, 1917–1931.* Ann Arbor: University Microfilms (66-7281), 1964. 233p. Dissertation, New York University.

Silver, Reuben. *A history of the Karamu Theatre of Karamu House, 1915–1960.* Dissertation, Ohio State University, 1961.

Simpson, Ralph Ricardo. *William Grant Still, the man and his music.* Ann Arbor: University Microfilms, 1964. 333p. Dissertation, Michigan State University, 1964. Library of Congress card Mic65-727.

Sjolund, James, comp. *The American Negro; a selected bibliography of materials including children's books, reference books, collections and anthologies, recordings, films and filmstrips.* Compiled by James Sjolund and Warren Burton. Olympia (Wash.): [n.p.?], 1969.

Southern, Eileen Stanza (Jackson). *The use of Negro folksong in symphonic form.* Thesis (M.A.), University of Chicago, 1941. [Note: Dr. Southern is publishing a book of source readings, and a historical study, both with W. W. Norton].

Spivey, Lenore. *Singing heart; a story based on the life of Marian Anderson.* Illus. by Howard and Thelma Hogan. Largo (Fla.): Community Service Foundation, 1963. 66p.

Stearns, Marshall Winslow. *Jazz dance; the story of American vernacular dance.* By Marshall Winslow Stearns and Jean Stearns. New York: Macmillan, 1968. xvi, 464p.

————. *The story of jazz,* with an expanded bibliography and a syllabus of fifteen lectures on the history of jazz. New York, Toronto: Mentor Books, 1958. 272p.

Stevenson, Janet. *Marian Anderson, singing to the world.* Chicago: Encyclopedia Britannica Press, 1963. 189p.

Still, William Grant. "The Negro musician in America" in *Music educators journal* (Washington), v.56, no.5 (January 1970), p. 100–101, 157–161.

Surge, Frank. *Singers of the blues.* Minneapolis: Lerner Publications, 1969. 63p.

Tallmadge, William H. "The responsorial and antiphonal practices in gospel song" in *Ethnomusicology* (Middletown, Conn.), v.12, no.2 (May 1968) p.219–238.

Thieme, Darius L. *African music; a briefly annotated bibliography*. Washington: Government Printing Office, 1964. xxvi, 55p.

———. *Social organization of Yoruba musicians*. Washington: Howard University. 1969. (Project in African music).

Thurman, Howard, 1899– *Deep river; reflections on the religious insight of certain Negro spirituals*. Port Washington (N.Y.): Kennikat Press, 1969, 1955. 93p.

Tones and overtones. Montgomery: Department of Music, Alabama State College, v.1– , 1954– .

Tracey, Hugh T. *Codification of African music and textbook project; a primer of practical suggestions for field research*. Roodepoort: International Library of African Music, 1969. 54p.

Trotter, James M. *Music and some highly musical people*. New York: Johnson Reprint Corporation, 1968(?), 1881. (Basic Afro-American reprint library).

Ulanov, Barry. *Duke Ellington*. New York: Creative Age Press, 1946.

Waterman, Richard Alan. " 'Hot' rhythms in Negro music" in *Journal of the American Musicological Society* (Princeton) v.1, no.1 (Spring 1948) p.24–37.

Waters, Ethel. *His eye is on the sparrow; an autobiography with Charles Samuels*. Garden City (N.Y.): Doubleday, 1951. 278p.

Wemen, Henry. *African music and the church in Africa*. Uppsala: Ludequistska Bokh., 1960. 296p. (Uppsala Univ. Arsskrift, Studia missionalia upsaliensa, 3).

White, Newman Ivey, 1892–1949. *American Negro folk songs*. Foreword by Bruce Jackson. Hatboro (Pa.): Folklore Associates, 1965, 1928. xxiv, 501p. Library of Congress card 65-1606.

Williams, Martin T., ed. *The art of jazz; essays on the nature and development of jazz*. New York: Grove Press, 1960. (Evergreen, E-272).

———. *Jazz masters of New Orleans*. New York: Macmillan; London: Collier-Macmillan, 1967. 287p.

———. *Jelly Roll Morton*. London: Cassell, 1962. 88p. (Kings of jazz, 110).

———. *King Oliver*. London: Cassell, 1960. 90p. (Kings of jazz, 8).

———. *Where's the melody?; a listener's introduction to jazz*. Rev. ed. New York: Pantheon Books, 1969. xvi, 205p.

Williams, Paul. *Outlaw blues; a book of rock music*. New York: E. P. Dutton, 1969. 191p.

Wilson, John S. *Jazz: the transition years, 1940–1960*. New York: Appleton-Century-Crofts, 1966. 185p.

Wise, Herbert H., ed. *Professional rock and roll.* New York: Collier; London: Collier-Macmillan, 1967. 94p.

Winter, Marian Hannah. "Juba and American minstrelsy" in *Dance index* (New York) v.6 (1947) p.28–47.

Work, John Wesley. *Jubilee.* New York: Holt, Reinhart & Winston, 1962. LC 62-12306/M.

Zenetti, Lothar. *Heisse (W)Eisen: Jazz, Spirituals, Beatsongs und Schlager in der Kirche.* München: Pfeiffer, 1966. 328p.

Sample Curricular Syllabi

The repertoires of Black music encompass virtually all styles and forms found in music by White composers of the past century. To this must be added, with proper emphasis, the *genres* shared by the two races (e.g., jazz and pop music), and those which are basically unique to Black culture. The development of class plans thus poses distinct challenges.

The teacher will have to decide if the course will integrate the new areas of study with those traditionally taught, or if specially designed courses will be dedicated to one, or to all, aspects of Black music. He will need to determine if the course should be directed to the non-music reader from Arts and Sciences, to the younger music major, or to the graduate student. In consideration of his students and the subject material, he will need to elect a strictly chronological approach, or one which is stylistic, or ethnic, or decide if he should guide his students first through that music which they already know. The decision of an Eastern urban teacher might not be satisfactory for one in the Midwest, or in the South, or in the Southwest. Each of these areas has a tradition and repertoire which may obligate special considerations.

The most "radical" and "student-oriented" approach (terminology favorably employed by the U.S. Office of Education early in 1970) which we have encountered is that of Professor Frank Suggs, at Illinois State University. He teaches music through participation, having the students prepare music from their immediate culture which is then tested off-campus, directly within the Black community.

Innovations within traditional classroom concepts are registered in the following course plans, kindly offered by the professors involved. This is a particularly generous and unselfish courtesy, especially in view of the fact that these ideas have not been in every instance tested in a classroom situation; some were merely talking papers for committee discussion, and the majority of these were drafted before 1969. Subsequent revision is thus a distinct possibility, but the patterns of their thinking should manifest stimulus for those engaged in music education.

Two outlines of contrasting natures have been seen which, because of length, cannot be reproduced here. Professor Johnnie V. Lee (Florida A. & M. University) has carefully developed a 28–page syllabus for the first six weeks of her course in Afro-American music, specifically designed for students at her school. Sister Mary Therese O'Neill, from the faculty of one of Chicago's parochial schools, has developed an exceptionally valuable document, *Curriculum for the Black-American Musical Heritage*, while working as a graduate student at Indiana University under the guidance of Dr. Robert H. Klotman.

This 107–page paper gives detailed consideration to all aspects of the religious and secular folk music, including serious examination of specific works and recordings, and provides the teacher with valuable philosophical direction as well. Plans are underway for this document to be published.

● As part of his work with the Contemporary Music Project, Dr. James A. Standifer of Temple University has developed two units to be used in his work in urban education. The first, presented below, is a remarkable compendium of data which should be on the agenda of any serious music student, regardless of the area under consideration.

TABLE OF EXPRESSIVE MUSICAL ELEMENTS

I. Tone color: the sounds of music.
    A. Quality.
        1. Medium.
            a. The voice.
            b. Groups of voices.
            c. The instruments.
            d. Groups of instruments.
            e. Other sounds of music.
        2. Use of medium.
            a. Usual—experimental.
            b. Thick—thin.
            c. Low pitch—high pitch.
        3. Dynamics (amount of sound).
            a, Soft—loud.
            b. Crescendo.
            c. Decrescendo.
            d. Accents.
II. Rhythm: the organization of movement.
    A. Tempo.
        1. Slow—fast.
        2. Ritardano—accelerando.
    B. Pulse.
        1. Grouping (meter): none, 1, 2, 3, 4, 5, 6, etc.
        2. Regular—irregular.
        3. Strong—weak.
    C. Quality.
        1. Notes.
            a. Long—short.
            b. Legato—staccato.
        2. Accents.
            a. Strong—weak.
            b. Regular—irregular.

3. Rubato: none—much.
4. Patterns: simple—complex.
5. Pace: static—active.

III. Melody: the organization of series of tones.
   A. Intervals.
      1. Length: small steps—large leaps.
      2. Organization: major, minor, others.
   B. Melodies.
      1. Length: short—long.
      2. Direction: upward—downward.
      3. Shape: jagged—smooth.
      4. Register: high—low.
      5. Pitch range: narrow—wide.
      6. Cadences: strong—weak.
      7. Structure: simple—complex.
      8. Usage.
         a. Motivic—complete.
         b. Continuous—interrupted.

IV. Harmony: the organization of tones sounded together.
   A. Structure: simple—complex.
   B. Tonality: tonal—atonal.
   C. Quality: consonant—dissonant.
   D. Density.
      1. Thick—thin.
      2. Block chords—harmonic patterns.
   E. Cadences: Strong—weak.
   F. Modulations.
      1. Few—many.
      2. Gradual—abrupt.
      3. Usual—unusual.
   G. Shape: jagged—smooth.
   H. Pace: infrequent changes—frequent changes.
   I. Prominence: accompaniment—main content.

V. Texture: the organization of melody and harmony.
   A. Monophonic.
   B. Polyphonic.
      1. Imitative—non-imitative.
      2. Blending color—contrasting color.
      3. Thin sonority—thick sonority.
   C. Mixed texture: polyphonic—homophonic.

VI. Form: the organization of all the elements.
   A. Principles followed by all forms.

       1. Unity.

       2. Variety.

B. Procedures used in all forms.

       1. Repetition.

       2. Contrast.

       3. Variation.

       4. Development.

C. Forms based on repetition (A, A, A, etc.).

       1. One-part song form.

       2. Round.

D. Forms based on repetition with contrast (A, B, A, C, A, etc.).

       1. Binary.

       2. Ternary.

       3. Rondo.

E. Forms based on repetition with variation (A, A1, A2, A3, etc.).

       1. Theme and variations.

       2. Continuous variations.

       3. Canon.

       4. Fugue.

F. Forms based on repetition with development: sonata form.

G. Free form (all contain repetition, contrast, variation and/or development).

       1. Impromptu.

       2. Prelude.

       3. Fantasia.

       4. Toccata.

       5. Étude.

       6. Rhapsody.

       7. Contemporary free forms.

       8. Others.

H. Combination of forms.

       1. Instrumental.

          a. Sonata.

          b. Symphony.

          c. Concerto.

          d. Suite.

          e. Others.

       2. Vocal.

          a. Opera.

          b. Oratorio.

          c. Cantata.

          d. Mass.

    e. Song cycles.
    f. Others.

● A second approach is a call chart which guides the music listener creatively through, in this instance, John Coltrane's recording of *Kulu sé mama*. During the playing of the recording, the instructor alerts the student to the inception of designated areas with reference to the call numbers.

Call no.

1 Cymbal; drum roll crescendo to fortissimo; accent; drum rolls; cymbals, drum rolls, percussion ad lib (prominent X X| X X| X X|, etc.); contrasting pitches on X X| X X| pattern; retardation; drum roll.

2 Voice (chant-like) enters: *Kulu sé mama*; soft; drum and double bass, finger piano in rhythmically free accompaniment.

3 Voice (loud); rattle added to tone colors of (2); cymbal roll; rattle shake leading to next section (4).

4 Voice now more melodic; strong, duple pulse giving way to shifting accents; cross rhythms; gong-gong prominent in emphasis of underlying 1̲ 2 3 4̲ 5 6 beat pattern.

5 Saxophone enters; thick texture; voice descant-like; bongo intrusion 1̲ 2̲ 3̲ 4̲ 5̲ 6̲; clashing harmonies; shifting accents, cross rhythms; polyphonic, each instrument does its own thing (listen!).

6 "Moaning" sax; strong pulse 1̲ 2 3 4̲ 5 6, ostinato rhythmic pattern; various tone colors; conch shell imitates "moaning" sax.

7 Piano solo prominent; atonal harmonies; chordal patterns thick and jagged; ostinato pattern 1̲ 2 3 4̲ 5 6 continues under shifting accents; irregular competing meters and accents.

8 Gong prominent on t̲i t̲i t̲i ta| t̲i t̲i t̲i ta| t̲i t̲i t̲i ta ta ta ta, etc.; sax and conch shell enter with "horn call." Indicate other things heard: _____

9 Double bass slows ensemble. Can you name the tone colors?

What happens with the rhythm? _____

● Professor Leonard Goines (York College of the City University of New York) had been concerned that student reactions to general music history survey courses were not satisfactory. Rather than regard this as the fault of the students, he blamed the course structure. His course still gives attention to Bach and Schönberg, but he considers other manifestations of music as well, and opens the course with illustrations of musical elements based on examples of that music which is already a part of his students' culture.

I. Basic musical concepts.
    A. Melody.
    B. Harmony.

     C.   Rhythm.
     D.   Texture.
     E.   Tone color.
     F.   Form.
     G.   Principles of musical organization.
     H.   Unity and variety.
     I.   Contrast and balance.
     J.   Instruments of the orchestra.
     K.   Voice quality.

II.   Twentieth-century music.
     A.   Jazz.
     B.   Popular music.
     C.   Latin music.
     D.   Country and Western music.
     E.   Folk music.
     F.   Rock.
     G.   Orchestral music.
     H.   Smaller ensembles.
     I.   Ballet.
     J.   Choral music.

III.   Jazz heritages.
     A.   European and African factors.
     B.   Field hollers.
     C.   Work songs.
     D.   Religious music.
     E.   Marching bands.

IV.   Chronological development of jazz.
     A.   Early New Orleans Dixieland.
     B.   Ragtime.
     C.   Chicago style Dixieland.
     D.   Boogie-woogie.
     E.   Swing.
     F.   Bop.
     G.   Cool jazz.
     H.   Funky.
     I.   Third stream music.
     J.   Soul jazz.

V.   The romantic period.
     A.   Absolute and program music.
     B.   Symphonic poem.
     C.   Music drama.

VI.   The classic and baroque periods.
     A.   Classical sonata form.

B. Symphony.
C. Concerto.
D. Concerto grosso.
E. Organ music.
F. Chamber music.

● More advanced students may wish to see Black music in the context of world music, such a course would provide information in those areas too frequently not considered in other music history courses. Such a class as outlined by Professor Henrietta Yurchenco (City College of the City University of New York) would develop deeper respect for the individual ethnic cultures of the world.

I. Western Mediterranean world.
    A. Spain, the Western and Eastern roots.
        1. Agricultural songs.
        2. Flamenco.
        3. The romances, children's songs, dances, and fiesta music.
    B. Latin America.
        1. The interplay of Indian, Spanish, European and Negro music.
        2. The national synthesis in Mexico, Guatemala, and South America.
II. The Slavic world.
    A. Music from Russia, Yugoslavia, Czechoslovakia, Hungary and other Slavic and Balkan countries.
    B. The epic poem, folk polyphony, keening (mourning) songs, ritual songs, instrumental and vocal styles.
III. Africa and the West Indies.
    A. Black Africa, south of the Sahara Desert.
    B. Polyphony, work songs, songs of political commentary and topical events.
    C. The world of rhythm.
    D. Religious cults in the New World, and their relation to Christian worship.
    E. British, American, Spanish and Portuguese influences.
IV. The Orient: folk music, chamber music, court music, music for the theater, influence of Western culture.
    A. Near East Islam.
        1. The maqam.
        2. Singing and instrumental styles from Iran to Morocco.
    B. India.
        1. The raga.

        2.   Hindustani style of North India, and Carnatic style of South India.

        3.   Sitar, vina, chenai, sarod, and tabla.

        4.   Singing styles.

        5.   Folk music, wandering minstrels, epic songs.

   C.   The Far East.

        1.   Kabuki, Gagaku and Koto music of Japan.

        2.   Opera and chamber music of China.

        3.   Western influence.

V.   The British Isles.

   A.   The traditional (Child) ballads, and broadside ballads.

   B.   Irish songs of rebellion, keening songs.

   C.   Occupational songs of miners, weavers, farm workers and tinkers.

   D.   "Mouth music."

   E.   Music of Lowland and Highland Scotland.

   F.   Street songs, instrumental music (fiddling, bagpipes).

VI.   The Germanic and Scandinavian world.

● As urban educators have long known, a study of Caribbean and Latin American music obligates consideration of European, African and Indian influences. Information coming from such a course, as outlined by Professor Yurchenco below, should be immediately practical and valuable to many inner-city educators and researchers.

I.   Spain.

   A.   Western and Eastern roots.

   B.   Agricultural songs.

   C.   Flamenco (dance, song and guitar).

   D.   Influence of religious (liturgical) music, music of the theater, the romances, children's songs, dances, etc.

   E.   Music of the Sephardic Jews of Morocco.

   F.   Western and Oriental vocal styles compared.

   G.   Circle and longway dances.

II.   Latin America.

   A.   The interplay of Indian, Spanish, nineteenth century European, and Negro music, from pre-Hispanic times to the present.

   B.   Mariachis, corridos, regional styles, Mexico, and the Andes.

III.   Africa and the West Indies.

   A.   Black Africa, south of the Sahara Desert.

   B.   Polyphony, works songs, songs of political commentary and topical songs from Africa and the New World (calypso, Plena, etc.).

   C.   The world of rhythm.

   D.   Music as an expression of every day life.

   E.   Religious cults in the New World, and Christian sects.

    F.   Influence of Islam, British, American, Spanish, and Portuguese music.

    G.   Study of musical styles, and vocal and instrumental techniques.

● Professor Eileen Southern (York College of the City University of New York) is interested in degree programs, both graduate and undergraduate, which have emphasis in Afro-American music, and expresses the following suggested requirements for this study on the undergraduate level.

I.   Music core courses (required):
1. Two years of harmony and counterpoint.
2. Two years of sight-singing and dictation.
3. One year of "European" music history.
4. One semester of music analysis.
5. One semester of twentieth century music.

II.   Music electives should include:
1. History of Afro-American music.
2. History of American music.
3. Jazz style and techniques.
4. Proseminar in Afro-American music.

III.   Performance courses.
1. African drumming.
2. Jazz ensemble.
3. Afro-American folk singing.

● Professor Raymond F. Kennedy (Brooklyn College of the City University of New York) has a detailed syllabus for his course in Afro-American music, including assigned and supplementary readings. Three texts are required: *Africa Yesterday and Today*, by Clark Moore and Ann Dunbar (New York: Bantam Books, 1968); *The Negro in the Making of America*, by Benjamin Quarles (New York: Collier Books, 1964); and *The Story of Jazz*, by Marshall Stearns (New York: Mentor Books, 1958). It might be noted that the latter book has an excellent syllabus for its own area.

I.   Fundamental concepts and problems of Afro-American music research; source and reference materials. The concept of Afro-American culture as a comparative base for the evaluation of African elements in Afro-American music. The oral tradition. Musical style and structure analysis. Musical syncretization.

   Readings:
      Nettl, Bruno.
          Folk and traditional music of the Western continents. Englewood Cliffs (N. J.): Prentice-Hall, 1965, p. 1–32.

Waterman, Richard A.
"On flogging a dead horse; lessons learned from the Africanisms controversy" in *Ethnomusicology* (Middletown, Conn.) v. 7 (May 1963) p. 83–87.
Supplemental readings:
Herskovits, Melville J.
"Acculturation and the American Negro" in *Southwest political and social science quarterly*, v.8, (1927) p. 211–225.
Herskovits, Melville J.
The myth of the Negro past. New York: Harpers, 1941.
Vansina, Jan.
Oral tradition: a study of historical methodology. Chicago: Aldine, 1965.
Wachsmann, Klaus P.
"Transplantation of folk music from one social environment to another" in *Journal of the International Folk Music Council* (Cambridge, Eng.) v.6 (1954) p. 41–45.

II. The musical heritage of the Afro-American: African elements in the New World music.

Readings:
Moore, Clark.
Op. cit., p. 1–202.
Quarles, Benjamin.
Op. cit., foreword and p. 7–32.
Stearns, Marshall.
Op. cit., p. 11–24.

Supplementary readings:
Chase, Gilbert.
America's music; from the Pilgrims to the present. Rev., 2d ed. New York: McGraw-Hill, 1966, p. 65–83.
Herskovits, Melville J.
The human factor in changing Africa. New York: Vintage Book, 1967, p. 441–447.
Merriam, Alan P.
"African music" in *Continuity and change in African cultures.* Chicago: University of Chicago Press, 1959, p. 49–86.
Nettl, Bruno.
Op. cit., p. 118–146.
Schuller, Gunther.
Early jazz; its roots and musical development. New York: Oxford University Press, 1968, p. 3–62.

III.   The musical heritage of the Afro-American; retentions and reinterpretations of African music in the Caribbean.
    Readings:
        Stearns, Marshall W.
            Op. cit., p. 25–32.
    Supplementary readings:
        Courlander, Harold.
            Negro folk music U.S.A. New York: Columbia University Press, 1963, p. 1–12.
        Herskovits, Melville J.
            "Drums and drummers in Afro-Brazilian cult life" in *Musical quarterly* (New York) v. 30 (1944) p. 447–492.
        Nettl, Bruno.
            Op. cit., p. 172–180.
        Roberts, Helen H.
            "Possible survivals of African song in Jamaica" in *Musical quarterly* (New York) v.12 (1926) p. 340–358.

IV.   The musical heritage of the Afro-American: retentions and reinterpretations of African music in the U.S.A.; cries, hollers, work songs, ring shouts, slave songs, spirited and secular spirituals.
    Readings:
        Chase, Gilbert.
            Op. cit., p. 232–258.
        Courlander, Harold.
            Op. cit., p. 13–220.
        Quarles, Benjamin.
            Op. cit., p. 33–108.
    Supplementary readings:
        Cray, Ed.
            "An acculturative continuum of Negro folk song in the United States" in *Ethnomusicology* (Middletown, Conn.) v.5 (1961) p. 10–15.
        Jackson, George Pullen.
            White and Negro spirituals. New York: J. J. Augustin, 1943 [note: a paperback edition was reportedly issued in 1965].

V.   Negro minstrelsy; the exploitation of the Negroes' music.
    Readings:
        Chase, Gilbert.
            Op. cit., p. 259–300.
    Supplementary readings:
        Wittke, Carl.
            Tambo and bones; a history of the American minstrel

stage. Durham: Duke University Press, 1930 [note: a reprint has been issued ca. 1969 by Greenwood Press in Westport, Conn.].

VI.   Abolitionist and jubilee songs.
      Readings:
            Greenway, John.
                  American folksongs of protest. New York: A. S. Barnes & Co., 1953, p. 87–105 [note: a reprint of the 1953 University of Pennsylvania Press edition was issued in 1970 by Octagon Books in New York].
            Quarles, Benjamin.
                  Op cit., p. 109-125.

VII. Blues; songs of social protest and discontent. The decades of dissappointment after the Civil War.
      Readings:
            Greenway, John.
                  Op. cit., p. 105–120.
            Stearns, Marshall W.
                  Op. cit., p. 75–81.
            Quarles, Benjamin.
                  Op. cit., p. 128–155.
      Supplementary readings:
            Chase, Gilbert.
                  Op. cit., p. 448–464, 719 (bibliography).

VIII. Ragtime; its history and forms.
      Readings:
            Stearns, Marshall W.
                  Op. cit., p. 104-110.
      Supplementary readings:
            Blesh, Rudi.
                  They all played ragtime. New York: Oak Publications, 1966.
            Schuller, Gunther.
                  Op. cit., p. 66–67, 139–145.

IX.   Growth of jazz; Dixieland.
      Readings:
            Chase, Gilbert.
                  Op. cit., p. 465–474.
            Schuller, Gunther.
                  Op. cit., p. 63–225.
            Stearns, Marshall W.
                  Op. cit., p. 111–139.
            Quarles, Benjamin.
                  Op. cit., p. 156–214.

X.   Growth of jazz; boogie-woogie; house-rent-party pianists.
　　　Readings:
　　　　　Chase, Gilbert.
　　　　　　　Op. cit., p. 462–464.
　　　　　Stearns, Marshall W.
　　　　　　　Op. cit., p. 122–123.
XI.   Growth of Jazz; urban blues (exodus from rural South to urban North).
　　　Readings:
　　　　　Shuller Gunther.
　　　　　　　Op. cit., p. 228–281.
　　　　　Stearns, Marshall W.
　　　　　　　Op. cit., p. 75–81.
　　　Supplementary readings:
　　　　　Jones, LeRoli.
　　　　　　　Blues people; Negro music in White America. New York: Morrow & Co., 1963.
　　　　　Keil, Charles.
　　　　　　　Urban blues. Chicago: University of Chicago Press, 1966.
XII.   Growth of jazz; the so-called Negro Renaissance.
　　　Readings:
　　　　　Stearns, Marshall W.
　　　　　　　Op. cit., p. 120–139.
　　　　　Quarles, Benjamin.
　　　　　　　Op. cit., p. 199–208.
　　　Supplementary readings:
　　　　　Schuller, Gunther.
　　　　　　　Op. cit., p. 245–397.
XIII.   Growth of jazz; the depression and its effects on jazz in the late Twenties and early Thirties.
　　　Readings:
　　　　　Stearns, Marshall W.
　　　　　　　Op. cit., p. 130–139.
　　　Supplementary readings:
　　　　　Jones, LeRoi.
　　　　　　　Op. cit., p. 117–121.
XIV.   Growth of Jazz; the swing era.
　　　Readings:
　　　　　Chase, Gilbert.
　　　　　　　Op. cit., p. 474-480.
　　　　　Stearns, Marshall W.
　　　　　　　Op. cit., p. 140-154.
　　　Supplementary readings:
　　　　　Shapiro, Nat, comp.

> *Hear me talkin' to ya; the story of jazz as told by the men who made it,* by Nate Shapiro and Nat Hentoff. New York: Dover Publications, 1966.

XV.   Growth of jazz; the Forties; the birth of bop; Afro-Cuban and the New Orleans revival.

    Readings:

        Stearns, Marshall W.

            Op. cit., p. 155–182.

        Quarles, Benjamin.

            Op. cit., p. 215–238.

    Supplementary readings:

        Hodeir, André.

            Jazz; its evolution and essence. New York: Grove Press, 1956, p. 116–136, 217–223.

XVIII.   Growth of jazz; the avant garde.

    Readings:

        Jones, LeRoi.

            Op. cit., p. 220–236.

    Supplementary readings:

        Jazz review. New York: v.1 (1958)–v.3n9 (1960). Various articles by Martin Williams, Nat Hentoff, Max Harrison, and Gunther Schuller. [Note: The full run of this periodical has been reprinted by Kraus Reprint Co., New York, in 1970].

XVIII.   The mid-twentieth century songs of protest.

    Readings:

        Carawan, Guy.

            We shall overcome!, songs of the Southern freedom movement, by Guy and Candie Carawan. New York: Oak Publications, 1963.

        Dunson, Josh.

            Freedom in the air. New York: International Publishers, 1965.

● A contrasting course plan for the same basic material is offered by Professor Eileen Southern:

I.   The African heritage.

    A.   The culture of West Africa.

    B.   The beginning and development of slave trade.

II.   Music in the ante-bellum period.

    A.   Folk music (the music of the slaves in oral tradition).

        1.   Song types.

       3. Texts.
       2. Musical style.
       4. Musical instruments.
       5. Musical performance.
  B. Influence of "Negro music" on the contemporary music of the time.
       1. Minstrelsy and blackface shows.
       2. Popular music.
       3. Art music.

III. Music in the post-war period.
  A. Folk music.
  B. Cultivated music.

IV. The emergence and growth of jazz.
  A. The New Orleans school (ca. 1880-1917).
  B. The dissemination of jazz.
       1. The Chicago school (early twentieth century).
       2. The New York school (1920's to 1950's).
       3. The West Coast group (1950's into the 1960's).
  C. The influence of jazz on traditional European style.

V. Cultivated music in the twentieth century.
  A. Black musicians in the early decades.
  B. Black musicians in the contemporary scene.

● A third syllabus, of even wider range, has been developed for his course "Black Music in the Americas" by David N. Baker of Indiana University.

I. Introduction: the African heritage.
  A. Early history of Africa's cultural areas:
       1. Northern Africa (Moslem Africa).
       2. Western Africa (True Negroes).
       3. Central Africa, or the Congo (Pygmies).
       4. Eastern Africa (cattle area; Nilotes).
       5, Southern Africa (Hottentots).
       6. Southwest Africa (Bushmen).
  B. Music as an expression of human experience and life in Africa:
       1. Polyrhythmic percussion techniques.
       2. Call and response patterns.
       3. Poetry of tom-toms; rhythm of life in Africa.
       4. Social and religious meaning of music and dance.
       5. Ritual music.

II. The early slave trade and African musical influence in the Americas.
  A. Slavery prior to the fifteenth century in Africa and Europe.
       1. Cultural traditions of slaves in travel, work and worship.
       2. Spain, Portugal, and the Moslems.

    B.   Survival of the musical attitudes of the African in the Americas.
        1.   Music, dance, story, and attitudes.
        2.   Reasons for survival of African cultural aspects.
III.   Music in the ante-bellum period; slaves and their music through oral
          tradition.
    A.   Song types (spirituals, shouts, gospel tunes, hollers).
    B.   Musical style.
    C.   Texts of dancing parties and praying parties.
    D.   Musical instruments.
    E.   Musical performance and the influence of Negro music on con-
          temporary music.
        1.   Minstrels and blackface shows.
        2.   Popular music.
        3.   Art music
    F.   Songs of the chain gangs.
    G.   "New Negroes" of Fisk University.
    H.   Black music with African, European and American elements.
        1.   Spirituals and work songs.
        1.   Cries and hollers.
        3.   Shouts and stomps.
        4.   Marches and slow drags.
IV.   The jazz era, the Black man's creation.
    A.   Origins.
        1.   The New Orleans school, circa 1880–1917.
        2.   The early performers, their instruments and sounds.
            a.   King Oliver.
            b.   Buddy Bolden.
            c.   Bunk Johnson.
            d.   Freddie Keppard.
            e.   Louis Armstrong.
            f.   Sidney Bechet.
            g.   Emanuel Perez.
            h.   Oscar Celestin.
            i.   Alphonse Picou.
        3.   Instrumentation and combination; acculturated rhythm;
           self-taught techniques of playing (vocal imitations, wail-
           ings, growlings, shoutings, moanings, laughing and
           throbbing tones).
        4.   Forms and textures (chorus and response, collective impro-
           visation, heterophony).
    B.   Dissemination.
        1.   Chicago school.

        2. New York school.

        3. West coast school.

    C. Influence of jazz on European music.

V. "Cultivated" music in the twentieth century.

    A. Black musicians in the early decades.

        1. Sacred music.

        2. Blues and other secular music.

        3. Jazz.

        4. Soul music.

    B. Contemporary Black musicians.

        1. Jazz.

            a. Mainstream jazz.

            b. Folk jazz.

            c. Liturgical jazz.

            d. Soul music.

            e. Avant garde jazz.

        2. Commercial music.

            a. Film music.

            b. Television music.

            c. Music for the theater.

        3. Religious music.

        4. Non-jazz music.

● Professor Henrietta Yurchenco has devised the following course plan which places music of the Black Americans in the context of general American folk music.

1. Traditional ballads and broadsides.

    A. British heritage.

    B. The Child ballads.

    C. Homegrown American ballads.

    D. Comparison of Negro and Anglo-American versions of traditional ballads.

II. Religious music.

    A. History since colonial times.

    B. White spirituals, lining-out hymns, Sacred Harp singing, the Great Awakening, hymns of various religious groups (Shakers, Methodists, Baptists, etc.).

    C. Negro spirituals, their African and European heritage.

    D. Pre-Civil War styles, Georgia Sea Islands, Primitive Baptists, rhyming style of the Bahamas.

    E. Gospel and the influence of jazz.

    F. Use of spirituals in freedom struggles.

III.   Secular music of the Negroes.
    A.   History of worksongs and the blues as poetry and specific musical
        forms, from the field holler to influence in jazz.
    B.   Blues content as a personal medium of social protest, and as an ex-
        pression of sexuality.
    C.   Country blues, classic period, urban blues, rhythm and blues of the
        '50's, rock and roll, soul music.
IV.   Country music from the Appalachians.
    A.   Instrumental music, from Irish fiddling and "Old-timey" music
        to Bluegrass.
    B.   Appalachian vocal styles, illustrated by such figures as Roscoe Hol-
        comb, Almeda Riddle, Frank Proffitt, Uncle Dave Macon, Dock
        Boggs, etc.
    C.   British traditions transformed on American soil.
V.   Children's songs, play party tunes, city street lore.
    A.   British, European, and American roots.
    B.   Folklore and folksongs of American cities.
VI.   Songs of industrial America, and the protest song.
    A.   Songs of the miners (hard and soft coal), migratory workers
        (from the I.W.W. to the Great Depression), Cowboys (the
        Bad Men), and the meatpacking industry, sailors (the whaling
        years) and the beginning of the urban folk song movement
        (1929–1941).
    B.   Outstanding personalities, including Leadbelly, Aunt Molly Jack-
        son, Woody Guthrie.
VII.   The urban folk song movement since 1936.
    A.   From Union songs of folk-rock.
    B.   Current revival of country music and blues.
    C.   New styles, new singers.
    D.   The role of Tin Pan Alley.
    E.   The young poets and protest song-writers, including Bob Dylan,
        Eric Anderson, Phil Ochs, Mike Settle, Tom Paxton.
    F.   Popular and controversial figures and their role in American folk
        music, including Pete Seeger.
    G.   The Beatles, the Incredible String Band, etc.

● In his outline for a history of jazz, originally prepared for use at George-
town University, Professor Ernest Dyson (Federal City College, in Washington) unites the subject to sociological and political influences without neglect-
ing the various historical manifestations of the jazz expression.

I.   Preliminary considerations.
    A.   Definitions.
        1.   Academic: e.g., Stearns.

        2.   Aesthetic: jazz as an art form and its cultural development in relation to the social sciences.

        3.   Musical: the basic rudiments of melody, harmony, rhythm; influences of European and African musical concepts with variations.

   B. Prehistory.

        1.   African musical heritage in the U.S.

        2.   Cultural background of two merging civilizations: Western Europe and Africa (West Africa, Haiti, Brazil, Cuba, Dutch Guiana).

II. Folklore.

   A. Blues.

        1.   The literature of folk expression and communicating about personal and social conditions.

        2.   Their musical development; the 12–bar blues structure.

        3.   Their influence on schools of jazz.

        4.   Biographical studies: Bessie Smith, Leadbelly, Big Bill Broonzy.

   B. Spiritual.

        1.   Adaptation of African ritual music to Christian liturgy.

        2.   Songs spontaneously created by a preacher and his congregation.

        3.   Negro variations on European ecclesiastical tunes.

        4.   Use of the spiritual element in jazz.

   C. Work song.

        1.   Field hollers, shouts, and street cries.

        2.   Work songs as documentation of commerce, transportation, etc.

        3.   Work song as a means of communication in Africa.

III. Early jazz.

   A. Ragtime.

        1.   Definition; its use in written piano compositions.

        2.   Styles in Sedalia, St. Louis, New Orleans and New York.

        3.   Dances inspired by ragtime: the cakewalk, the Charleston, etc.

        4.   Scott Joplin and other exponents.

   B. Boogie-woogie.

        1.   Boogie-woogie as an aspect of the blues (fast blues).

        2.   The musical concept of boogie-woogie.

        3.   Socio-economic use in rural and urban areas (i.e., rent parties, railroad camps, etc.).

        4.   Jimmy Yancey, Meade Lux Lewis, and other exponents.

5. The Harlem school of stride piano: James P. Johnson, Luckey Roberts, "The Lion", and others.

IV. Schools and idioms of jazz.
    A. Traditional.
        1. New Orleans.
            a. Social, economic and political backgrounds.
            b. The role of the marching bands.
            c. The use of the blues, Protestant hymns, and Afro-European dances.
            d. Instrumentation of New Orleans jazz.
            e. Buddy Bolden, Jelly Roll Morton and other exponents.
            f. The revival at Preservation Hall and the Eureka Brass Band.
        2. Chicago.
            a. The exodus from Storyville in 1917.
            b. Socio-economic conditions of the exodus.
            c. The racially divided urban locales.
            d. Vice and corruption in jazz.
            e. Musical and social influences of South Side Negroes on North Side Whites.
            f. North Side jazz developments (NORK, Bix, Austin High Gang).
            g. South Side jazzmen (Joe Oliver, Louis Armstrong, etc.).
        3. San Francisco traditionalism.
            a. The general social climate of the Bay area.
            b. Distinctive instrumental sound and blues innovations.
            c. Turk Murphy, Bob Scobey and other exponents.
    B. Swing.
        1. Big bands.
            a. Structure, function and principal aims of the big band.
            b. The impact of live, recorded and broadcast performances.
            c. Commercialization.
            d. Style analyses of the Black and White bands.
            e. Fletcher Henderson, Benny Goodman, Duke Ellington and other exponents.
            f. Detailed consideration of the accomplishments of Duke Ellington.
            g. Outstanding sidemen in the big bands.

2. Kansas City establishment.
   a. The Pendergast political machine from 1927 to 1938.
   b. The immigration of Southwestern musicians.
   c. The Kansas City formula of rhythm, riffs, and other elements.
   d. The Kansas City approach to the blues (urban blues).
   e. The contribution of Count Basie.
   f. The influence of Kansas City sidemen ("Pres," "Hawk," Mary Lou, etc.).
3. The jam session.
   a. Definition.
   b. Spontaneous improvisation as a vital source for jazz.
   c. The jam session as a proving ground for new expressive forms.
   d. Live and recorded jam sessions, including the JATP and Commodore series.

C. Contemporary jazz.
   1. Bop.
      a. Culture and its socio-economic status in the U.S. during and after World War II.
      b. The effect of the sessions at Minton's Playhouse and the result of these new concepts.
      c. Jargon, dress and other fads with respect to the public response.
      d. The musical structure of the bop era.
      e. Charlie Parker, Dizzy Gillespie, Thelonius Monk, Charlie Christian, Kenny Clarke and other innovators.
   2. Cool jazz.
      a. The effect of bop on the cool style.
      b. The emergence of technically skilled composers and musicians.
      c. The intellectuals and the appeal of cool jazz.
      d. Miles Davis, Lennie Tristano, Woody Herman and their contributions.
      e. The "West Coast" school.
   3. Hard bop.
      a. The Negro in the '50's and his search for identity.
      b. The translation of this identity with the return to the blues.

      c. The influence of the commercial forces, recording companies, A & R men, and critics.

      d. The death of the Bird.

      e. Horace Silver, Clifford Brown, Sonny Rollins and other new stars.

    4. Third stream jazz.

      a. The academic approach to jazz in schools.

      b. The merger of jazz elements with those of the "classical" idiom.

      c. John Lewis and the Modern Jazz Quartet.

      d. An appraisal of the works of John Lewis, Gunther Schuller and Jimmy Giuffre.

      e. The effect of the concert image on jazz.

    5. The avant-garde.

      a. The Civil Rights movement of the '60's.

      b. The emergence of the new Negro.

      c. The new method of free expression.

      d. The influence from literature of James Baldwin, LeRoi Jones, Nat Hentoff and Claude Brown.

      e. John Coltrane, Ornette Coleman, Archie Shepp, and other exponents.

V. Summary; the aesthetic role of jazz in the development of American culture.

    A. The humanities and the innovations of jazz.

    B. Jazz as an international art.

    C. Bibliographic development of materials related to jazz.

    D. Discographical developments and the basic jazz record library.

● The matter of contemporary jazz and soul music is outlined by Professor David Baker, giving attention to the influences and important peripheral figures.

I. Jazz.

    A. Mainstream.

      1. Swing.

      2. Dixieland.

      3. The big bands.

      4. Post-bebop.

    B. Soul jazz.

    C. Influences on jazz from other ethnic music.

      1. Spanish.

      2. Eastern.

      3. Indian.

      4. Caribbean.

          5. Gypsy.

          6. Others.

    D. Liturgical music.

          1. Reasons for origin.

          2. Cultural, moral and religious implications.

    E. Experimental jazz (Third stream and symphonic jazz).

          1. Forms.

          2. Media.

          3. New instruments.

          4. New uses of old instruments.

    F. Avant garde.

          1. Cerebral.

              a. Extensive ordering of music.

              b. Restrictive forms; extreme scale techniques.

          2. Intuitive.

              a. Return to the organic.

              b. Re-introduction of simplicity (primitivism).

              c. Major-minor triadic harmony.

              d. Emphasis on melody and harmony.

          3. Unique relationships of this music to the Black culture.

          4. Nationalism and jazz.

          5. Avant garde jazz in relationship to the "Academy."

              a. Birth of theoretical systems.

              b. Teaching methods.

II. Soul music (rhythm and blues).

    A. General definition.

    B. Origin and debt to gospel music.

    C. Relationships to the Black community.

    D. Influences on American music.

    E. Rhythm and blues since the Twenties.

    F. Representative figures.

          1. Performers.

          2. Writers.

          3. "A & R" men.

          4. Recording co-owners (including Motown, Atlantic) and their influence.

    G. Influences on the current popular scene.

    H. Economics.

          1. Black music exploited by Whites.

          2. Economic advantages to the imitators.

          3. Constant revitalization by the innovators.

    I. Bibliography and discography.

● A final example is Professor Baker's course plan for a study of contemporary non-jazz Black music, based to a large extent on the original research conducted with funding provided by the National Endowment for the Humanities.

I.   Introduction.
    1.   The Black aesthetic.
    2.   Impositions and errors of stereotypes in Black music.
II. The Black composer.
    1.   Biographical identification.
    2.   Media and styles.
    3.   Cultural, economic and social influences.
    4.   Philosophy and attitudes.
    5.   Representative works.
III. The relationship of Black music to general American music.
    1.   Definitions of Black music.
    2.   Unique qualities of Black music.
    3.   Innovations by Black musicians.
    4.   The relationship of Black music to the Black community.
    5.   The future of Black music.
IV. The Black performer in Euro-American music.
    1.   Singers.
    2.   Pianists.
    3.   Instrumentalists.
    4.   Conductors.
V.   Goals, programs and other activities of Black musical societies.
    1.   AACM.
    2.   BAG.
    3.   Society of Black Composers.
    4.   National Association of Negro Musicians.
    5.   Composers' Guild.
    6.   AAMOA.
VI. Religious music.
    1.   Composers (biographical and bibliographic data).
    2.   The Black composer as, essentially, a creator of jazz or religious music.
    3.   Representative scores and performances.
    4.   Performers and performance practices.
    5.   Liturgical jazz (definitions, figures, and compositions).
VII. Incidental music (film, television, Broadway, theater).
    1.   Composers.
    2.   Media.
    3.   Particular problems.
    4.   Relationships of jazz to non-jazz.
    5.   Representative works.

VIII. The Black music critic.
    1. Musical commentary.
    2. Social commentary.

A List of Registrants

Those persons who were registered for Indiana University's seminar, *Black Music in College and University Curricula* (June 18 to 21, 1969) are listed below. Addresses are given only in those instances of institutional affiliation. Persons who are known to have changed this affiliation are indicated according to currently available information.

Abbott, William W., Jr. (River Falls, Wisconsin)

Adkins, Prof. Aldrich W. (Huston-Tillotson College, Austin, Texas, 78702)

Adoff, Stephen (Bronx, New York)

Allison, Dr. Roland L. (Spelman College, Atlanta, Georgia, 30314)

Anderson, Dr. Thomas Jefferson, Jr. (Composer-in-Residence, Atlanta Symphony Orchestra, Atlanta, Georgia)

Baker, Prof. David N., Jr. (Indiana University, Bloomington, Indiana, 47401)

Baker, Mrs. Jeannie (Bloomington, Indiana)

Banulis, Mrs. Carolyn (South Bend, Indiana)

Banulis, T. Brent (South Bend, Indiana)

Bastin, Prof. Ernest E. (Ohio University, Athens, Ohio)

Beadell, Prof. Robert M. (University of Nebraska, Lincoln, Nebraska, 68510)

Belt, Lida M. (Bloomington, Indiana)

Blum, Sister Madeline M. (Xavier University, New Orleans, Louisiana, 70125)

Bower, Dr. George (Wenatchee Valley College, Wenatchee, Washington, 98801)

Brandt, Prof. William E. (Washington State University, Pullman, Washington, 99163)

Bumgarner, Prof. Roy J. (Flint Community Junior College, Flint, Michigan, 48503)

Bunton, Irving (Public Schools, Chicago, Illinois, 60649)

Caswell, Dr. Austin B. (Indiana University, Bloomington, Indiana, 47401)

Caswell, Mrs. Judith (Bloomington, Indiana)

Chapman, Mary Helen (Bloomington, Indiana)

Clemens, Marc D. (Chicago, Illinois)

Cole, Prof. William S. (University of Pittsburgh, Pittsburgh, Pennsylvania, 15206)

D'Angelo, Prof. Nicholas V. (Hobart & William Smith Colleges, Geneva, New York, 14456)

de Lerma, Dr. Dominique-René (Indiana University, Bloomington, Indiana, 47401)

Dillard, Dr. James A. (Winston-Salem, North Carolina)

Drossin, Dr. Julius (Cleveland

State University, Cleveland,
Ohio, 44115)

Dyson, Prof. Ernest F. (Federal
City College, Washington,
D.C.)

Edwards, Bessie May (Fort Valley
State College, Fort Valley,
Georgia)

Evans, Dr. Jesse G. (Cornell College,
Mount Vernon, Iowa, 52314)

Feist, Leonard (National Music
Publishers Association, 460
Park Avenue, New York, N.Y.
10022)

Finnell, Romona M. (Bloomington,
Indiana)

Foster, Rachel E. (Hampton,
Virginia)

Fritschel, Dr. James E. (Wartburg
College, Waverly, Iowa, 50677)

Fritschel, Mrs. James E. (Wartburg
College, Waverly, Iowa, 50677)

Fuller, Dr. O. Anderson (Lincoln
University, Jefferson City,
Missouri, 65101)

Fuller, Mrs. Edith (Jefferson City,
Missouri)

Gidney, William (Cleveland State
University, Cleveland, Ohio)

Gould, Prof. Glen H. (Chambersburg,
Pennsylvania)

Grossman, Mrs. Carol (Irwin-
Sweeney-Miller Foundation,
Columbus, Indiana)

Hammond, John (CBS Records, 51
West 52 Street, New York, N.Y.
10019)

Hancock, Dr. Eugene W.
(Detroit, Michigan)

Hawk, Marcellene (Cleveland Music
School Settlement, Cleveland,
Ohio, 44106)

Hebb, Christopher (Beloit College,
Beloit, Wisconsin)

Henderson, Dr. Hubert P.
(University of Kentucky,
Lexington, Kentucky, 40506)

Hinderas, Natalie L. (Temple
University, Philadelphia,
Pennsylvania)

Howe, Prof. Richard E. (Grinnell
College, Grinnell, Iowa, 50112)

Johns, Prof. Altona (Virginia State
College, Petersburg, Virginia,
23803)

Kaufmann, Dr. Henry W. (Rutgers
University, New Brunswick,
New Jersey)

Kirton, Prof. Stanley D.
(Wilberforce University,
Wilberforce, Ohio)

Klinge, Paul (Indiana University
Foundation, Bloomington,
Indiana, 47401)

La Brew, Arthur R. (Detroit,
Michigan)

Lee, Sylvia (Curtis Institute of
Music, Philadelphia,
Pennsylvania)

McCall, Prof. Maurice (Hampton
Institute, Hampton, Virginia,
23368)

MacDonald, Dr. John A.
(University of Akron, Akron,
Ohio 44304)

Mack, Prof. James L. (Loop College,
Chicago, Illinois)

McKernan, Dr. Felix E. (Occidental
College, Los Angeles,
California, 90041)

McLin, Mrs. Lena (Kenwood High
School, Chicago, Illinois)

Malin, Don (Edward B. Marks Music
Corporation, 136 West 52 Street,
New York, N.Y., 10019)

Marquis, Dr. James H. (Albany State

College, Albany, Georgia,
31705)
Martin, Sister Maryann (Buffalo,
New York)
Maultsby, Portia K. (Madison,
Wisconsin)
Merrifield, Norman L. (Indianapolis,
Indiana)
Morris, Robert L. (Bloomington,
Indiana)
Morrison, Mary Etta (Indianapolis,
Indiana)
Mosier, Mrs. Martha (Indiana
University, Bloomington,
Indiana, 47401)
Oatts, Helene (Bloomington,
Indiana)
Owens, Robert G. (Jackson,
Tennessee)
Perkins, Marcia (Chicago, Illinois)
Preuter, Bruce A. (Oshkosh,
Wisconsin)
Sanjek, Russell (Broadcast Music,
Inc., 589 Fifth Avenue, New
York, N.Y., 10017)
Schlaefer, Sister Ann (Alverno
College, Milwaukee, Wisconsin,
53215)
Schuller, Prof. Gunther (New
England Conservatory, Boston,
Massachusetts)
Shandler, Gail E. (Skokie, Illinois)
Shurr, Sister Janet (Alverno College,
Milwaukee, Wisconsin, 53215)
Smith, George (Indianapolis,
Indiana)
Smith, Hale (Freeport, New York)
Solano, Dr. Robert P. (State
University of New York,
Oneonta, New York, 13820)
Southern, Dr. Eileen J. (York

College of the City University
of New York, Flushing, N.Y.)
Standifer, Dr. James A. (Temple
University, Philadelphia,
Pennsylvania)
Still, Mrs. Verna Arvey (Los
Angeles, California)
Still, Dr. William Grant (Los
Angeles, California)
Suggs, Frank, Jr. (Bloomington,
Indiana)
Suthern, Prof. Orrin Clayton, II
(Lincoln University,
Pennsylvania, 19352)
Thompson, Bruce A. (Bloomington,
Indiana)
Thompson, Mrs. Sharon B. (Indiana
University Music Library,
Bloomington, Indiana, 47401)
Turner, Prof. Richard M., III
(Fisk University, Nashville,
Tennessee, 37203)
Van Solkema, Prof. Sherman
(Brooklyn College, Brooklyn,
New York, 11210)
Ward, Dr. C. Edouard (Tuskegee
Institute, Tuskegee, Alabama,
36088)
Waters, Mrs. Emily E. (Montclair
State College, Upper Montclair,
New Jersey, 07043)
Weidner, Dr. Robert W. (Eastern
Illinois University, Charleston,
Illinois)
White, Prof. Don Lee (California
State College, Los Angeles,
California)
Whitworth, Prof. Louis (Chicago,
Illinois)
Wilson, Dr. Olly (University of
California, Berkeley, California)

Index to the Text